A
DREAM
DEFERRED

A
DREAM
DEFERRED

America's Discontent
and the
Search for a New Democratic Ideal

Philip Slater

BEACON PRESS
Boston

Beacon Press
25 Beacon Street
Boston, Massachusetts 02108-2892
www.beacon.org

Beacon Press books
are published under the auspices of
the Unitarian Universalist Association of Congregations.

First digital-print edition 2001

Library of Congress Cataloging-in-Publication Data
Slater, Philip Elliot
A dream deferred : America's discontent and the search for a new democratic ideal / Philip Slater.
p.   cm.
Includes bibliographical references (p.   ) and index.
ISBN 0-8070-4304-4 (cloth)
ISBN 0-8070-4305-2 (paper)
1. Authoritiarianism—United States 2. United States—Social conditions—1945– 3. United States—Politics and government—1945– 4. Democracy. I. Title.
HN65.S5649 1991
306´.0973—dc20   90-22592

*for Denny Palmer, Felicity Slater,
and Simon Von Elgg*

Contents

Acknowledgments

This book is an attempt to integrate a number of ideas I have been mulling over and writing about for the past thirty years. It has been influenced by many people, the most important of whom was Mary Parker Follett, whose writings are always a source of fresh excitement.

My interest in democracy was triggered long ago by Warren Bennis's work on industrial bureaucracy, and led to our *Harvard Business Review* article, "Democracy Is Inevitable."

A number of ideas in chapters 7, 9, 10, and 13 were purloined from the restless and fertile mind of Melita Cowie, whose unbounded curiosity has always been helpful in tearing down the maze of Berlin walls that immure academic knowledge.

Valerie Kuletz provided invaluable assistance to an aging and unretentive memory in tracking down coy references and fugitive bits of data.

I am grateful to friends for their criticism of early drafts of the work, especially Melita Cowie, Glenn Lyons, Andrew Schiffrin, and my agent, Susan Zilber. I also owe an overdue debt of thanks to Arnold Tovell, who edited *The Pursuit of Loneliness*, and whose skeptical laughter still echoes usefully in my mind at times.

Special thanks are due Wendy Strothman, who took time from her administrative responsibilities to edit the book, and whose suggestions were invaluable. Whatever failings the book has are entirely my own.

What happens to a dream deferred?
    Does it dry up
    like a raisin in the sun? . . .
    Or does it explode?

—Langston Hughes, "Harlem"

Introduction:
The End of an Era

We have not yet tried democracy. . . . We have not even a conception of what democracy means.

—Mary Parker Follett, *The New State*

Twenty-five years ago, Warren Bennis and I predicted that democratization would overtake the communist nations, and indeed the entire world, within fifty years. We suggested, in a paper called "Democracy Is Inevitable," that the rate of change in the modern world—the need for flexible responses and maximum adaptability—would force these nations to dismantle their authoritarian structures in order to survive. We suggested that in the earlier stages of industrialization dictatorial regimes might prevail in the less-developed nations but that after a generation or two democratization would become unavoidable. Each authoritarian government, groping toward modernization, would thereby sow the seeds of its own destruction, and democratization would gradually engulf it.

This prediction is coming true, not only in the communist world, but in many of the notably unfree segments of the so-called free world as well. South Korea, the Philippines, Taiwan, much of Latin America—all are feeling the pressure.

What Bennis and I did *not* predict was that the United States, in its obsession with the Cold War, would bargain away pieces of its own democratic heritage and, as a result, begin to lose its pre-eminence—not only as a world economic power but also as a civilized nation and a model of democracy, falling far behind many of the Western European democracies for whom we once proudly pointed the way.

What do these changes mean? What is happening in the world? Why are so many nations embracing democracy and why do we seem to be retreating from it? Perhaps it is time to stop being smug about changes in the communist world and take a hard look at our own relation to democracy. What is it? And how do we really feel about it?

USING OUR CULTURAL TELESCOPES

Human beings live only a short time relative to the pace of cultural change. We are like some tiny insect species the members of which live for only a few hours, half of them believing there is no night, the other half assured there is no such thing as day. But we have the advantage of our imaginations, and can use them to propel ourselves beyond the limitations of our abbreviated experience.

Suppose this entire century, and the next one, and the previous one—all that we have ever experienced or will experience in our lives, all of modern history, all that our children and grandchildren will ever experience—suppose all this is just a brief period of transition between one human era and another? How likely is it that we would immediately grasp the significance of our position?

This book assumes that we are, in fact, in such a period. It is designed to help us understand the transition we are going through and envisage the future toward which it points. It presents no new data, but merely tries to bring together some observations about twentieth-century life that have heretofore been forced—by the passion for compartmentalization that dominates the authoritarian mentality—to languish in separate cells.

PROPHETS OF DOOM

As the century draws to an end the air is full of gloomy forebodings. Every day we hear news and commentary suggesting that the world around us is deteriorating. Nuclear destruction, ecological disaster, economic collapse, moral decay—we have a whole menu of depressing scenarios to choose from.

But what is coming to an end is not the world but only an era: the era of authoritarianism. It is an era that has lasted for over five thousand years—virtually all of recorded history—and still dominates our ideas and customs. The aura of decay that envelops us like a suffocating smog is only an effect of this cultural expiration, a sign that a global social system—a shared way of looking at the world and organizing our relationships—is winding down. This cultural system is so old and so familiar that we tend to mistake its customs and habits for human nature. Our anxious feeling of impending doom reflects the fact that we cannot imagine life without it or envision what will take its place.

I call such pervasive social systems *megacultures*. A megaculture is a core of attitudes, practices, and beliefs shared by a wide range of vastly differing cultures, and covering most of the globe. Megacultures are formed as a result of generalized changes in human evolution, and hence tend to transcend local differences. The authoritarianism of Tokugawa Japan, the Ottoman Empire, the Wehrmacht, and a Marine boot camp may take interestingly different forms, but there is a recognizably common core.

Some of the more visible timber of our current megaculture, authoritarianism, is rotting and crashing all around us, but the thousands of tiny roots that permeate our psyches are still very largely intact and will take longer to disappear. Many of the agonies and upheavals of our time result from our efforts to move into a new era while still toting a huge load of emotional and intellectual baggage from the old one. Yet a new megaculture is being born as fast as the old one dies, and each sign of decay is also a sign of new life. Our present sufferings are birth pangs—part of the agony attendant on all transitions.

This emerging megaculture is democracy.

Everyone talks about democracy, but few people have any idea why it exists, why it is happening now, or where it will lead. Most people see it as a merely political phenomenon—which is a little like seeing TV as merely an electrical phenomenon.

MISCONCEPTIONS ABOUT DEMOCRACY

Americans are prone to four fundamental misconceptions about democracy:

(1) *That democracy is created by idealistic strivings—"a yearning for freedom."*

In fact, democracy exists because under modern conditions it is the most efficient form of social organization. It exists because it is a flexible and sophisticated system for maximizing group effectiveness and speed of adaptation under conditions of chronic change and cultural complexity.

(2) *That democracy is synonymous with capitalism.*

In fact, democracy as we know it can exist with or without capitalism. Our own allies over the past few decades have included both socialist democracies like the Scandinavian countries and capitalist dictatorships such as those in much of Latin America. Capitalism and communism may both be considered transitional structures blundering toward full democracy.

(3) *That we are living in a democratic condition today.*

In fact, we are barely holding our own in the global movement toward democracy. While cheering the emergence of democratic movements in the communist world, we ourselves are losing ground. We who began as leaders and innovators of the new megaculture—the inspiration of the democratic world—no longer seem to be convinced that it was a good idea. Our media are entranced with authoritarian imagery; our foreign policy—under the guise of "fighting communism"—has been devoted to crushing democratic movements all over the Third World; and our democratic heritage—of which we are rightly proud—has been so thoroughly redefined by anticommunist fanatics that the values for which we once stood are now viewed as subversive, while "patriotism" has come to mean not a love of the democratic principles on which this nation was founded, but a worship of authority, militarism, autocracy, obedience, and rigidity—all the vestiges of the authoritarian era the rest of the world is desperately trying to leave behind.

And although we may have a sturdier democratic tradition than most nations, we still tend to see life through authoritarian lenses. Our economic organizations, educational systems, thought patterns, religious ideas, literary and artistic products, media, myths, relationships—even the way we deal with ourselves and our bodies—are still dominated by authoritarian assumptions. We may have some democratic institutions, but we are a long way from being democratic in spirit.

(4) *That democracy has to do only with forms of governing and the relation between the governors and the governed.*

In fact, democracy is a vast social movement embracing every aspect of human existence—from family life to religion, from the rigors of economic survival to the free-floating creations of mythology. The democratic forms we are familiar with are merely the first harbingers of this megaculture which will eventually permeate every aspect of human thought and behavior, just as authoritarian ideas do today. All our assumptions, habits, and preoccupations will be transformed by it, and in future generations these new patterns will themselves become so deeply ingrained as to be considered "just human nature."

Democracy does not stop at the borders of politics: it only begins there.

The democratic megaculture is a newborn infant. It is beginning to uproot a way of life that has existed without serious interruption for thousands of years. We are living on the threshold of the most radical transformation of human organization in recorded history. We have no precedents. The ways of "primitive" humanity cannot help us. The ways of chimps, baboons, dormice, dolphins, ants, bees, or praying mantises cannot enlighten us—except to point out the infinite possibilities open to us. The struggle between the emerging megaculture of democracy and the dying megaculture of authoritarianism is taking place within every society in the world today, whether capitalist or communist, socialist or fascist, democratic or plutocratic. And it has only begun.

It has been said that in a sense *all* government is government by the people. The most repressive dictatorship is held in place by the complicity of its populace—by inertia, awe, submissiveness, terror, and greed. A passive populace is governed by the few; only an active one can legitimately be called democratic.

But to *be* active, to reclaim our democratic heritage, to join constructively in the immense transformation that is sweeping the earth, we need to understand the true nature of what we already possess, and of the new megaculture growing around us.

PART I

Megacultures

Life is reduced to a rivulet under dictatorship.
But in freedom it becomes a boundless ocean.

—Iqbal

CHAPTER 1

Why Democracy Happens

Democracy is just stumbling along to the right decision instead of going straight forward to the wrong one.

—Laurence J. Peter

Americans stand firmly behind democratic reform as long as it occurs somewhere else. As soon as it gets close to home people begin complaining about government by committee, and how you can't stop to take votes when you're trying to get a job done.

But democracy is not just a matter of taking votes or forming committees, any more than major league baseball is just a matter of scratching one's testicles and spitting. Democracy is a system of organizing human relationships, and it is spreading through the world today for a very simple reason: *It is the most efficient way of organizing those relationships under conditions of chronic change.*

A MODERN NECESSITY

Americans tend to think of democracy as a charming but expensive and somewhat inconvenient luxury, like an English mansion with no central heating, or an overbred horse subject to frequent ailments—something only the well-to-do can afford. As is the case with so many of the possessions of the rich, our pride in democracy comes less from an appreciation of its intrinsic merits than from our ability to afford it. (Thorstein Veblen would have said that we enjoy democracy as a form of conspicuous consumption.)

Government officials, for example, often complain about how "handicapped" a democratic government is in dealing with a dictatorial regime. They complain about not being able to embark on every military adventure that takes their fancy. They complain about not being able to hide their actions from the public as fully as they would like. They complain about the aggressiveness of the press and about "uninformed dissent"—arguing that if the people only knew all the facts that their leaders decline to tell them, they would not only applaud these secret schemes but acknowledge the wisdom of allowing themselves to be deceived.

When confronted with the fact that fascism was an abysmal failure and that communist regimes around the world are being forced to institute democratic reforms in order to survive, these same officials will suddenly wax sentimental about "the yearning for freedom"—as if yearning ever created anything by itself. (People have been yearning for happy marriages since time immemorial, but we don't see them suddenly springing up everywhere.)

To understand the recent burgeoning of democratic movements, we need to know what democracy *does*, what it's *for*. No form of government exists for long just because people think it's fun. If democracy really conformed to the pleasant-but-inefficient stereotype we have of it, it would have died out long ago. In order to survive, a social system has to *work* in some way—to put bread on the table—and this is what Americans, for all our alleged practicality, have the most difficulty comprehending about our own democracy.

WHY AND WHEN IT WORKS

Just after World War II Alex Bavelas, a researcher at M.I.T., carried out a study that cast light on why democracy works. Bavelas was interested in the effects of different communication networks on task performance in small groups. He arranged some groups so that each subject was able to communicate only with his or her immediate neighbors, forming a kind of circular chain. These he called democratic groups, since there was complete equality of communication access. Another set of groups was arranged in a starlike pattern—one person could communicate with all of the others, but they in turn were able to send messages only to this focal person, not to each other. Bavelas called these groups autocratic.

The initial results of this experiment, which involved the carrying out of very simple mechanical tasks under static conditions, tended to confirm popular assumptions: the autocratic groups were more efficient in solving the task but had poorer morale—only the leaders seemed to be enjoying themselves. Democracy emerged as the "pleasant but inefficient" luxury of our stereotyped beliefs.

But when the tasks were made more complex, more subtle, and subject to changing conditions, the outcome was entirely different. Under these circumstances the decentralized groups not only had better morale but solved the tasks more rapidly and with fewer mistakes. Democracy, in other words, was superior *because it worked better*.

The fundamental flaw in the centralized groups was their rigidity. The "leaders" in these groups failed because they were too busy to pay attention to vital information coming from their peripheral "subordinates"—information suggesting that the leader's assumptions might need to be reexamined. The leaders were so absorbed in plowing ahead with their given agendas that they were apt to discard or ignore a valuable idea from the periphery—seeing it as impractical or tangential. These leaders tended to make a mistake very common among heads of state—to assume that because they had access to information from several sources they could see the masked face of the future.

The power and centrality of the authoritarian leader blinds him—renders him unable to respond flexibly to changing conditions. It was this rigidity, for example, that kept Nazi Germany from developing the atom bomb during World War II. Fortunately for the world, Hitler had his own agenda, and this new, "impractical," "tangential" idea from the periphery didn't fit into it.

It is this same rigidity that has crippled the Soviet economy for decades and has kept Eastern Europe in a backward condition relative to the West. And it is this same rigidity that has made generals throughout history so notoriously reluctant to abandon prearranged battle plans in the face of inhospitable terrain, unexpected events, or new weaponry.

Nor have American presidents been immune to this chronic disease of authority. It was this rigidity that caused the fall of Richard Nixon, for example. During the Watergate crisis, Nixon and his aides saw themselves not only as above the law but as beyond the reach of the public, and acted on this assumption at a time when a simple admission of misdemeanor would have ended the crisis with little damage. But the messages from the periphery were ignored, the damage escalated, and the entire regime was brought down.

The current crisis in Iraq can also be attributed in part to this reluctance of people in positions of centralized authority to respond to negative feedback. The Bush administration was averse to hearing anything that cast doubt on its policy of encouraging Iraq's military buildup and ignored clear signs of the impending invasion of Kuwait. According to government officials themselves, "the intelligence community provided adequate warning that Iraq was capable of attack but . . . policymakers chose to discount the alert."

The same rigidity has caused equivalent failures in private industry. Often the very success of the original entrepreneur so calcifies the organization that it is soon bypassed by alert competitors. The decline of Wang computers in 1989 is a recent example, but the history of American business is full of such incidents. It was this same rigidity that led the Big Three auto makers to lose a large share of the American market to foreign car manufacturers. It was this rigidity that gave us the Edsel.

The necessary overhauling of basic assumptions required in these situations always seems too drastic to be considered seriously by those comfortably embedded in the status quo. Their favorite term for such a procedure is "unrealistic." In a bureaucracy, "realism" means doing nothing this year too markedly inconsistent with what was done last year. If it was done last year, it is "our policy," and no matter how inane and unsuccessful it might have proven, flying in the face of it becomes "unrealistic."

THE UNAVOIDABLE BLINDNESS OF AUTHORITY

The story is always the same: the authoritarian leader is warned of approaching danger by a subordinate, but disregards it and may even punish the bearer of the alarm. He pursues his own course in the blind conviction that power resides permanently in himself. But power is always rented, never owned—even during the age of monarchies it was at best a long lease. The Achilles' heel of authoritarianism is that the leader *by the very nature of his position is able to ignore the wisdom of anyone "below" him*—that is, anyone who stands between him and the real world. This is what authority means: immunity from competence. The authoritarian leader need not be wise or knowledgeable or skilled. By the nature of his *position* he has the right to be as stupid, insensitive, and blind as he chooses and still be obeyed. This is one of the many reasons power so inevitably corrupts. No individual used to being automatically obeyed can retain his or her flexibility, balance, adaptability, and judgment—like unused muscles these capabilities will eventually atrophy.

This effect is cumulative, for the longer one remains in power the more automatically he or she will be obeyed, and the more automatic the obedience, the greater the atrophy. As Loren Baritz points out in his book on the Vietnam War, "it is an iron law of bureaucracy that the higher one is in an organization, the more optimistic one is"—the principle apparently being that "if *I* am in charge things *must* be going well." Thus "the more senior one is, the more one is subject to the disease of being 'hard-of-listening.' "

The authoritarian leader is insulated from his environment. *All his information is filtered through people whose well-being depends on his approval*, hence they tend to tell him what he wants to hear—that his decisions are correct and everything is going well. Bad news—that is, news suggesting his policies are misguided and he needs to make drastic changes—tends to be received as a personal affront. The messenger is shot, the whistleblower fired, the loyal dissenter accused of treason.

Those closest to an authoritarian leader tend to make the same mistake. Since they believe that power resides *in* him—that the closer they are to him the more power they have—they are reluctant to give credence to any information suggesting that his power is eroding, or that he is pursuing a fatal course. Anxiety merely drives them closer to what they believe is the source of power, and they ignore or punish those who challenge this belief. But you can always tell when an authoritarian leader is about to fall: it is the moment when subordinates suddenly become aware that power, like beauty, fame, the value of stocks, or the existence of Tinkerbell, is in the eye of the beholder—it is the moment they suddenly stop competing like suitors to be closest to their leader, and begin instead to profess a purely formal acquaintance.

The blindness of the authoritarian leader has nothing to do with his or her ability or character. It comes with the job—an occupational hazard, like pesticide poisoning or brown lung. The most intelligent, creative, popular, pragmatic, and effective leaders eventually become rigid and inflexible if they remain in office too long. Washington analyst Hedrick Smith argues that our worst failures as a nation have come from "presidential overreaching," and that *reelected* presidents have a special susceptibility to this weakness: "Lyndon Johnson, Richard Nixon, and Ronald Reagan seemed to share a temporary illusion of presidential omnipotence." Such men seem to find it impossible to hold firmly in mind the borrowed and temporary nature of their powers. They begin to see all questioning or opposition as malicious.

Democratic government *requires* the incorporation of a range of opinions, including contrary ones. As Mary Parker Follett says, "our 'opponents' are our co-creators, for they have something to give which we have not."

This is the heart of democracy.

VIETNAM: A CASE STUDY

American foreign policy is largely shielded from public input. Democratic or Republican, the White House jealously guards its authoritarian dominion over foreign matters, its obsession with secrecy often achieving Kremlinesque proportions. The American people are viewed by White House and State Department officials as too stupid and uninformed to be allowed to influence foreign policy in any way, and to fulfill this prophecy, they are routinely misinformed and kept in the dark as much as possible.

Even under these unfavorable conditions it is difficult to imagine the American public collectively coming up with a policy as ignorant, silly, and uninformed as the bizarre patchwork of knee-jerk anticommunism, presidential machismo, obsolete military strategies, cultural solipsism, blind habit, and bureaucratic obfuscation that composed official American policy in Vietnam during the three decades following World War II. It will serve as an example of the inefficiency of centralized power structures.

At every point in the history of this tragic fiasco there were intelligent minds in Washington who recognized the folly of American policy in Vietnam. As Richard Goodwin, a Johnson adviser, remarks, "almost everyone knew the war was unwinnable," except for the president and a few who "served to fortify his disastrous self-deception." But those who suggested the necessity of a change in policy were one by one omitted from the decision process and increasingly denied access to data that cast doubt on the official line. Dissenting voices were barred from the Oval Office, and Vietnam policy was clutched tightly in the hands of a dwindling group of sycophants. Those who sought change were fired or exiled or resigned. Congress was systematically deceived. Intelligence reports from the CIA were routinely ignored because they conflicted with White House rhetoric, and the reluctance of CIA officials to fabricate positive evidence of the war's satisfactory progress was denounced as disloyalty. Ultimately the agency was forced to cave in and give the president the false reports that he wanted to hear, in order not to lose its position in the Washington power hierarchy. This strangulation of information sources is typical of authoritarian power structures.

Few American presidents have wielded the power Lyndon Johnson did, and by the time he left the presidency he had been insulated from reality for so long that some people close to him were convinced that he had become clinically paranoid—a view supported by the psychiatrists whose advice they sought. He believed that everyone was "out to get him," that those who disagreed with his policies were part of an elaborate communist conspiracy. He railed at the Kennedys, at Harvard men, at the *New York Times*. On occasion he would interrupt work to make long, confused speeches to White House tourists.

Paranoia is another occupational hazard of those in positions of great political power. Most people who have the overweening ambition necessary to attain such power are deeply unconvinced of their innate ability to elicit love and respect from others, and are driven to extreme measures to ensure them. They have excessive needs for control, and are under constant and severe stress. Worst of all, they are surrounded by other power junkies who, to further their own ambitions, tend to tell them only what they want to hear. Personality and situation thus conspire to maximize the threat of paranoia. Power, like many other things, is healthy when evenly distributed, and highly toxic in heavy concentrations.

Johnson's advisers tended increasingly to tell him that he was a "strong" president (that is, as macho as Kennedy), that his policies were correct, and that he was winning the war. Those bold enough to criticize his policies were banished. (Vice President Humphrey was excluded from foreign policy discussions for a year for opposing the bombing of North Vietnam; and when previously hawkish Defense Secretary Robert McNamara told LBJ to stop the bombing, he was hustled off to the World Bank.) Statistics were invented, massaged, and reinvented to underestimate the strength of Vietcong forces and make the war seem winnable. By the time plans for the Tet offensive of 1968 had been revealed in captured Vietcong documents, the Pentagon had become so befuddled by its own mendacity and rhetoric that the documents were "dismissed as *unbelievable*," and the offensive took American forces completely by surprise.

By the end of 1965, input on Vietnam was limited to a small "loyal" group that met for Tuesday lunches to discuss the progress of the war. None of them knew anything about Vietnamese culture and politics, and Goodwin remarks that none of them knew much about the United States either, so insulated were they from the public—as if they were "gathered in some space capsule." The narrowing of focus in these meetings is typical of authoritarian structures: the group discussed bombing targets, helicopter capacities, and waterproof boots, with no mention of what they were trying to accomplish or whether it was worthwhile. "Someone once said as he watched Dean Rusk hurrying to the White House . . . 'If you told him right now of a sure-fire way to defeat the Vietcong and get out of Vietnam, he would groan that he was too busy to worry about that now; he had to discuss next week's bombing targets.' "

Under Nixon there were few changes. Increasingly cut off from reality by his obsession with secrecy and his demand for unquestioning loyalty, Nixon became more and more dependent on Henry Kissinger, who lost no opportunity to flatter and appease him. The invasion of Cambodia—opposed by the secretaries of state and defense and most of the American people—was masterminded by Kissinger to endear himself to Nixon and establish his credentials as a macho bureaucrat.

Meanwhile the military, struggling with the problem of trying to wage this unpopular and ill-advised war, was cruelly hampered by its own rigid and unwieldy authoritarian structure. U.S. troops in Vietnam were managed by career-oriented officers who were anxious to please their superiors and get good ratings at any cost. A study undertaken by the army itself concluded that officers in Vietnam were too busy trying to flatter their superiors with rose-colored statistics to pay attention to their subordinates, who had to deal with the real war going on around them. Officers were rewarded for falsifying records that made their superiors look good on paper (as in all bureaucracies there was an obsession with paper products and things that could be quantified), thus enabling the Pentagon to prove mathematically that the war was being won, right up to the very day it was lost.

Goodwin calls the Vietnam War "a fearsome lesson in the potential power of the modern presidency to ignore and override the process of democracy." This presidential authoritarianism, which has become even more extreme in the last decade, is captured in a remark made by Lyndon Johnson during the latter years of his reign. He complained that the people of America "don't realize that the leaders are the ones who've got the secrets, and that's something they should respect." He spoke wistfully of "Catholic followers," who (in his mind, at least) did exactly what the Pope told them to do and believed whatever the Pope told them to believe. This from the mouth of a man who considered himself a bulwark of democracy.

DEMOCRACY EQUALS FLEXIBILITY

Authoritarianism has an undeserved reputation for efficiency—based largely on the achievements of a handful of charismatic leaders. But these rare moments pale to insignificance beside the dreary norm—soldiers driven mechanically to their deaths by rule-bound generals following antiquated strategies, dictators chaining their people in misery and backwardness while the world passes them by, bureaucrats plodding through corridors swollen like clogged arteries with proliferating regulations.

One of the most highly touted examples of authoritarian "efficiency" in its day was the Third Reich, which did manage to accomplish a great deal of harm in a very short time but then destroyed itself. Nazi Germany is the perfect model of authoritarianism at work and of the inherent flaw that limits its effectiveness for good or evil—its tunnel vision. It achieves its narrow short-run efficiency by ignoring the broader, long-range variables that eventually destroy it. Authoritarians tend to win battles and lose wars. They perform successful operations in which the patient dies. They know how to construct elegant and intricate houses of cards, but always seem to forget about the open window.

In biological evolution, a successful species is one that is (a) finely tuned to its environment and (b) quick to adapt to changing conditions. Authoritarian structures, because they limit the responsive power of those in most direct contact with the environment, fail on both counts.

Military analyst James Gibson shows how the effectiveness of U.S. ground troops in Vietnam was hamstrung by irrelevant commands from distant officers. Several tiers of commanders might be circling in their helicopters at a safe distance above the ground, each countermanding the orders of the one beneath. Unable to distinguish friend from foe, or to assess the nature of the terrain through which the ground troops had to move, these armchair quarterbacks would instruct troops to attack guerrillas airily referred to as "a few minutes away" in impenetrable jungle or to shoot at flares that were completely hidden behind intervening hills.

What makes authoritarianism so inefficient is the long vertical chain of command through which information has to travel before a decision can be reached. In a static environment this may be manageable, and provides consistency and uniformity. But in a world like ours, in constant flux, it is a severe handicap. By the time the news travels to the top and down again—even if it manages to avoid being distorted, ignored, or discarded—the situation has probably altered.

Democracy is efficient, despite its slovenly exterior, because its decision-making power is decentralized. Changes can be recognized and responded to immediately, at the source, without referring to rule books or calling headquarters.

DEMOCRACY AND INNOVATION

Decentralization makes democratic systems receptive to innovation. Historians and anthropologists have frequently commented on the fact that major cultural breakthroughs rarely come from societies that already enjoy positions of eminence in the world—those deeply invested in things as they are. If they did, Egypt would still be the center of the Western world. Cultural dominance has always shown a tendency to hop around the globe—the hicks and barbarians of one age are the rulers and aesthetes of the next. This has been called "the law of local discontinuity of progress"—the tendency for the cultural advances of the future to come from the cultural boondocks of the present.

The same is true of technological change. Our major innovations have come not from corporate behemoths but from individuals or small groups working outside traditional frameworks. Corporations are forever congratulating themselves on their large staffs of inventors, but their purpose is to invent elaborations on what they already do. Marshall McLuhan was exaggerating only slightly when he said, "No new idea ever starts from within a big operation. It must assail the organization from outside, through some small but competing organization." Walter Adams and James W. Brock observe that very small firms produce *twenty-four times* as many innovations per research and development dollar as large corporations.

One key to democratic efficiency, then, is *the rapid acceptance of new ideas*. People in highly centralized positions of authority have internalized patterns that have brought them success, and are not likely to be receptive to ideas that might undermine this state of affairs. Their minds have a prior engagement. When change comes, it is people less invested in the status quo who are in the best position to take advantage of that change, and it is these "agenda-free" individuals who are most likely to come up with the new ideas in the first place.

In societies with primogeniture, for example, it was the younger sons who became the adventurers, explorers, entrepreneurs, and artists, while their elder brothers managed the estates and chased foxes. "In Japanese folk wisdom," says William Goode, "it is the younger sons who are the innovators." For similar reasons it seems likely that the most important social innovations of the next century will come from women, who are freer from the male-dominated agendas and patterns of the present era, and hence in the best position to break the tedious cycle of competitive male narcissism that has spread such a pall of frantic stagnation, angry repetition, and belligerent decay over all areas of human endeavor today.

In nature, species adaptation to changing conditions is made possible through mutation. Authoritarianism allows for change only through death or conquest. The political forms of democracy provide far more flexibility. Each time a new slate of candidates is elected, an opportunity is created to abandon any obsolete policies and strategies to which the previous incumbents might have been committed. Wars can be ended, policies reversed, new programs initiated, and so on. (The willingness of the people to avail themselves of this opportunity, however, depends on how much the underlying assumptions and beliefs of the democratic megaculture have taken root—institutions will not do it alone.)

Democracy, then, is a cultural mechanism for maximizing the accessibility of agenda-free individuals—a way of more rapidly exposing such individuals to new situations as they arise.

CRITERIA OF DEMOCRACY

Democracy is harder to describe than any other form of organization because it is not imposed, not fixed. Democracy is created anew every day or it is not really democracy. Democracy is not laid down like a blueprint; it grows like a forest. *Democracy is self-creating.* It is a permanent state of self-reinvention. Thinking and doing are not separate steps but part of the same self-correcting process. Mary Parker Follett insists that "no conception of democracy is sound which does not take this into account."

Democracy is *decentralized*—power is diffused to the widest possible constituency. In a true democracy, power—military, political, or economic—is not concentrated in the hands of a few—not at any time and not for any reason.

Decentralization means that (a) individual participants have maximum input into all decisions that concern them; (b) authority and responsibility for decisions are vested to the maximum degree in those who apply them; (c) leadership is situational, formal hierarchies do not exist; and (d) there are no impediments to communication from any part of the system to any other part.

Finally, democracies are *self-governing.* This concept is difficult for people to grasp. *Government* or *rule* suggests control from "above"—the terms are derived from our authoritarian heritage and their roots go much deeper than our experience with democratic institutions. For many people democracy means only that if we don't like our elected "king" we can throw him out after four years. Which is certainly a step in the right direction but a far cry from what democracy is about.

The idea of people acting together, stumbling along toward collective decisions and being responsible for them, is still foreign to us. Lacking confidence in ourselves, we shudder at the mistakes that might be made. (The catastrophic errors of kings, generals, and presidents over the ages don't seem to faze us.)

Authoritarians often object that democracy means giving the people what they want, and people often want what isn't good for them. The democratic approach to this problem is to allow people to learn what isn't good for them by making their own mistakes. The authoritarian solution is to give absolute power to *one* of these people who don't know what's good for them so that he can impose his own peculiar brand of benightedness on everyone else.

This is not to say that people acting in concert cannot make stupid and vicious decisions. Numbers certainly do not guarantee wisdom, and *there is no system of government that is mistake-proof.* But people tend to learn best from their own mistakes, not from other people's. Mistakes are an inevitable part of learning and growth, and the advantage of *self*-governing is that the consequences of foolish decisions fall directly on those who make them.

Under our present system, leaders seldom suffer from the results of their own stupidity; these misfortunes descend on the population as a whole, or on its more powerless segments—the soldiers who get killed, the workers who get poisoned, the poor who are made poorer. Authoritarian leaders are insulated by their position from the consequences of their folly. (When was the last time a general died in an ill-advised battle?) And when they can hide their blunders from the public under the cloak of "classified information," what is to prevent them from blundering indefinitely?

PARTICIPATION

For the individual, democracy means *participation*. It demands that we leave as little decision making as possible in the hands of people who are not in direct contact with the situations that concern us. It means taking active responsibility for the issues that affect our lives. Americans have an unfortunate tendency to assume that freedom means being left alone. We are surprised and outraged when we stumble across the mammoth bureaucracies we have created through our abdication of political responsibility.

In my own community, for example, there is a chronic furor over the local planning department. Every homeowner has a horror story about trying to get some bit of construction accomplished in the face of a convoluted mass of red tape. People who live in such a community want to preserve its beauty. They want open space, slow growth, nature unspoiled. They want pleasant surroundings—a nice-looking neighborhood with houses well constructed, not too close together, and in forms that will enhance rather than detract from the community's ambience. But on top of all that they want the freedom to do whatever they please with their own property. They want to build their own house on their own land to their own taste and specifications.

Like people everywhere, they are reluctant to face the contradictions between these sets of desires, nor do they want to take the trouble to negotiate with their neighbors on a day-to-day basis. They want the freedom to do their own thing without being bothered with "politics." Hence their representatives are kept busy passing contradictory laws and ordinances of ever-increasing complexity, in an effort to encompass these opposing needs. It is pleasant to withdraw and be private, but we need to recognize that red tape is a direct consequence of this withdrawal. Whenever we are unwilling to deal with our neighbors on a direct case-by-case basis, we empower a bureaucracy to deal with us on a one-size-fits-all basis.

We want to drive to work at highway speeds but don't want the highways going through our own neighborhoods. We want to preserve the environment but don't want to give up any of the toys that destroy it. We dump these insoluble dilemmas in the laps of our representatives and are so annoyed at their inability to resolve them that we refuse to pay them salaries commensurate with their responsibilities—squealing like punctured livestock if anyone tries to bring those salaries in line with those of private industry. And those who complain most vociferously about "politicians" often decline to exert even minimal influence on the political process by voting.

DEMOCRACY IN AMERICA TODAY

Although some democratic institutions seem firmly entrenched in our society, the attitudes, values, and beliefs that support these institutions are not to be taken for granted. Democracy has penetrated only a limited segment of our collective consciousness. Most of our public and private organizations are still authoritarian in structure—our corporations, professions, and educational institutions have yet to feel more than the palest breath of democratic influence. The authoritarian era, after all, embraces most of recorded history—most of what we think of as civilization—and it is still deeply embedded in our psyches. Our most popular legends are rooted in it, our deepest beliefs have been shaped and colored by it. We need now to take a look at this decaying system—to see how it came into being and what is causing its decay.

CHAPTER 2

The Rise and Decline of Authoritarianism

We no longer live as part of nature, content to be one species out of many making up the whole fabric of life; we must be the only species, and all others must serve us or die.

—Elspeth Huxley, *The Red Rock Wilderness*

Some years ago William Stephens, a crosscultural analyst, discovered that while the simplest and most complex societies tended to be democratically organized, the intermediate ones were overwhelmingly authoritarian. This seems to suggest that authoritarianism is merely some kind of transitional phase in human development—an interruption of humanity's natural predilection for decentralized forms of organization.

Groups that depend entirely on gathering and hunting for their subsistence have no centralized authority—no chiefs, kings, nobles, or structured hierarchies of any kind. Informal leadership may accrue to the wise, the elderly, or those who are particularly proficient in some way, but they do not have power over others. Chiefs and kings appear—along with armed power, social classes, and hereditary rule—only when tribes begin to conquer one another.

Hunter-gatherer tribes are not warlike. Quarrels are more apt to result in separation than in battle, and no one would think of conquering anyone else, since no one owns anything and there are no fields for slaves to till. Hunter-gatherers live off the land—it would never occur to them to try to control or coerce it. They do not see themselves as separate from the rest of life. They take what nature offers, and don't try to squeeze more out of it by planting or breeding.

SOMETHING TO FIGHT OVER

For most of human history people lived in such hunter-gatherer bands. But at some point this began to change—we can only guess why. Perhaps it started with agriculture—humanity's first lapse of faith in nature. Perhaps it began with irrigation, which made slavery cost effective.

In *The Chalice and the Blade*, Riane Eisler argues, following Marija Gimbutas and others, that a full-fledged gynocentric civilization sprang up during the Neolithic period and was then overrun by patriarchal hordes from the fringes of this civilization. But while the evidence for such a civilization is convincing, the reconstruction of its demise leaves many questions unanswered. Who were these patriarchal hordes and how did they get that way? If they were powerful enough to conquer a civilization, it seems unlikely that they were merely some straggly band of deprived barbarian nomads.

This question is not of particular concern to Eisler and Gimbutas, who are interested primarily in documenting the existence of this early civilization and the harshness of the culture that

Megacultures

replaced it. But I am inclined to believe that the seeds of what Eisler calls "the dominator model" were already sown the moment gathering and hunting gave way to agriculture and animal husbandry—when humanity, in other words, first tried to control and manipulate nature. This need to exercise control over life—to push nature in certain directions—is what led to the dominator model. It seems more plausible to me that as all these communities developed and became more civilized, some of them drifted into specializations that took them apart. Perhaps the males in some communities (for it seems obvious, from later events, who went astray) became intoxicated with the power potential of animal breeding—which is almost universally associated with authoritarianism and the oppression of women—and took to the plains and a cruder, more bellicose life.

Whatever the causes, authoritarianism began to appear as a dominant social form in many parts of the world five or six thousand years ago—in the Far East, North Africa, India, and the Middle East—and has continued to be the prevailing megaculture ever since, spreading to Europe, Africa, Meso-America, and most of Asia. We begin to find kings, social classes, slaves, standing armies, weaponry, torture, and human sacrifice. Gods are put over goddesses, wives begin to pay deference to husbands, sons begin to pay deference to fathers. Making war becomes the most interesting thing in life, and "honor"—a word applied to everything that serves to nourish masculine narcissism—the central value.

The original and principal function of authoritarianism was to manage and control enslaved tribes—*people who would not voluntarily participate in the society or carry out its tasks.* And although it has broadened its range somewhat over the centuries, it has never lost this coercive focus. Authoritarianism may in fact be defined as *a highly centralized social organization developed in order to exercise coercive control over unwilling participants in the community.* It is characterized by fixed vertical hierarchies of power and status, pyramid-like organizational structures, a rigid system of control, and an exclusive reliance on competition as a motivational tool.

TAKE ME TO YOUR LEADER

When small groups of friends get together to enjoy themselves or engage in some activity, we don't usually talk about who their leaders are. Some groups have a person who seems central—who "makes the group happen." He or she may be particularly popular, or may simply be the person who cares most whether the group exists or not. Other groups are essentially leaderless. When the group engages in some special activity, a leader may emerge for that situation—the group hikes to an area known only by one member, or tries a new skill already mastered by one of them, or learns a new game. Leadership, in other words, is situationally specific—the boat owner becomes the leader on the water, the homeowner in his or her kitchen. Anyone who tries to generalize leadership beyond these momentary occasions of expertise is considered a tiresome egotist and a bore.

Yet sociologists and retired military men sometimes talk about leadership as if you couldn't ever get three people together without electing officers. There are, of course, small groups in which recognized formal leadership seems to be extremely important—where an established pecking order exists. But what sorts of groups *are* these?

The most commonly cited example is the street gang, and if we ask what it is that differentiates the street gang from an ordinary circle of friends, the obvious answer is that it makes war. It exists to fight.

In a hunter-gatherer tribe, leadership tends to be—as with ordinary groups of friends—informal and situationally specific. The better hunters tend to take the lead in hunting. The better singers take the lead in singing. Those who have lived longer and know more, or who are particularly sensible or likeable or capable, are respected and listened to for these reasons.

But once war becomes a major focus of life, leadership tends to become fixed—otherwise the constant battles for primacy within the group would wreak more destruction than the enemy. The unfortunate thing about martial skills is that, unlike most other forms of expertise, they are *inherently* competitive. To show you are good at fighting you have to fight. Leadership therefore has to be decided by physical combat, and since this is destructive to the cohesiveness of the group, such decisions have a strong tendency to become permanent. Command becomes habitual, obedience becomes a virtue. That which was amassed by sheer force is retained by custom. Leadership and its perquisites become hereditary.

Social classes are established in the same way—by battle. The winning tribes become the aristocracy, the losers become slaves or serfs. The serfs till the soil while the nobles practice bashing each other with weapons. The upper classes "protect" the serfs by taking the fruit of their labor and leaving them enough to keep them from dying in the fields.

Megacultures

A powerful myth now evolves to shore up this clumsy system: the myth of legitimacy. This means that any goodies acquired in an act of brutality will be redefined as God-given if they can be successfully passed on to heirs for a few generations.

THE PILLARS OF AUTHORITARIANISM

Authoritarianism is also sustained by certain customs:

1. *The practice of deference or submissiveness.*

The trick here is to get people to give automatic obedience and unearned respect to any person "higher" in the social order (we will see later how important verticality is in the authoritarian worldview). For although it is often assumed that behavior follows beliefs, the opposite is also true: if you can force or trick people into behaving long enough in a certain way they will eventually begin to believe in its rightness and appropriateness. It isn't easy, for example, to "stand up to" someone you've been bowing to for decades; the habit is too deeply ingrained, the self too deeply disparaged by such constant abasement.

2. *Systematic oppression through brutality and terror.*

From a slaveowner's viewpoint, the big problem with slaves and serfs is that if you feed them enough for them to do the work you want done, they may have enough strength left over to kill you (which is also why warrior aristocracies always hold a monopoly on the most sophisticated weapons). Some of these serfs and slaves may not buy the myth of legitimacy and there are, necessarily, more of them than there are of you, for it takes many peasants slaving in the sun to support one glorious warrior with colorful armor. Therefore you need to terrorize them every now and then to keep them off balance: beatings, torture, and occasional executions are useful whenever there's a hint of challenge to the system. The right-wing death squads prevalent in parts of Latin America today are remnants of this ancient system.

3. *Secrecy.*

If you're trying to maintain control over a group that outnumbers you, it's a good idea to corner the information market. You need to establish an efficient communication network from which they are excluded—a different language, or a code of some kind. The invention of writing was probably motivated in part by this need—if you use slaves to run your messages it's best for them not to know what they're carrying. (Mythology and folklore are full of tales in which the illiterate hero unwittingly carries a note with instructions to have him killed.) Special languages, codes, arcane symbols, secret rituals, and other forms of mystification are all helpful for keeping serfs in their place.

4. *Deflection.*

It is also important to deflect your serfs' hostility and resentment onto other targets. If they seem to be getting restless, you set them against some foreigners. Most tyrannies are sustained by war or the threat of it and deflection is an important aspect of military training.

These four patterns—institutionalized submissiveness, systematic oppression, secrecy, and deflected hate—are the four pillars of authoritarianism. We tend to notice tyranny only when there is highly visible oppression—death squads, secret police, torture, and so on—and pay far less attention to the other three. Yet any leader who talks frequently about obedience and loyalty, who tries to hide his acts or those of his subordinates under a cloak of secrecy, or who tries to whip up hatred against an outside group is creating the conditions under which more visible forms of oppression are likely to appear.

DEAD WEIGHT

Some view the history of authoritarianism as little more than a dossier of human calamity—a "bloody five-thousand-year dominator detour," as Riane Eisler puts it—a wrong turning with no socially redeeming value, a violent interruption of the gentle progress of the species toward true civilization. Others would condemn such a wholesale rejection of Western civilization as frivolous. We could argue forever whether Bach, Shakespeare, and the microchip were worth two World Wars, the Inquisition, and the Holocaust, but it doesn't seem very useful. Nor can we even guess whether we could have reached the place we are now—or some far better place—by some more benign pathway. The important thing is not to argue about the past but to find the best path to the future. Even if authoritarianism *was* necessary to bring us to this place, it is necessary no longer. Even if—like a first-stage rocket—it got us off the ground, it has now become a dead weight.

Authoritarian history had a certain rhythm. Bellicose tribes conquered more civilized ones, became civilized themselves, then were conquered by new barbarians who in turn became civilized, and so on. Natural selection favored the barbarians as long as the world was spacious and divided, with most tribes and nations unknown to one another. The most warlike and competitive peoples survived, reproduced, and made the widest linkages. And as long as conquered civilizations continued to swallow up the conquerors and "civilize" them, there was a kind of lurching and stuttering sense of human progress. But now civilization is global, and conquest has become meaningless.

Although war has always been destructive and wasteful, in the past one could persuade oneself that there were gains to be made from it. Territory could be added, slaves acquired, treasure stolen. Something could be *won*. Now it is no longer possible to gain an advantage from war. The "losers" of the last major war—Japan and Germany—are the most prosperous nations in the world, while the "winners"—the United States and the Soviet Union—are sinking into mediocrity, crippled by the crushing burden of their defense budgets.

Today the world is a unit. For all its incredible variety, for all its quarrels and hatreds, for all its bizarre inequalities, it is a single functioning interdependent economic system. We have global communication and, increasingly, a shared civilization, enriched by infusions from all the diverse cultures of our planet. Satellites serve to link even our fantasy worlds. We are, as never before, a single family—a nasty, squabbling family, to be sure, racked with feuds and contested wills, but a family nonetheless.

War no longer has any evolutionary value whatever, and the traits we have worshipped for so many thousands of years have suddenly become not merely obsolete but an acute liability. What we need to do now is not to look around for someone new to fight but rather to find ways to integrate more fully this confused mass of conflicting claims that we call humanity.

Conflict will never be eliminated from human affairs. Conflict is simply the active expression of difference, and an essential part of human development. Without conflict change would be impossible. Our goal as a species at this point in our development is to mold a world in which conflict can be contained within a larger embracing understanding—the realization that we share certain goals and aspirations in common, no matter how much we scream at each other about procedures.

DISTANT EARLY WARNINGS

Social change is never tidy. Successive megacultures have no clear lines of demarcation, but overlap each other like runners in a relay race. The authoritarian megaculture began to decay well before it reached its peak, and began to be infected with democratic viruses before anyone had any idea what democracy was really about. The Athenian democracy of the fifth century B.C.E. was a very minor sniffle indeed—embracing only a tiny fragment of the population and with very little effect on underlying values and attitudes—and was thrown off very quickly by the surrounding social tissue. It left us with Plato, the ultimate apologist for authoritarianism, and Aristotle, whose rigid, pyramidal thought processes were the foundation of authoritarian ideation for the next two thousand years.

A few hundred years later the early Christians embraced radically democratic values and practices, but they, too, were soon engulfed by the universal authoritarianism of the age. It wasn't until the eighteenth century that democracy was able to get any kind of foothold in the world, and to this day two of the largest nations in the world—China and the Soviet Union—have never experienced any kind of real democracy, while most of the "democracies" of Asia, Africa, and Latin America are such in name only.

Still, the process has continued unabated, despite setbacks and hesitations. The reasons are not difficult to see. The cumbersomeness of authoritarianism becomes more and more glaring as the rate of change speeds up. The very success of authoritarianism was its undoing, for as each society expanded, its communication problems increased geometrically. To maintain control, rulers needed not only more rapid communication but also more communicators. Literacy was essential for this, and as literacy increased the rate of change increased, and the entire edifice became harder to keep under control.

We are seeing this all over the world today. There is an extremely high correlation between tyranny and what we call backwardness. Authoritarian systems simply cannot cope effectively with the information explosion, and more and more nations are realizing they must either democratize or fall behind. The epidemic of democratization in Eastern Europe is a symptom of this, and in 1992 most of Europe will become a single economic and democratic entity—an event that would have seemed like the most woolly and optimistic daydream a mere fifty years ago. We can only hope that our own country will participate in this vital trend, instead of slumbering in the comforting illusion that we have already completed a democratic transition that in fact has barely begun.

CHAPTER 3

The Warrior Mentality

Disguise fair nature with hard-favoured rage!

—Shakespeare, *Henry V*

Napoleon brought the highest genius to victory, only to show how little victory could achieve.

—Hegel

The myth of the macho primitive hunter dies hard. I don't know who invented him—that burly caveman so popular with cartoonists, protecting his woman from the wild beasts or dragging her around by the hair—but he is a most convenient fiction. Men seem to seek in him some kind of biological justification for authoritarian habits, but he is in fact completely anachronistic.

In the first place most hunter-gatherer societies would more appropriately be called gatherer-hunter, since the gathered food is usually the more essential of the two. The roles of men and women are not as differentiated as in more complex societies, and the social position of women is much stronger. The crucial factor in specialization by sex is not size or strength but mobility—the men being unhampered by pregnancy or nursing children and hence better suited for activities like hunting which require rapid and wide-ranging movement.

If natural selection were determined by size and strength, humanity would have thrown in the towel a million years ago. Survival under natural conditions is a case not of the strong and the weak—that favorite dichotomy of the authoritarian personality—but of the quick and the dead.

Brute strength is very useful in war but of little value in hunting, especially under primitive conditions. A primitive hunter needs to be fast, have keen senses—be "sense-itive," in other words—and possess a great deal of intelligence, knowledge, and intuition. The beefy caveman of cartoon fame, with the scraggly hair and the shillelagh, might make an excellent soldier, but he couldn't catch his dinner if he fell over it.

SPLITTING THE UNIVERSE

Hunter-gatherers are not acquainted with our concept of fences and boundaries. Their world is a unified whole. The hunter's prey is not an enemy but a partner in this totality. Each depends on the other: the hunter must not kill too many of his prey or his food supply will be gone; yet if the prey escapes every time, it will overpopulate and outstrip its own food supply. The "primitive" hunter has an understanding of this fundamental unity of purpose—an understanding he begins to lose the moment he starts dabbling in animal husbandry.

It is only when authoritarians come on the scene that hunting begins to be viewed as antagonistic. It is the military mentality that sees hunting as a *battle* between hunter and prey—the same ignorant pseudo-Darwinism that prevailed in the Victorian Age ("Nature red in tooth and claw") in which each species supposedly lives in lethal competition with all others so it can one day starve by itself in glorious isolation.

Like other species, hunter-gatherers ate what they killed. For the hunter-gatherer, killing his prey was no more an act of aggression or competition than cutting a lock of his own hair. Primitive hunting is a negotiation. It recognizes a common destiny. The hunter woos his prey—calls to it, prays to it, begs its forgiveness, and later dances a dance of gratitude to it for having allowed itself to be killed that he might live. The hunter sees himself and his prey as parts of the same organic whole.

War, on the other hand, demands a dualistic mental attitude—us versus them. The soldier is taught to deny himself any relationship to the enemy. Fraternization is treason. The enemy is not to be seen as a part of the same whole. Every effort is made to define the enemy as irretrievably *other*—alien, evil. To facilitate slaughter, the enemy is best defined as not even human.

The primitive hunter seeks to *merge* with his prey. He identifies with it, tries to enter into its psyche, imitates its movements, dresses up in its hides and feathers, and seeks in ceremonies and dances to become one with it. The soldier tries to *separate* himself from his enemies, to depersonalize and erase all connection with them.

But the soldier must not only split himself off from the enemy, he must split himself off from *himself*—from his own emotionality, from his vulnerability, from his fear. He must become a block of wood, enduring and unfeeling. Obeying and killing.

The primitive hunter has no need to repress or deny fear. He is in no greater danger from lethal animals, reptiles, and insects than the women who wander in search of other edibles. And when danger does strike, the best possible thing for him to do is to respond to his fear and make himself scarce—what nature designed for survival works very well. It was only when some human beings began to specialize in killing each other that denying one's feelings came to have any social utility. The "fearless hunter" is a meaningless concept. The fearless soldier is an absolute necessity for an authoritarian leader in search of an expendable killing tool.

Eisler points out that no warriors or weapons of war appear in the art of pre-authoritarian times. The very notion of conquest was alien to the hunter-gatherer worldview. It was as meaningless then as it has become today.

European colonial rulers had difficulty making servants out of hunter-gatherers. They complained that they were lazy and had no discipline, that as soon as they received wages they would disappear. They were "untameable."

Not all natives fell into this category, however. Many of the peoples conquered by Europeans had already "advanced" into the authoritarian era. These societies already had kings, social classes, armies, and slaves. They made good soldiers and servants—as good as the Europeans themselves—because they had already developed the appropriate mental attitudes. Since they already had classes they recognized "superior" and "inferior" and were able to accept their conquerors as "superior" to themselves. They understood the game, just as the Egyptians understood the game when they were conquered by the Romans, and the Anglo-Saxons when they were conquered by the Normans.

HIGHER AND LOWER

We are so used to the authoritarian equation of *higher* with *better* that it seems natural to us. Yet there is nothing inherently superior—morally, socially, or intellectually—about being farther removed from the center of the earth. In an age of space exploration this entire equation of "up" and "better" seems quaint and primitive. Yet it is built into our language: *superior* and *inferior* are based on Latin roots reflecting height, and simple words like *above* and *below* are, in most European languages, loaded with evaluative meanings.

It is often assumed that these added meanings derived from religion—that "higher" meant closer to heaven, closer to God. But it was only a few thousand years ago that God was put in the sky. For the hunter-gatherer, God was everywhere—in the earth, in the water, in all living and inanimate things. It was authoritarians who invented the distinction between heavenly and earthly qualities. For the hunter-gatherer the ground was as holy as the sky, because God was everywhere. It was authoritarianism that turned the universe into an organization chart, with God representing not the whole, but merely the chief bureaucrat at the top. The earth ceased to be the home of God because it became contaminated, in the eyes of the conquerors, by its association with the gestures of the conquered.

Bowing, kneeling, prostrating oneself—these are all gestures of submission, and they all have the side effect of making one lower

Megacultures

in height. So much so that we might be led to assume that this was their intent, but the original purpose of these gestures was simply to signify surrender by rendering oneself powerless. An ethologist would probably say that they derive from the common mammalian practice of offering the back of one's neck to an opponent to indicate surrender and end the hostilities (a signal that usually works between animals but frequently fails between humans).

If surrendering tribes always made themselves lower in height, then, and were subsequently enslaved, it isn't hard to see how the idea of *lower* and the idea of *socially inferior* came to be associated. Social superiority, furthermore, was soon translated into moral superiority—as we know from words like *villain, rascal, knave, blackguard, churl, varlet,* and so on, which originally were merely terms used to designate the "lower" classes; or from the use of *noble* and *gentle* to refer to positive human qualities (found all too infrequently among the class to which they were originally applied); or from the modern practice of calling a good-hearted man "a prince."

Bit by bit, then, as hunter-gatherer tribes lost ground to warlike authoritarians, the world came to be seen not as an organic whole in which every being played an equally significant part, *each uniquely different,* but as a collection of ranked classes, one piled on top of the other. Within each category people were more or less lumped together—their uniqueness being less important than their class membership. Every member of a given class was defined as "superior" to every member of the class "below" it and "inferior" to all those in the class "above" it.

Animals, once so important to human appreciation of the spiritual, were placed below the lowest class, and ultimately came to be rank-ordered according to how close to humans they were thought to be. Bit by bit, all of existence was squeezed into this ranking system, until today many people find it hard even to think without arranging nature on a ranked scale of some kind. The world is seen not as a great sphere of life, but as some kind of graduated pyramid.

Finally the earth itself came to be disdained, through association with those lowly beings who lived by tilling it. And because of this same contamination, God ceased to embrace all of life and was reduced to being the most upper of the upper class: Lord of lords, King of kings—no longer to be associated with anything as plebeian as the earth—consigned to a kind of government-in-exile in the sky.

THE STRONG AND THE WEAK

Artificial social arrangements, such as class systems, demand a great deal of psychological and social energy to keep them in place. Yet a not insignificant part of this energy is expended in the attempt of the participants to convince themselves that the system reflects a natural order of things. The more artificial the system is, the more people will insist on its "naturalness"; and the more they insist that it's "just the way the world is," the harder they work to prop it up and keep it in place.

People of the authoritarian persuasion, for example, like to argue that the world is divided into two categories: the "strong" and the "weak." (By "strong," they seem to mean rigid and emotionally impacted, and by "weak" they seem to refer to any awakening signs of intelligence, flexibility, or responsiveness.) In their view, "the strong" were put on earth to rule over "the weak," and one might expect that those who hold this view could comfortably sit back and let nature take its course; yet they seem to be concerned about some insidious conspiracy among "the weak" that manages to keep propelling these inferior types into positions of power. They complain rather petulantly that although "the strong" *should* be ruling "the weak," it just isn't happening. This argument for some reason seemed very compelling to nearly half of the German people in the early 1930s.

EVIL

Authoritarianism created a divided world. What had once been a unified whole was now a set of stratified layers and rigid dualities. The final division was the division of Good and Evil.

In the hunter-gatherer world there were natural forces that were frightening and destructive. There were large animals not to be toyed with. There were poisonous insects and reptiles and sea creatures. There were powerful and unfriendly spirits. There were people with nasty tempers and selfish habits—people with all the foibles and failings that have always characterized the species. But none of these things led people to believe that there was some organized negative force in the world engaged in a protracted war against an organized positive force. The idea that life is a battleground between the armies of Good and the armies of Evil had to wait for a time when armies actually existed. Life was no piece of cake for the hunter-gatherer, but it was a struggle, not a war. And although people were undoubtedly as complex and troublesome as they are now, they were just "poor ornery people," not cannon fodder in some cosmic artillery duel.

Evil as an independent, organized force was a *military* concept, evolved by people who spent much of their time at war and thought of life as a battleground. It was a concept nourished and watered daily by rulers trying to cast their enemies in the worst possible light so that their subjects would be more willing to kill them.

This idea of an evil force trying to drag humanity "down" also helped correct an awkward flaw in the class system—the fact that the class at the bottom had nowhere to fall. It's always dangerous to have a large group of people around who have nothing to lose. The system needed something the bottom class could fall into if they didn't play their proper role—something lower than the low. The invention of Hell as a special underground retreat for the punishment of those who fail to live up to society's rules provided a convenient solution to this problem. No longer was the earth the bottom rung on the ladder, and no longer was tilling the soil the "lowest" occupation. Worse things could happen if you didn't behave yourself—not only would you join the lowest imaginable social class, but your time there would be spent enduring miseries even worse than those in your everyday life. And while none of these terrifying thoughts seem to have made anyone behave any better, they did serve to keep people in their place.

Finally, since ideas are most easily conveyed by being personified, it was useful to have a Devil. Today we're so used to seeing our most horrible atrocities perpetrated by faceless bureaucrats "just doing their job," or energetic entrepreneurs "just trying to make a buck," or enthusiastic scientists "trying to make the world a better place," or soldiers "with God on their side" that we find it hard to get excited about some fellow with a sardonic laugh and too much testosterone. But to authoritarians he continues to provide a useful object of fear.

THE ENEMY

The idea of Evil warring with Good goes far beyond the mere observation that there is a lot of unpleasantness in the world. It implies (a) that Good and Evil can be disentangled from one another and located spatially, (b) that Evil is an organized entity, a kind of cosmic conspiracy, and therefore, (c) that we can eliminate Evil if we are willing to engage in mass murder. People are attracted to this concept because it simplifies life: you don't have to worry about integrating a confusing array of groups with different values and goals—all you have to do is kill people.

This simplicity is so appealing that people are willing to overlook the fact that very little is ever settled by war. When peace comes the underlying problems are still there, compounded by the additional misery and destruction of war. Yet peace is so complicated that simple minds find it irresistible to divide the world into good and bad people and to envision some sort of ultimate battle that will end all these difficult problems without anyone ever having to think about them. If there is hunger in the world, for example, and the poor have become resentful that a few rich people own all the land, those in power can reduce this complex problem to a kindergarten level by defining the poor people as evil communists and sending soldiers in to kill them and burn their houses and crops. Unfortunately, this tends to increase both the poverty and the resentment. Yet it makes the world seem like a simpler place, and we should never underestimate the seductive appeal of this mental minimalism.

When something goes wrong, our authoritarian heritage leads us to ask who is to blame. The hunter-gatherer would suspect some spiritual imbalance, but when the world is seen as a battleground, trouble tends to be personalized: some soldier is being disobedient and must be punished. It is often assumed that once the punishment is administered the problem will go away. Many organizations—especially governments—operate on this principle.

THE ROAD TO ATROCITY

Once an Evil Enemy has been designated, its members are fair game. Since they are motivated not by ordinary human passions but by some mysterious determination to destroy all Good, they must be exterminated at all costs. Since the human beings we know have conflicting motives, some kindly, some not, these Enemies clearly do not belong to the human race and can be killed with a clear conscience. The Enemy is heartless and cannot be reasoned with or bargained with because he is fanatical, devious, untrustworthy. The Enemy will stop at nothing until the world is his. The Enemy is fiendishly clever and places no value on human life (and therefore *we* don't need to, either). Most important of all, the Enemy is *monolithic*. All individual members of the Enemy are exactly alike. Whatever is true of the most extreme of these Enemies is true of them all. Even children.

At this point, as we well know from our own experiences in Vietnam and Nicaragua, the stage is set for atrocity. Mutilation, rape, torture, and the mass slaughter of innocent people, including children, becomes permissible because, after all, they are the Evil Enemy. In ancient Rome the designated Evil Enemies were the

Christians, in the Middle Ages in Europe they were the heretics and Saracens, in the Reformation they were the Protestants, in nineteenth-century America they were the Indians, in Hitler's Germany they were the Jews, in Vietnam they were the Communists, in South Africa they were the Blacks. (Minorities and people of other races are especially likely to be chosen.)

Individuals commit atrocities under any system, but mass atrocities and genocide are a by-product of authoritarianism. People in hunter-gatherer tribes quarrel and occasionally kill one another, but systematic persecution demands an authoritarian worldview. Atrocities are invariably committed by people who believe they are on the side of the Good.

Atrocities are built into our culture, not into our genes—the ancient authoritarian claim that human beings are innately aggressive was effectively demolished years ago by the anthropologist Ashley Montagu. Atrocities are made possible by (a) the need to deflect hostility from rulers and ruling classes, (b) the encouragement of blind obedience, (c) a dualistic way of looking at the world, and (d) the frustrations inherent in a military lifestyle. A soldier is *trained* to be a mass murderer, and if he manages to transcend this training in the field it is a victory of humanity over culture. We may be particularly horrified by the atrocities of some particular group in some particular situation, but the phenomenon is hardly unusual. Massacres like the one at My Lai were a commonplace occurrence in Vietnam, judging from the reports of Vietnam veterans themselves. *Any* army in civilian territory is an atrocity waiting to happen.

Riane Eisler observes, with remarkable understatement, that "times of war usually are also times of greater authoritarianism." War is democracy's greatest enemy. The weapon most commonly used by authoritarians to destroy democratic institutions is the phrase "but we are at war!" Freedoms are then curtailed, legislatures become rubber stamps, foreigners become spies, criticism becomes treason, and nonviolent protesters become terrorists. The war may exist only in the two-dimensional minds of authoritarian leaders, but it always carries the power to limit democracy and push us back toward authoritarianism.

WOMEN AT THE BOTTOM

One of the most drastic changes accompanying the rise of authoritarianism is a sharp decline in the position of women. When the world is an integrated whole, the unique parts that people play in it are of equal significance. But once the world is split into higher and lower, everyone must be assigned a category and a ranking. Who you are becomes less important than *what* you are, and women as a class are downgraded for the obvious reason that they are not soldiers.

Once women have been determined to be "lower" by virtue of their mediocre skills at homicide, it becomes vitally important to men not to be mistaken for women. They feel obliged to demonstrate their manhood *negatively*, by never being nurturant, sensitive, or emotionally alive. A vicious cycle is now set in motion: the more rigidly the men adopt this stance, the more a vacuum is created that women must work hard to fill, and the more women concentrate on these integrative functions, the more inferior they will seem to men, and hence the more rigidly men will avoid being like them.

Women are seen as belonging to the "lowly" domain of the earth. They take care of earthly things like food, childbirth, clothing, feelings, and so on, so that men are able to concentrate on the more spiritual and cerebral issue of population control. It is expected that women will recognize the triviality of their pursuits and be submissive and deferential to males, and women who fail to do this (most often older women who have nothing to lose) provoke great terror in the authoritarian male psyche.

Since men must maintain a fighting stance at all times, women are obliged to spend a great deal of time mediating. Within the family, for example, they are kept busy even today communicating ordinary human feelings that emotionally crippled males are unable to express: "Your father loves you, dear, he just doesn't know how to express it." "Your father was very hurt by what you said the other day." "Sonny worships you, dear, he just doesn't know how to express it."

Were it not for all this caring, nurturance, and mediation, it is doubtful if an authoritarian society could survive, since these are vital functions in any community, and authoritarian systems tend to ignore them in favor of coercion and bureaucratic obedience. Yet even though this traditionally "female" behavior helps make it possible for the males to run about numbly bashing each other and competing, they tend not to value it.

It is these "female" traits—flexibility, creativity, sensitivity, understanding, emotional honesty, directness, warmth, realism, and the ability to mediate, to communicate, to negotiate, to integrate, to cooperate—*that are precisely those most needed to successfully maintain a democratic society.* But they are traits that must be developed in the entire population, not merely in half of it. You can *stand* on one leg, but you cannot *walk*, and while authoritarian societies are designed for stasis, democratic ones are designed for movement.

Hence not only is equality of the sexes inconceivable within the framework of an authoritarian society, *no real democratic tradition can take root in a society in which the macho tradition holds sway.*

PART II

Authoritarian Survivals in American Society

What has made it impossible for us to live in time like fish in water, like birds in air, like children? It is the fault of empire! . . . . Empire has located its existence not in the smooth recurrent spinning time of the cycle of the seasons but in the jagged time of rise and fall, of beginning and end, of catastrophe.

—J.M. Coetzee, *Waiting for the Barbarians*

CHAPTER 4

Military Myopia

Every gun that's made, every warship launched, every rocket fired, signifies a theft from those who hunger and are not fed, those who are cold and not clothed. This world in arms...is spending the genius of its scientists, the sweat of its laborers, the hope of its children—it is humanity hanging from a cross of iron.

—Dwight Eisenhower, 1953

The United States does not have kings, or landed aristocrats, or serfs, or slaves, or a warrior class that exists only to fight. Yet it does have the most gigantic military machine the world has ever known and has sent its troops onto foreign soil more often than any other nation since World War II ended. At the same time, the disparity between classes is growing, and the power of the executive branch of the government is less and less subject to democratic control.

A democratic society is decentralized, yet much of the everyday business of our lives is transacted in huge, unwieldy, authoritarian organizations over which we have almost no control. A democratic society requires universal participation, yet the American people have one of the lowest voter turnouts in the world. A democratic society requires an informed, educated public, yet our news media no longer perform this function and our schools and universities have been systematically despoiled in order to maintain a gargantuan defense budget. A democratic leader must be flexible, open, and capable of knitting together disparate groups, yet we often seem to place the highest value on leaders who are rigid, secretive, and belligerent.

These are holdovers—authoritarian traditions we have not yet outgrown. The ten chapters in this section will attempt to identify the most important of them. Some are being challenged today, but all are deeply ingrained, perhaps none more so than militarism.

OBEDIENCE SCHOOL

It is often remarked that the one institution where democracy has no place is the military. Yet it is also maintained that "democracy must be defended," and that the only way to do this is through a conventional authoritarian military force, backed by conventional military training.

But military training creates a real dilemma in a democracy. On the one hand, if the soldier is fighting for his country, he would presumably do a better job if he valued the democratic traditions that make his country what it is; on the other hand, military training as it is generally practiced requires the systematic demolition of democratic beliefs, values, and practices.

Most of the time this reeducation is successful, and many men who have undergone extensive military training have had any democratic tendencies pretty well knocked out of them and can be expected to embrace authoritarian values thenceforward. Not all, of course—there are true democrats and pacifists even in the heart of the Pentagon. But it requires a certain inner security to admit that surviving an unpleasant experience does not automatically make that experience worthwhile, and those who can maintain democratic values and behavior in the face of this indoctrination are to be admired.

Boot camp training has been portrayed countless times in books, plays, and films, either to pillory its unremitting brutality or to eulogize the molding of hardened soldiers out of raw recruits. Marine training is usually regarded as its most extreme form, and every decade or so a recruit succumbs to its rigors, usually expiring in the course of a severe punishment of the sort often found in the reports of Amnesty International. An outcry occurs, there is an investigation, the sergeant responsible is transferred to other duties for a time, and things return to normal. People seem to feel that the Marine Corps should be allowed to train people as they see fit.

The main purpose of such training is to inculcate unquestioning obedience to authority. This is done by obliterating the self-esteem of the individual recruit and substituting pride of membership in the Corps. The recruit is bombarded continually with the message that he (or she in our time) is nothing, the lowest of the low, that only the greatest effort will permit him to be accepted into membership. A hole is created in the ego, and into this hole is stuffed a message—the message of loyalty and obedience.

The hostility aroused by this procedure must be deflected, but deflecting resentment onto "the enemy" is a little abstract in a boot camp, where the "enemy" is far away and the drill sergeant nearby. This is one reason why, when a dereliction occurs, the drill sergeant will punish everyone *except* the culprit, thus turning the rage of the group onto a scapegoat.

The drill sergeant himself is a scapegoat of sorts. It seems to be extremely difficult for the human mind to see beyond an immediate agent of misery to the more remote person who gave the order for it to be inflicted. We are always ready to see the sergeant, the foreman, or the nurse as personally responsible for our troubles— projecting onto the colonel, the manager, or the doctor our desire for a benign authority. These more distant authorities, if they know their business, convey a benevolent aura that suggests they would have forbidden such harshness on the part of their subordinates had they but known—had they not been distracted by the press of extremely important concerns about which we can know little.

Exposure to random punishment, stress, fatigue, personal degradation and abuse, irrational authority, and constant assertions of one's worthlessness as a human being—all tried-and-true techniques of "reeducation" used by totalitarian regimes—are in most cases effective in creating and maintaining an obedient killing machine. But the cost of this training is high. We are so used to living amidst the psychological deformities of authoritarianism that we have come to take their oddness for granted. But what could be more unnatural than to ignore the counsel of one's own intelligence and repress one's survival instincts?

Systematic domination and submission have been an important part of civilization for thousands of years, so that we have come to view them as normal; and while we have not all been to boot camp, most of us have received some form of authoritarian indoctrination—in schools, families, or other institutions. We accept sadism and masochism as mere variations in human sexual temperament, for example, yet they are not found in societies that have never experienced authoritarianism in any form; and they are most highly developed in countries that have built authoritarianism into their educational systems.

THE INEFFICIENCY OF BUREAUCRATIC ARMIES

Any form of military activity will erode democratic attitudes in the long run. But an army is an organization, and therefore more efficient when arranged democratically. So while there is an irresistible tendency for democratic armies to become more rigid, centralized, and bureaucratic over time, they have a great advantage over conventional military forces until this sclerosis sets in.

The superiority of guerrilla bands—their ability to prevail against traditional armies even when greatly outnumbered and facing prodigious superiority in firepower—is partly a result of being decentralized and hence able to respond more immediately to the unexpected. They know when to fight and when to run away. They know the terrain and can trust their own instincts—they don't need to deal with the ignorant and irrelevant orders of a distant commander. Soldiers in regular forces who trust their instincts run a great danger of being court-martialed for it, even if later proven correct. Conversely, many of the worst military disasters in history were suffered by troops whose discipline was impeccable.

Yet most people—even proponents of democracy—still cling to the idea that bureaucratic armies are efficient. They say you can't stop to have discussions and take votes in the middle of a battle. (For some reason they have no difficulty with the concept of stopping to call headquarters for instructions.) Yet in the heat and chaos of actual fighting, arguments over tactics can and do occur, and hated officers are often "voted out of office" by drastic means. In Vietnam the killing of officers by their own men took place at the astonishing rate of one every other day.

Democracy is not a matter of taking votes on every occasion. An organization is democratic to the degree that those who give orders enjoy that privilege by the will of those ordered. A democratic army is one in which maximum decision-making power rests with those on the front line rather than with those sitting at desks far away. It is one in which incompetent leaders can be replaced with better ones by those they lead. This notion will send chills up and down the spine of the authoritarian, but it reflects the reality of guerrilla armies. No guerrilla army would put up with the kind of ineptitude that would offer, as its only strategy, a war of attrition.

The Department of Defense is one of the largest bureaucracies on the planet, and behaves like very other bureaucracy in the world. Searching for a way to describe the Soviet economic system to a fellow American, a military attaché could find no more apt comparison than our own military establishment. And although the United States Army once had a reputation for flexibility and efficiency—precisely because it placed more reliance on the soldier in the field—this edge has long since been eroded by decades of bureaucratic bloat and the inevitable withering that any democratic tradition will suffer in a military setting.

THE INEFFICIENCY OF MILITARY SOLUTIONS

A more serious misconception about defending democracy is the idea that an army is the only way to do it. Our exclusive reliance on this method has not only increased the threat itself but has also crippled our ability to defend ourselves by more effective means.

The rhetoric of "defense" assumes that we ourselves are passive in the international arena, quietly minding our own business until some threat arises to galvanize us into action. This is the myth of America the Sleeping Giant—popular in the past but beginning to lose credibility as the public becomes better informed. A sleeping giant that has managed to overturn more than a dozen governments since the century began must be suspected of playing possum.

Like any major power, we are actively engaged in manipulating world events, and the worst foreign crises we have faced since World War II are those we have brought upon ourselves. Since 1948 we bear the dubious honor of being the only nation in the world that has used force to overturn the democratically elected governments of other countries—in Iran, Guatemala, and Chile, for example.

To the military mind the best defense is offense, and arming oneself leads sooner or later to acts of aggression. To "defend itself" after being invaded by Germany in World War II, the Soviet Union sent troops into all of Eastern Europe and, decades later, into Afghanistan. To "defend itself" from hostile Arab neighbors, Israel sent troops into Egypt and Lebanon and annexed the West Bank and the Gaza Strip. To "defend itself" from communist invasion, the United States sent troops to Vietnam, on the other side of the globe, and to the tiny island of Grenada.

During the Cold War we consistently responded to ideological challenges as if they were military ones. Instead of trying to capture the allegiance of popular movements, we tried to suppress them. Instead of persuading them to move in democratic directions, we exerted ourselves heroically to drive them into the arms of the Soviet Union.

We are a capitalist nation. One would expect us to look at the world in economic terms: if a new regime went in search of foreign aid one would expect us to compete, to say, "We can offer you a better deal than the Soviets—work with us." Especially in situations where it was clear to everyone that we could offer more—that our support would be more valuable and the lack of it more inconvenient. But our thinking on this question has been unrelentingly military—the fact that a new regime negotiated with our opponents for the aid we refused to give them was viewed as "consorting with the enemy" and therefore as a cause for permanent hostility. We surrendered the marketplace before the competition had even taken place, declared ourselves beaten before even making an offer, and called in the troops.

When Fidel Castro, for example, overthrew the brutal dictatorship of Batista with overwhelming popular support, his first move was to visit the United States and make a series of speeches begging for U.S. aid and support. It was denied—plans were already being made to mount the ill-fated Bay of Pigs invasion—and Castro was forced to depend entirely on Soviet support.

Anticommunist fanatics make no distinction between the armed invasion of one country by another and a popular insurrection led by leftists of any kind. A democratic election won by a Marxist candidate is viewed as a communist invasion in disguise. Henry Kissinger's comment about Chile, that "we're not going to stand by and let a country go Communist through the irresponsibility of its own people," exemplifies the shallowness of the rabid anticommunist's commitment to democracy. Rightists have tried to persuade the

American people that any change in a leftward direction in any government anywhere in the world by any means is equivalent to an armed invasion of the United States—an attitude as self-defeating as it is unimaginative.

It may be objected that the collapse of communist regimes in Eastern Europe is proof that our foreign policy has been on the right track all along. This is a little like the rooster believing that his crowing made the sun come up. These regimes did not collapse because of our enmity. They collapsed because they were authoritarian—for the very same reason, in other words, that dozens of right-wing dictatorships have collapsed over the past several decades—dictatorships that our own government propped up (and in many cases installed) at huge expense to the American people. Dictatorial regimes are no longer viable in the modern world, whatever their political hue.

For anyone who believes in democracy, there is no difference between the overthrow of a brutal communist dictator like Ceausescu and that of a brutal capitalist one like Batista or Somoza, and it behooves a democratic nation to support both upheavals with enthusiasm.

IS AMERICA MORALLY BANKRUPT?

People become violent when they feel powerless or when they have no answer to the mental or moral challenges being put to them. We are certainly not powerless—are we then mentally and morally bankrupt? Our military approach to foreign policy makes the tacit assumption that democracy has nothing to offer the world. Yet democracy is more vital today than it has ever been—sweeping Eastern Europe and making inroads even in South Korea and Taiwan. It seems that everyone in the world is coming to appreciate its value except our own government.

The militaristic approach has not only involved us in continual violations of the sovereignty of our neighbors, it has also placed us in direct opposition to their efforts to raise their own standard of living. Instead of helping people build schools and hospitals, we have sent men to blow them up as soon as they were built. Instead of helping people stamp out illiteracy, we have sent men to shoot the teachers. Is this spreading freedom? Can we find no other response to change in the world than to shoot at it? Cuba sent three thousand doctors to Nicaragua when Somoza fell. We sent the Contras.

The core of our foreign policy since World War II has been anti-communism, and this is its primary flaw. Our government knows what it is against, but what is it *for*? What is our program for raising the level of health and literacy in the Third World? What is our program for creating an integrated planet? What is our program for ecological recovery? We have something to offer the Third World beside dictators, death squads, and the economic exploitation of the many by the few—the openness and flexibility of our society has excited the imagination of other countries for two centuries. Why have these positive aspects played so little role in our foreign policy?

The military approach is also undermining our economic health. Most government spending is recycled through the economy and comes back in taxes. Social security, welfare, and unemployment benefits, for example, are spent to buy food, clothing, and other goods and services, maintaining the economy on an even keel. Educational programs and funds spent for the health and development of children create lasting human assets. But in the area of defense we get almost nothing for our money. Salaries paid to soldiers overseas increase our trade imbalance, and the trillions spent on weaponry is money that might just as well be burnt. The products, if used, are destroyed; if not, they become obsolete and are junked. It is often assumed that defense industries create jobs, but in fact defense industries are not labor-intensive and peacetime conversion would ultimately create hundreds of thousands of jobs.

Pouring our assets down the rathole of military expenditure has drained our strength as a nation in ways that will be felt for decades—possibly forever. It is one of the great ironies of history that our obsession with maintaining our position as the world's greatest power is bringing about the loss of that position. While we have had our eyes glued to the world's keyholes to see what the "Evil Empire" was doing, other nations in the Western world have been hurtling past us—economically and socially. Japan, having failed to conquer the United States by force, seems to have realized it would be simpler to buy it. In their exaggerated concern with "defending" America, our anticommunist zealots have ended by mortgaging it. The Cold War was in essence a war of economic attrition—with national budgets as the hapless soldiers dying in the trenches.

For what have we been doing to raise the health, education, and welfare of our own population? Or to facilitate the arts and sciences so that history may look back on us and say that this was a great culture that finally lived up to its potential? Will future generations look back on us and say, "By the end of the twentieth century their

Authoritarian Survivals in American Society

civilization was already in decline, as they sacrificed their economy, their landscape, their infrastructure, their arts, their sciences, and the welfare and future of their children to the manufacture of arms?''

In recent years the percentage of the Japanese national budget spent on education was almost twice that of the United States, the percentage spent on housing three times as great; while in Germany the percentage spent on social security and welfare was three times that of the United States and the percentage spent on health six times as great. These are investments that bring long-range returns, while we have been squandering our resources on useless military toys.

In 1987 the federal budget for *all* the arts in America—music, dance, painting, sculpture, theater, and so on—was lower than the amount allocated for military bands in the defense budget. Is this an accurate reflection of our national priorities?

THE HIDDEN PURPOSE

Militant anticommunists show a profound disbelief in the power of democracy. Authoritarianism is crumbling all over the world, yet for decades they managed to persuade the American people that democracy was losing ground and could only be preserved by force. It is with this argument that they betrayed themselves. For when they claim that democracy can only be saved by becoming more authoritarian, should we not be suspicious of their motives?

The truth is that once a democracy has been established for a generation or two it is extremely difficult to dislodge. What the anticommunists failed to mention is that *communists have never overthrown a single well-established democracy; most of their gains were at the expense of right-wing dictatorships or monarchies.* In Russia they replaced the oppressive tyranny of the tsars, in China the dictatorship of Chiang Kai-shek, in Cuba the dictatorship of Batista, in Nicaragua the dictatorship of Somoza, in Vietnam a succession of dictatorships and three foreign powers, and so on around the world.

Isn't it rather suspect, then, that anticommunists have consistently elected to crush incipient democratic systems and set up right-wing dictatorships in their place, knowing as they must by this time that the latter are far more vulnerable to communist takeovers? This demonstrates rather clearly, I think, that *the true agenda of the zealous anticommunist is not so much to compete successfully with communism as it is to crush democracy,* both at home and abroad. It was none other than Robert Welch—the founder of the zealously anticommunist John Birch Society—who said that "democracy is the worst system of all forms of government." Hitler came to power as an anticommunist, after all, as did Mussolini, Franco, and most of today's non-communist dictators.

Anticommunism has been the justification for almost every assault on democratic liberties in this country since the end of World War II (just as the fight against "bourgeois imperialism" has been the excuse for the tyrannies of leftist governments). Americans have been forbidden, for example, to hear the ideas of speakers and writers from other countries. Anticommunists have so little faith in the viability of our own democratic institutions that they apparently believe that mere exposure to different ideas will lead to mass conversions to communism. Recent documents have revealed that the list of forbidden visitors to the United States numbers well over 350,000 men and women from 146 countries. The list includes Nobel Laureates Gabriel Garcia Marquez and Pablo Neruda, as well as Graham Greene, Doris Lessing, and many other notable authors, writers, actors, and so on. All but a few thousand of these were forbidden because of their political beliefs, and over two-thirds of them were banned by the Reagan administration, which scarcely let a day go by without using the word *freedom*.

THE "LESSON OF HITLER"

Right-wing militarists are fond of talking about the "lesson of Hitler"—the futility of appeasement, the folly of the Munich Treaty in 1938, the necessity of strangling aggression in its infancy so we don't have to combat it full-grown on our own soil. This popular and plausible anticommunist slogan has been revived by President Bush to justify an American invasion in the Middle East (although not even the most hysterical militarists claim that Saddam Hussein is a serious candidate to conquer the Western Hemisphere).

The irony of the "lesson of Hitler" argument is that the anticommunists who popularized it immediately after World War II were in many cases the very people who had cheered the Munich Pact at the time. During the 1930s the right wing in America argued that we should stand aloof from Europe's conflicts—"America First!" was their slogan. Many American businessmen were very taken with Hitler and Mussolini—how they had "pulled their countries together" and brought order out of chaos. Henry Ford and John D. Rockefeller were among Hitler's fans, and in the privacy of the golf course and club room many corporate leaders expressed the

Authoritarian Survivals in American Society

opinion that we were getting into the war on the wrong side—that we should be allied with Hitler and Mussolini fighting communism. They hoped the Munich Pact would permit Hitler to concentrate on Russia and leave the West alone.

These "enemies of appeasement," in short, were all for it at the time. Their real sympathies were revealed by the haste with which Nazi war criminals were smuggled out of Germany and into our own intelligence agencies after the war. How much these Nazis influenced our foreign policy is unclear, but the influence of the men who hired them cannot be denied. They were the architects of the Cold War: rabid anticommunists like CIA head Allen Dulles and his brother, Secretary of State John Foster Dulles, who together dominated American foreign policy under Eisenhower, worked hand in glove with Nazis and Nazi collaborators throughout the 1950s. They had no use for democracy and were contemptuous of the American people. And George Kennan, the architect of America's "containment" policy toward the Soviet Union, thought America would be better run with a right-wing dictator like Portugal's Salazar.

PERSONALITY DEFECTS BECOME VIRTUES

Another unfortunate effect of the militaristic worldview is that it places a high value on certain personality defects: rigidity, paranoia, and an inability to see things from anyone else's viewpoint. Through these lenses, as Thucydides said long ago, "frantic violence" becomes the proof of masculinity and moderation a sign of cowardice.

Leadership—especially in a democracy, and most particularly under modern conditions of chronic change—demands flexibility and a breadth of vision. Yet candidates for national office in America seem to compete with each other to see who can appear the most rigid, brittle, and narrow-minded. In a democracy the role of a leader is to mediate, to negotiate, to accommodate the needs of opposing groups; but we find our candidates advertising themselves as blocks of granite and lumps of concrete, trying to prove they are not "soft." Women candidates have been questioned on their ability to "stand up to" the Soviets, as if international politics involved nothing more complicated than the ability to push and shove. President Bush, a former head of the CIA, had to invade Panama in order to overcome his "wimp" image. John Kennedy first sent troops to Vietnam to show Nikita Khrushchev he "had balls," and a few years later fifty thousand Americans and a million Vietnamese had to lose their lives to prove that Lyndon Johnson had balls as big as Kennedy's.

Mikhail Gorbachev seems to have forsworn the sandbox diplomacy that has characterized Soviet-American relations since World War II, and we can only hope that one day our own leaders will be mature enough to follow suit. For machismo is contagious. Authoritarians tend to define masculinity as including a large component of mulish belligerence, and the mere sight of some male acting this way seems to provoke it in others, until all the males in the vicinity are bleating and butting their heads together. This is useful for hard-liners in the United States and the USSR: if those in one country begin to lose ground they can usually count on their counterparts to rattle some sabers and get the head-butting going again.

THE FOUNDING FATHERS' WISDOM

It was said long ago that "power corrupts, and absolute power corrupts absolutely." Yet despite our democratic tradition, Americans have a touching faith in the myth of the Incorruptible Man. In this scenario a hero rides out of the West, assumes absolute power, cleans up the town, and then rides off into the sunset. He is simple and unaffected and good, and after he leaves, everything is all right, and everyone lives happily ever after. It was the power of this fantasy that maintained Ronald Reagan's popularity through eight years of one of the most undemocratic regimes in American history.

We have been indoctrinated with the culture of authoritarianism for thousands of years, and a century or two of semi-democracy is not enough to make us immune to it. Our Founding Fathers, whose commitment to democracy was rather narrow, were nevertheless entirely clear about one point: democracy cannot survive if any one person or group is given too much power. Power is like alcohol—if everybody gets a little, a good time can be had by all, but if a few people consume the whole supply you can count on a bad night.

Authoritarians are trying very hard today to increase the power of the presidency and reduce that of Congress, in order to free the commander in chief from the restraining influence of the people's representatives and permit him to undertake military adventures at will. But it was the Democratic party under Roosevelt that began this process—not to further military goals but to achieve more quickly the entirely democratic aim of increasing equality in our nation. It was only a means to an apparently democratic end, but as so often happens with means, it eventually *became* the end, and American democracy has suffered from it ever since.

There are no shortcuts to democracy, certainly none that pass through the quicksand of centralized power—the history of communism is ample proof of that. The seeds of the antidemocratic institutions of today—the National Security Council, the covert operations divisions of the CIA and the Army—were planted by well-meaning liberals in the thirties.

One of the most stubborn delusions in the vast reservoir of human fatuity is the belief that if you just give the right sort of person a whole lot of power everything will turn out all right. Consider the history of communist states around the world—the Soviet Union, China, Cuba—each beginning with equalitarian aspirations and significant social reforms, all ending in tyranny and stagnation. What is a centralized socialist state, after all, but a giant corporation with a standing army and police powers?

We keep imagining that someone with good intentions, someone committed to democracy—especially someone with a fresh memory of their own oppression—will be able to handle power in a benign way. But power has a devastating effect on memory. We are the children of a revolution, and came into being by freeing ourselves from the control of our mother country. Yet we have fought against virtually every revolution in this century, and have attempted to impose our will on the political life of countries in every corner of the world, often by military force. The Soviets are also the children of revolution, and were born repelling foreign troops who were trying to stamp it out. Yet they themselves have suppressed popular movements in Czechoslovakia, Hungary, Poland, and Afghanistan with their own invading forces. European Jews were victims of ethnic persecution on an unparalleled scale by a militaristic regime, yet Israel today is engaged in militaristic persecution of the Palestinians.

The examples are endless, for the amnesiac effect of power is universal. It is not a matter of any particular individual or any particular group or any particular ideology. *It is the wielding of concentrated power itself that breeds evil*, that has an irresistibly corrupting influence. It is the power of one adult to decide what's best for another and to implement that decision against the other's will. *It is authoritarianism itself that creates brutality toward others, not any particular expression of it.* The Founding Fathers, however limited their vision may have been in other respects, had a complete understanding of this point, and many of the complexities of our Constitution derive from their efforts to implement that insight.

Richard Goodwin, who served in both the Kennedy and Johnson administrations, also observes that only institutional restraints on power can preserve democracy:

> I have worked with many powerful men. They were all convinced
> that their goals were righteous, that their sole objective was the

public good; and they all resented obstacles to their will. Yet those obstacles are essential to preserve democracy, not against the depredations of the corrupt, but the deeds of those who believe their objectives benign or even, in Johnson's words, "essential to the security of the free world."

PATRIOTISM

Authoritarians have always tried to make patriotism synonymous with hatred—as if one couldn't love one's own country without wanting to murder some stranger. Through their all too successful efforts, patriotism in America has come to be associated with the very opposite of democracy—with militarism, secrecy, and slavish obedience. Citizens bold enough to assert that America stands for something other than greed have been called unpatriotic, and if they have tried to put their democratic beliefs into practice have been harassed and investigated.

The authoritarian tradition is still strong enough that we tend to equate patriotism with war rather than with our constructive accomplishments. We celebrate our battles more than our integrative achievements—the creation of the Constitution, the absorption of millions of immigrants, the gradual expansion of our freedoms to embrace more and more segments of the population, our continuing struggle for social justice, our inventions, our liberties, our culture.

The democratic worldview is focused, not on "enemies," but on the resolution of conflict. It is *integrative*—seeking to accommodate the needs of all participants in the community (and the world is now a single community whether we like it or not). It is our ability to unite diverse elements that is admired around the globe—our ability to maintain a loose decentralized community of disparate interests, cultures, and races. Our flag is a symbol of this—of the inclusion of separate and unique entities. It is perhaps the only flag that expresses this ideal. It is also a flag that allows for change—for new integrations. This is what our flag stands for, not glaring rockets and bursting bombs.

CHAPTER 5

The Private Sector

[Corporations] feel neither shame, remorse, gratitude, nor goodwill.

—William Hazlitt

The emergence of free markets in Eastern Europe is a form of democratization, insofar as capitalistic institutions in these settings represent a movement away from monolithic government bureaucracies which stifle initiative, innovation, and creativity. If small businesses like those emerging in Eastern Europe were the dominant form of economic organization in the West, the equation between capitalism and democracy so often made by conservatives would have considerable merit. But they are not; the increasingly dominant form of economic organization in non-communist countries is the giant corporation—a huge centralized bureaucracy, usually as stifling, stodgy, and uncreative as its communist counterpart. While the communist world is becoming less centralized, we are becoming more so.

The major defect in communism, overwhelming its humanitarian ideals and aspirations, is the authoritarianism of its huge centralized bureaucracies. The major defect in capitalism, overwhelming its freedom, initiative, and creativity, is the authoritarianism of overblown corporate behemoths. What is needed on both sides of the disintegrating Iron Curtain is decentralization.

We are much more aware, however, of the changes needed to fix up our neighbor's house than of those needed to fix up our own. Mammoth corporations—wielding more power than most of the nations in the UN—have successfully passed themselves off as agents of democracy, when in fact (in the Western world at least) they are its principal enemy. When 1 percent of the corporations account for 87 percent of the sales—the kind of lopsided distribution of wealth and power we usually associate with Latin America—it is a mockery to call the United States a democratic society.

WHAT AUTHORITARIANS MEAN BY "FREEDOM"

Many people have wondered what U.S. government spokespersons mean when they designate right-wing military dictatorships—devoid of the most elementary human rights, characterized by press censorship, death squads, secret police, imprisonment without trial, the use of torture, and the disappearance of dissident persons—as representatives of the free world. Is it mere hypocrisy, or is there some coded significance to the term *freedom?*

There is indeed. What authoritarians have in mind is not personal freedom, not human freedom. What they have in mind is *corporate* freedom. In these right-wing societies (in Latin America particularly) American corporations are far less constrained by government regulation than they are at home. For corporations it's not only a "free world" in these repressive dictatorships, it's a free lunch. They are able freely to pollute the air and water and soil, when complex evasions would have been necessary at home. They are free to dump toxic chemicals there—forbidden pesticides, polluted foods, banned drugs—that they have been prevented from unloading at home. They are free from taxes, free to pay workers nineteenth-century wages, and free from inconvenient rules about worker health and safety.

The multinational character of the modern corporation tends to put it beyond the reach of democratic influence, since no single government can exercise effective control. To talk of competition from Japan or Taiwan or Korea is highly misleading, since, as Bluestone and Harrison point out in their book on corporate emigration overseas, American corporations are deeply involved in financing this competition.

The power of these corporations and the fact that most people in America work for them make it vital for us to understand their impact on the democratic process. This impact takes two forms: an external one, their impact on public policy; and an internal one, the effect of corporate structures on the values of the people who work in them.

THE MANY FACES OF THE CORPORATION

We need first to understand exactly what corporations *are*—a question that is far from easy to answer. For the corporation is protean—a shapeshifter, a master of disguise. The moment you try to confront it in one of its personas, it will instantly transform itself into another.

The original legal fiction—the source of the corporation's enormous power and license—is that it is an individual, with all the rights and privileges pertaining thereto. This is the ideological launching pad for the homilies of right-wing economists and politicians, all of which rest on the assumption that a giant corporation like Exxon and an unemployed black maintenance worker have equal power in the marketplace, the legislature, and the courts.

But does any private citizen have the power to finance a course in conservative economics for one hundred federal judges, paid for a few years ago by several large corporations? Or to introduce pronuclear-power propaganda into the public schools, as utility companies did? Or to persuade members of Congress to pass special interest bills opposed by a majority of the population? Or to hire spies to infiltrate environmental groups? Or to mount multimillion-dollar advertising campaigns to fight popular initiatives, as oil, chemical, and liquor corporations have done in California? Or to emasculate such initiatives in the courts when they are voted in, as insurance corporations have done?

The Private Citizen mask is the one that corporations like best and employ most often, especially when the public expresses concern over some potentially nefarious activity, or one with a destructive social or environmental impact; corporate leaders react as if the police were peering in their bedroom windows and talk of their privacy being invaded. They want to "get government off 'our' backs"—as if they, the corporations, and we, the people, were all in the same boat.

Yet let one of these giant "individuals" begin to lose money and the Private Citizen mask is whisked away faster than you can say "bailout," to be immediately replaced by the Public Institution mask. Suddenly the corporation is not private at all, but a noble service organization providing the community with employment and a product which has long been part of the American tradition and should be treated with all the respect due an endangered species. As a "public institution," it obviously deserves a handout from the government: the failure of a badly managed bank would threaten the economic stability of the entire community; and if a badly run manufacturing company were allowed to collapse, what would happen to all the workers? The success of this mask is apparent: small businesses may rise and fall by the thousands, but above a certain size no major corporation is allowed to collapse, no matter how badly it performs.

But suppose we were to take them up on this pose and say, "Yessiree, you surely do employ a lot of workers, and maybe you ought to give us sixty days notice before you suddenly pull up stakes and transfer your whole operation to Mexico or Taiwan where the labor's so much cheaper." Whisk! The Public Institution mask is gone faster than you can say "profit margin," and we find ourselves contemplating a brand new face: the struggling-small-business-that's-gotta-do-what-it's-gotta-do-to-make-a-buck. If they have to bother about the welfare of their labor force, they protest, it's goodbye to profits. They are a private business, and they shouldn't be forced to contend with all these rules and regulations.

Whenever they have to deal with federal regulatory agencies, corporations like to dress up in short pants and beanies and masquerade as the little-guy-fighting-against-big-government. This is a hard one to carry off, given that the corporation has a squadron of expensive lawyers and accountants to stare down a handful of underpaid functionaries who represent—however inadequately—the will of the public.

When all else fails, corporations will pull out the Avuncular-Institution-For-Widows-And-Orphans mask. They will plead for all the "little people" who have entrusted their hard-earned pennies to the corporation and deserve a return on their investment. (Such people, of course, are a tiny minority of the stockholders, and have little or no impact on its policies.)

Large corporations shuffle these disguises with consummate skill, and, given their extraordinary wealth and power (and the highly paid lawyers, accountants, lobbyists, public relations experts, and advertising firms they retain), it isn't surprising that they are so often able to frustrate and negate the will of the people by their ability to manipulate legislatures, public officials, the media, and the courts.

The legal fiction that the corporation is an individual is an absurd anachronism. The social and economic role of corporations in modern society is more like that of the great feudal landholders of medieval Europe and Japan. No organization that has thousands of employees, billions in assets, and giant tracts of land can lay any claim to being private. These corporations are public institutions, and as such should be subject to democratic control. Their decisions affect every one of us, not just their stockholders. If they want to be private, let them be smaller. We can no longer afford the luxury of encouraging our corporations to do whatever they can get away with and letting them off with a slap on the wrist on the rare occasions when our woefully inadequate enforcement agencies happen to surprise them in a major crime.

Early in 1990 the Justice Department proposed a set of guidelines for sentencing corporate criminals. An intense lobbying campaign by those most likely to be affected—oil companies, defense contractors, and Fortune 500 firms—persuaded Attorney General Thornburgh to withdraw his support and the effort died. The argument put forth by the potential felons was that if stiff fines were imposed on convicted corporations, it might drive them into bankruptcy. We can imagine the reaction if a convicted mugger or burglar tried to use this argument, but apparently the "highest" law enforcement official in the land saw nothing odd in this insistence that corporate felons should not have to pay for their crimes.

Faced with criminal prosecution, large defense contractors have created yet another corporate mask: the Essential-For-National-Security mask. Twenty-five of the nation's biggest defense contractors have been convicted of various kinds of procurement fraud— bribing officials to obtain confidential Pentagon documents, failing to test equipment or falsifying test results (an important cause of accidental deaths in the Services), overcharging, and so on. Some corporations are repeated offenders. Yet none of these corporate giants have been barred from doing business with the government (the punishment usually administered to small firms), despite the fact that they continue to rob taxpayers of billions of dollars each year. Beyond a certain size, defense contractors seem to be above the law.

"GOVERNMENT WASTE"

It is the function of a democracy to mediate among the conflicting desires of its citizenry. This means it must move slowly and make complex adjustments, for it has many different needs to consider and must negotiate with all parties concerned on any issue. The corporation, which has no such obligation, is impatient with this complexity and calls it inefficient. A small boy who wants to open all his Christmas presents at once, before anybody else, probably sees his parents as inefficient in much the same way.

Donald Regan, for example, comparing his Washington and Wall Street experiences, was quoted as saying that "the 'get-along' atmosphere in Washington is a shock for a 'get-results' business executive," and offered as an example how much harder it was to get rid of government employees. But the fallout from these "quick results" in the world of business lands on government. The burden of social responsibility doesn't disappear, it is simply shifted—dumped in the lap of those who can't obtain "quick results" because they are held responsible for their actions.

The irony in this corporate rhetoric is that much of the "inefficiency" of government is caused by the corporations themselves. Through lobbyists, campaign contributions, and discreet forms of bribery and influence, they obtain handouts of land, resources, and equipment and then accuse the government of waste. They pollute the environment without restraint, send the cleanup bill to government, and are then bold enough to complain of the taxpayer's burden. They are like an alcoholic husband who smashes all the dishes in a drunken fit and then complains to his wife that the house is a mess.

Much of what is referred to as "government waste" is in fact corporate waste—waste for which corporations refuse to take responsibility. The government picks up the tab for corporate pollution, corporate bad management, corporate overseas protection, and corporate irresponsibility with regard to occupational health and safety, consumer protection, and employee job security. Not

Authoritarian Survivals in American Society

to mention an enormous health bill, since corporations are responsible, directly or indirectly, for more American deaths annually than all our designated enemies since World War II.

When a pesticide is found to have a lethal impact on consumer health, for example, does the corporation immediately take it off the market? Rarely. The product is phased out gradually, which means that the company would rather kill more Americans than lose a few dollars. Once it is "phased out," it is usually sold overseas, often in countries growing products that will be exported back to the United States.

In 1987 the Reagan administration actually introduced a bill requiring the Environmental Protection Agency to *reimburse* any pesticide manufacturer if an emergency halt to the production of a lethal pesticide was required. The amount sought for a single such reimbursement was 50 percent higher than the entire annual budget for the EPA.

Corporations have never paid their own way. As a group, they are reminiscent of the proverbial spoiled teenager: they take whatever they want without paying, expect everyone to clean up after them, have a million excuses when caught in wrongdoing ("You didn't *tell* me I couldn't"), and when asked to take responsibility for their actions will expend more energy (and money—on lawyers, lobbyists, and misleading advertising) arguing and dragging their feet than they would have spent had they simply gone ahead and cleaned up their corporate room.

Exxon's handling of its massive oil spill in Alaska is a case in point. After a token effort—when it became clear that to do the most rudimentary job of cleaning up its mess would affect its profit structure—Exxon's executives simply threw up their hands and pulled out, leaving local government and volunteer organizations to do a job they were not equipped for. Exxon spent millions on public relations "damage control" that might have been applied to the cleanup (not to mention the money spent trying to block enactment of the structural requirements affecting tanker construction that would have prevented the spill). By refusing to take proper responsibility for the transportation of a potentially destructive cargo, Exxon's executives put money in the stockholders' pockets and sent the bill to Alaska. Unlike the "welfare bums" conservatives are so fond of talking about, corporations seem to feel that the world owes them not just a living but a handsome profit as well.

Consider also the social cost of our national addiction to alcohol and tobacco. Corporations have spent billions to hook Americans on these lethal drugs, and they have succeeded. The price of these addictions is astronomical—the physical, mental, and emotional damage not only to the addicts themselves but to family, lovers, and friends; time lost from work, medical expenses, fires, automobile accidents, industrial accidents—not to mention the sub- sidies paid to tobacco growers. And who pays these costs? We all do, in taxes and higher medical and insurance rates. To suggest that corporations bear any fraction of responsibility for the results of their own actions raises the cry of "communism."

Unfortunately, as a people we seem to identify with this rapacity—we fantasize that some day we'll be on the lion's side of the fence and tolerate the real and oppressive burdens that we bear in the here and now in exchange for this illusory future. When Union Carbide caused the deaths of thousands in India there was very little public outcry against Union Carbide; the brunt of the criticism fell on the lawyers who went to India to take on Union Car- bide's own highly paid attorneys in court. Our admiration of organized avarice keeps us in the role of janitor, continually sweep- ing up after corporate carouses.

Many Americans entertain the belief that third-world peoples place a low value on human life—a reflection, perhaps, of the fact that many Americans place a low value on the lives of third-world peoples, or anyone who doesn't own many possessions. Corpora- tions, however, put a very specific value on human life: if taking one will cause a lawsuit, it is worth the cost of that lawsuit; if not, it is worth nothing. And if the cost of the lawsuit resulting from a lethal action is less than the money saved by taking that action, the action will and must be taken if the management is to discharge its responsibility to its stockholders. This is the beginning and end of corporate morality—an all but inevitable result of the legal fic- tion that insulates them from public responsibility.

THE AUTHORITARIAN WORKPLACE

Conservatives in our country often talk about reducing the size and power of the federal government. I am in complete agreement with this goal, since decentralization is the kingpin of democracy. Unfor- tunately, however, those who advance this position are often pro- foundly silent on two issues:

First, they usually have nothing whatever to say about the seg- ment of the federal government which is the *most* overgrown, powerful, corrupt, extravagant, and wasteful—the defense establish- ment. They want to eliminate government where it is least threaten- ing to our freedoms (that is, in the areas of health, education, wel- fare, services for children, the aged, the handicapped, the poor, etc), while enlarging it in precisely those areas where it is *most* threatening—the military, law enforcement, and covert operations, the three pillars of a police state.

Second, this opposition to bloated bureaucracies seems to evaporate when it comes to corporations. If decentralization is a good thing in government, why isn't it a good thing in industry and finance? Why are corporations gobbling each other up like piranhas in a feeding frenzy, generating overstuffed bureaucracies headed by executives more and more removed from, and with less and less knowledge of, the businesses they are supposedly running?

Centralization is the basic flaw in traditional socialism and communism. It is also the basic flaw in capitalism as it is practiced in the United States today. There is no real difference between a large government bureaucracy and a large corporate one, as any consumer knows who has had occasion to be the victim of a computer error or to fall outside one of their conceptual pigeonholes. A bureaucracy is a bureaucracy, and its titanic ineptitude will betray its identity wherever it tries to hide. If you want to rip the mask from a closet authoritarian when he's busy talking democracy, ask him to apply it to his own organization.

Authoritarianism in industry is viable only when the work to be performed consists of specialized functions carried out in a routine way by unskilled workers under unvarying conditions. But these are the tasks that lend themselves to automation. *Any situation in which an authoritarian structure is efficient is ideally suited to the replacement of humans by robots.* Or, to put it another way, there is no work setting requiring *humans* that would not be rendered more efficient by democratization.

Tom Peters's insightful book, *Thriving On Chaos*, states the argument for industrial democratization: "The times demand that flexibility and love of change replace our longstanding penchant for mass production and mass markets, based as it is on a relatively predictable environment now vanished." He points to the unwieldy, unresponsive, and non-innovative character of our giant corporations and argues that in order to function effectively in today's chaotic world they must decentralize—operate with "flatter" structures, more local autonomy, more labor participation in decision making, sharing "virtually all information with everyone."

Technology itself has encouraged this change. Automation and the computer have had a "flattening" effect, eliminating some levels of the management hierarchy and creating more direct lines of communication between the "top" and "bottom" of an organization. Their use has also tended to reduce the size of the workforce, create more flexible working hours, and eliminate the narrow, routine, mechanical tasks that lend themselves to authoritarian structures. All this has encouraged the emergence of small, decentralized working units with little or no hierarchy, making democratic participation in organizational decision making both more likely and more manageable.

Richard L. Harris points out that "multiple levels of hierarchy and bureaucratic procedures inhibit both innovation and successful adaptation to a rapidly changing . . . environment," and many large corporations have begun to create smaller units in order to encourage innovation and employee involvement. Workplace democratization is far more advanced in Western Europe, however—another example of our having fallen behind those we once led.

BACK TO THE SALT MINES

However poorly it may perform, bureaucracy is still the dominant species in the American economy. Most Americans work in settings that are resolutely authoritarian. This is particularly true of the working class, for whom democracy is more of a slogan than a fact of everyday life. What is the effect of this constant, grinding authoritarianism on the psyche of the average American worker? Can we expect democratic attitudes and responses from citizens who so rarely experience it in their daily lives? How can the reality of the workplace be reconciled with the democratic visions of our heritage?

We spend almost a third of our lives in the workplace, most of us in settings that are structurally antiquated, unfulfilling, uncreative, and antidemocratic. (Recent polls have suggested that more and more people are putting personal fulfillment ahead of money when considering a job, but other polls suggest that only a minority are finding it.) Perry Pascarella has shown that some of the most successful corporations are those that make work humanly fulfilling—that *empower* those who work in them—but these are still a small minority. We can never call ourselves a true democracy until the values of our heritage are reflected in the reality of our daily lives.

RICH AND POOR

Democracy cannot survive inequality. If power and wealth are concentrated in the hands of a few, the fact that poor people can vote means very little. Only the wealthy can mount expensive advertising campaigns, lobby effectively, bribe legislators, conduct protracted legal battles, and so on. It takes money to run for office. Poor people do not hobnob with judges, diplomats, or U.S. senators. Given these circumstances the vote is little more than a fingerhold on democracy.

The last decade has witnessed an increase in the gap between rich and poor in America—enlarging the power, wealth, and immunity of the former and disenfranchising the latter. Even by the rosy-hued statistics of the Reagan administration, we have more poor people (in what was once the world's wealthiest nation) than most industrialized countries. Income figures show a consistent increase in the number of extremely wealthy individuals and in the very poor, while the middle class—once considered the bulwark of a healthy democracy—has been severely eroded. Instead of helping Latin America realize our democratic and equalitarian ideals, recent administrations seem to be trying to turn the United States into a replica of Guatemala or El Salvador.

During the last decade millions of people have slipped into the ranks of the destitute. Exactly how many we cannot determine, since so many of these people never get counted in the census and do not appear on voter registration rolls or any other official statistic. These people have literally been dumped out of our society. This is one of the great inventions of the Reagan era—the statistical forgetting of disaffected portions of the population. Unemployment figures remain low because those whose unemployment benefits run out are no longer classified as unemployed. People who have lost their homes and are living on the street often go uncounted and cannot vote to express their dissatisfaction because they have no addresses and are not registered.

And because the people who suffer under this regime are unlikely to mingle with the perpetrators of it, the latter are able to pretend they don't exist. Although for years millions of Americans have been eating in soup kitchens and out of garbage cans, officials proclaim that the "economy" is basically healthy. What is this "economy," that it can thrive on so much misery? What does it mean that the "economy" is basically healthy when there is more poverty in the United States than at any time since the Great Depression? This "economy" seems to consist of the exchange of goods and services merely among the well-to-do. Fewer and fewer Americans can afford to own a home, but the "economy" is basically healthy. Fewer and fewer Americans can afford a college education, but the "economy" is basically healthy. The infrastructure of our nation has deteriorated, our states, cities, and towns no longer can afford to provide any but the most rudimentary services, our schools have been starved into mere custodial institutions, and only the wealthy or heavily insured can afford medical care, but our "economy" is basically healthy.

This "economy" has very little to do with ordinary people. In theory it is supposed to benefit everyone, through the mysterious workings of the infamous "trickle-down theory"—the supply-side version of "the check is in the mail"—but since few supply-side economists ever bother to inspect a poor person's mailbox (and in the post-Reagan era the poor may not *have* a mailbox), they never discover that nothing is trickling down. How much, after all, is likely to slip through the fingers of people whose religion is greed?

The justification for all this is the archaic notion that giving more money to the rich will "encourage investment," which is supposed to "stimulate the economy" in ways that will "benefit everyone." Since "everyone" is very narrowly defined by those who advance this idea ("everyone who is anyone" would be a close translation) it isn't too surprising that the gap between rich and poor invariably widens when this view prevails. From a societal viewpoint the rich are poor investors—most likely to put their surplus dollars into corporate takeovers and other get-rich-quick schemes that will yield still more dollars for them and have a fundamentally destructive impact on the society as a whole; least likely to invest in anything of long-range benefit to the nation. We don't need to encourage them to find ways of making more money for themselves—they are addicted to it. To offer inducements—such as a lower capital gains tax—is like passing a law to encourage alcoholics to drink more.

The alarming increase in the gap between rich and poor is one of the most severe threats to American democracy today. Recent studies have shown, for example, that having affluent parents automatically adds an average of about twelve points to the IQ of a growing child. One result of supply-side economics, then, is to reduce the intelligence of future millions. Those who advocate policies that have this result can have no other goal but to reinstate the authoritarianism of centuries past.

CHAPTER 6

Learning the Ropes

[Schools are] machines for forcing spurious learning on children in order that your universities may stamp them as educated men when they have finally lost all power to think for themselves.

—George Bernard Shaw

In the education of our young people it is not enough to teach them their "duty," . . . there must be created for them . . . a world of high purpose to which their own psychic energies will instinctively respond.

—Mary Parker Follett, *The New State*

Cultural patterns are imbibed in infancy. What the child learns in the mini-society of the family is often accepted as the way the world is, even in the face of radically new experiences later in life. A child raised in an authoritarian family—where unquestioning obedience is demanded, discipline is severe, the parents secretive, and the child encouraged to hate various kinds of strangers—may grow up, even in a democracy, believing that authoritarianism is normal and psychological slavery a sign of character and moral rectitude.

People brought up in this way are uncomfortable with democracy and never really accept its premises. Yet they are too well trained in obedience to rebel overtly against their society's principles. Their solution to this dilemma is to pay the most fervent devotion to the words and subvert the principles themselves. We see this a great deal today: self-proclaimed superpatriots talking raptly of democracy while opposing its principles in practice.

THE AUTHORITARIAN FAMILY MYTH

In our society it has long been believed that at some time in the past this strict authoritarian family was the norm, but that at some recent date some benign or misguided (depending on your viewpoint) person persuaded American parents to become "child-oriented" and "permissive." What is peculiar about this myth is that it has existed ever since the Pilgrims landed. There is no time in the history of our nation when Americans didn't believe that previous generations were brought up with a severity only recently abandoned—each generation believing itself to have newly discovered, or been newly victimized by, "permissiveness."

Foreign visitors to American shores, on the other hand, exclaim with horrified unanimity—from 1650 to the present day—that American children are spoiled, overindulged, demanding, intrusive, and rowdy—even in the "best" families—and that their presence makes intelligent adult discourse impossible.

In each period there have been many individual families structured on authoritarian lines (several million, after all, would still be a tiny minority today). But most American parents have tended to act from a conviction that children represent the future, and should be allowed to grow into that future with as little archaic baggage as possible. This conviction is based on a realistic assessment of American conditions. Ever since the first settlers arrived, parents have noticed the ease with which their children were able to adapt to life here, having known no other. They spoke the language better, understood the culture better, felt more at home with technological change and the increasingly man-made environment.

Authoritarian Survivals in American Society

It is folly, in other words, to bring up children in rigid accordance with some parental formula when conditions are changing so rapidly that by the time the children grow up that formula may no longer apply. Children will always be better adapted to a changing environment than their parents—less committed to obsolete agendas. The democratic family—like democracy itself—is a system that maximizes the availability of agenda-free individuals. In a democracy, as Follett says, the goal of education is to train citizens in "the power to make a new choice at every moment."

In the past decade this characteristic American child-orientedness has undergone a severe decline. According to a recent congressional study, we now stand last among industrialized nations in providing for our children.

"THE PEOPLE ARE CHILDREN"

Authoritarian individuals like to use the parent-child relation as a model for political relationships—the rulers seen as parents who guide, protect, and discipline the silly, unruly masses, who are so very likely to do the wrong thing because the simple creatures don't know what's good for them.

This analogy is badly flawed, for the authoritarian ideal is static—masters remain masters and slaves remain slaves—but children grow up and in time supersede their parents.

Democratic families try to facilitate this process and prepare their children for self-mastery. Authoritarians resist it in both the family and the body politic. Authoritarian parents try to maintain social inequality even with middle-aged children, and authoritarian rulers are antagonistic to anything that will help the public "grow up"—such as the exposure of secrets or the expenditure of funds for education.

This difference reflects the contrasting educational goals of democrats and authoritarians. In a democracy, the fundamental goal of education is *development*. For authoritarians it is *obedience*. What authoritarians want children to learn is their "place" in society. The idea of children becoming curious, creative, or original gives them hives.

To the authoritarian mind the world is permanent and fixed—any departure from their rectilinear concept of it is seen as decay. Society is a series of slots, and education a process of molding people to fit into those slots. To the authoritarian, children are not complex beings of infinite and uncharted potentiality—they are simply a sloppy throng of round pegs in desperate need of being squared up.

THE "BASICS" IN AN AUTHORITARIAN SOCIETY

This is the reason why authoritarian educators call for "a return to basics," and the elimination of "educational frills." The "basics" are the basics of two centuries ago, the "frills" are attempts—some successful, some not—to involve students in the present and the future. Underlying these so-called frills is the idea that the natural curiosity and motivation of the student should be kept alive at all costs. For boredom is the greatest enemy of learning, and when the brightest students find school boring—as they usually do in traditional authoritarian schools—it is an incalculable loss.

But there is a hidden agenda in this concern with "basics." What characterizes "the basics" above all is that they are fixed and arbitrary. The student is told how to write, how to spell, how to add and subtract, what to read and how to interpret what is read. There is very little room for exploration, for discovery, for putting together old facts in new ways. There is no need to think, only to remember. It is the intellectual equivalent of boot camp.

The call for "a return to basics" has a covert message, which can be translated simply as "we should spend less money on education." The authoritarian senses intuitively that an ignorant populace is more likely to be an obedient one. Less money for education means larger classes. Larger classes mean that less time will be spent learning and more time keeping order. Students in such classes will learn little except how to take orders and how to keep quiet.

Children learn by doing. This is how we learn to walk and talk, to ride a bike, to drive a car. We don't learn by sitting straight in a chair and having someone tell us how to do it. "As we perform a certain activity," Mary Parker Follett reminds us, "our thought towards it changes and that changes our activity." But in a large, authoritarian classroom there is very little opportunity for doing, only for rote repetition and the application of unanalyzed principles and formulae. There is little true education here—students are merely taught to take a great deal of nonsense on faith. This will prepare them to live in the kind of society in which authoritarians feel comfortable—where people know only what their ruler chooses to tell them and authority is never questioned—but it is an abominable preparation for life in a free democratic society.

A first-grade teacher once told me about going into a new school and finding the students all sitting mutely at their desks. "It was so *quiet!* How can they learn anything if they're not talking?" Her response was based on the democratic approach of learning by doing, by experimenting and testing the world and making knowledge your own.

Democracy is based on participation, and if students are not in a position to participate, what are they being prepared for? Democracy also depends on informed and independent minds, and how can they inform themselves if they are taught from their earliest years to remain passive no matter what nonsense is being stuffed down their throats?

The thrust of our current educational system—the obsession with product, with SAT scores, with grade-point averages—leads naturally to the mentally moribund college student who asks continually, "Will this be on the exam?" and thence smoothly forward to the bureaucrat who wants everything in writing so he can "cover his ass," and who trusts only what can be quantified and manipulated statistically. The kind of bureaucrat who compiled body counts in Vietnam. The kind of bureaucrat who can't see people in front of him—only their files, ID numbers, and constructed résumés. The kind of bureaucrat who is skilled at finding flaws and imperfections, but couldn't recognize a new idea if it bit him on the neck and drew blood.

Early in 1989 the National Assessment of Educational Progress reported that students taught by traditional methods were unable to reason or think for themselves, and that teachers would have to become less authoritarian for more sophisticated learning to occur. This was no news to good teachers, and will probably be ignored by the authoritarians who so often make educational policy.

The middle-class American child has at least a chance of receiving an education in which this kind of active, participatory learning is possible. But most working-class children are packed into classrooms that are run like boot camps and help track them into authoritarian work situations. Our educational system—despite all the rags-to-riches myths attached to it—seems designed to maintain a rigid class structure with as little movement between the classes as possible. Our schools—especially as crippled by the authoritarian policies of the last decade—seem designed to keep people stuck in the social stratum into which they were born.

The Carnegie Foundation for the Advancement of Teaching found in a recent study that more than two-thirds of the nation's teachers instruct children who live in poverty, who are undernourished, in poor health, abused, or neglected. This is a sorry record for a democracy, for a nation that believes itself to be child-centered, for a nation that pretends to believe in the future.

EXTRACURRICULAR "BASICS"

School isn't the only way children learn. The world is brimming with information, available to any active, curious person. Even TV, our most loathed and yet most used source of information, probably gives the child more information in a week about the society he or she lives in than the average authoritarian school does in a year. It is a distorted and unreal picture, but in comparison with the average American history text it comes off rather well. Both contain more fantasy than reality, but the TV fantasies are at least current.

The big problem with TV (as so many critics have pointed out) is that, like the authoritarian school, it encourages passivity. If participation is the soul of democracy then anything that encourages spectatorship is to be viewed with mistrust, and it cannot be denied that TV has replaced innumerable participatory activities. While the *content* of TV is ambiguous from a democratic viewpoint the *process* of TV watching is inherently destructive to democracy.

Another unfortunate trend is the increasing bureaucratization of athletic activities for children (Little League, etc.). When children play by themselves they are training for democracy. The uncertainties and imperfections of available playing fields ("if it hits the tree it's a double"), and the fluctuating numbers of players ("you got Louie so we get the extra player") call for the continual making, modifying, and discarding of rules. This is done collectively, by agreement. No adult is around to hand down edicts or resolve disputes. All free play, physical and otherwise, is democracy in action, and has been since the beginning of time.

Much of this is now gone. Adults have usurped the play of children and converted it into an authoritarian activity. Adults establish the rules and enforce them; there is no democratic negotiation. In many contests I have seen, the adults seem more obsessed with the outcome than the players. They scream with rage over the failings of their own and other people's children. The games do not seem to be played for pleasure, only to win—perhaps to bring some vicarious triumphs into the unsatisfying lives of the parents. The children learn to be competitive and follow orders—excellent training for the army—but they do not learn how to live in a democratic society. From a democratic viewpoint, the intrusion of adults into the play of children must be deemed an unqualified disaster.

Children raised with a basically democratic vision can survive many authoritarian experiences without altering that vision. I myself was educated in traditional schools, and although I was intensely bored, I can't say I was marked by it. It was simply a waste of time and a lost opportunity for learning. I played the game and succeeded, but it never once occurred to me that there was any connection between the avid reading I did on my own and what went on in school. (Like many people, I developed an almost permanent loathing for authors whose books we had to read in school.) That school could be a place where ideas were exchanged—where you could think and talk about important questions—was inconceivable.

For me the authoritarianism of school was balanced by the democracy of play. But if *all* a child's experiences are framed in an authoritarian mode, some of it will begin to rub off; and it is disconcerting that the typical American childhood seems to be drifting in that direction.

ADVANCED "BASICS"

For the rapidly decreasing number of Americans who are able to afford it, college is supposed to restore a modicum of democracy to the educational process, but this is true in only a very small number of settings. For students at many universities—especially the larger ones—college is simply high school all over again, one more dehumanizing bureaucracy. As Baritz points out, "higher education is as bureaucratic in its form and substance as the military."

Authoritarianism in education takes forms so familiar to us that it seems almost persnickety to call attention to them. My intent is merely to show how deeply and comfortably embedded we are in our authoritarian past, not to argue that this or that pedagogical custom will stunt growth or engender political masochism. Each may in and of itself be harmless.

The most obvious authoritarian holdover in education is the obsession with ranking—with placing individuals above and below one another on some sort of scale. We do this first of all by the system of consecutive classes—first grade, second grade, junior, senior, etc.—which takes no account of the fact that people do not learn in numbered increments, but in bursts, and at uneven and unpredictable rates. Nor is intelligence measured out in years, or in accumulated obedience. Yet people are defined this way, by category ("she's a senior"). And within each "class" (the word itself is revealing) students are ranked by grades, and defined as such ("she's an A student").

In addition, the material to be learned is arranged in artificial categories, and artificial rankings are created within these. This system is a vestige of the slaveholding tradition of keeping information hidden from the subject classes—protecting it with esoteric jargon. Medicine, law, and many of the sciences, for example, disguise very commonplace ideas in Greek and Latin terminology whose only function is to hide understanding from the "common" people.

ACADEMIC BORDER GUARDS

The division of knowledge into departments or disciplines is a holdover from feudal real estate customs and the obsession with classification that afflicted the medieval clergy. James Gleick, in his book on chaos theory, points out that this system is a serious impediment to scientific progress and tends to block the acceptance of new ideas. Scientific revolutions, he observes, tend to arise from people "straying outside the normal bounds of their specialties." Chaos theorists—the current revolutionaries in science—were all interdisciplinary mavericks, and all met with resistance and hostility. For years their interests were considered illegitimate, their research proposals turned down, their thesis prospectuses rejected, their articles refused for publication.

Each discipline, furthermore, is structured hierarchically, so that the student is forced to learn the material in certain order. In many cases this order is completely arbitrary. There are some areas of knowledge that presuppose others, but this is the exception rather than the rule. The main function of this rigid control is to ensure that the student learns to look at reality through the lenses of that particular discipline—absorbing its conventions, prejudices, and worldview.

This is not a conscious goal, of course. Most academics sincerely believe that there is only one path to the truth and the student must be led carefully along it. But fashions change, even in the sciences, and the truth of one decade becomes the quackery of the next, as when doctors say, without a shred of embarrassment or diminution of arrogance, "Oh, we no longer do that operation—we *now* believe...." or a scientist says, "No reputable biologist (chemist, physicist, palaeontologist, or whatever) thinks *that* anymore."

But the discarding of useless academic fashions and outmoded theories would take place a lot more quickly if students weren't required to absorb information in quite so controlled a manner. Learning at a university is a little like being taken through the spook house at an amusement park—one has the sense of going on a long twisting road, but when you turn the lights on it's just one little room with a lot of corners and a winding bit of track. To turn on the lights—to learn things in the "wrong" order—would shake up traditional arrangements of ideas. It is no accident that some of the most creative and radical thinkers in every era have been self-educated.

This turnstile approach to education—which says, in effect, that if you want to go to New York or San Francisco you must first spend specified amounts of time in Memphis, Indianapolis, Oklahoma City, Butte, and Phoenix—is not only cumbersome but demotivating. Why not let the student go where he or she wants?

It will be objected that the analogy is unfair, since you don't have to know Butte to understand San Francisco, but you do have to know math to understand physics. But a person who plunges into physics, eager to learn, and discovers this need, will approach math with a very different attitude than one who is simply told that you must learn X before we will even let you look at Y. No one had to persuade me to take statistics in graduate school once I had tried to make sense out of some research data without it.

Adults as well as children learn by doing—by trying things out, making mistakes, failing, and trying again. This is the democratic approach to learning. The authoritarian way is to say, "We already know the Truth, and hence every conceivable error that can ever be made, and we will save you from the humiliating experience of failure; simply follow our directions and we will lead you along the Only True Path."

Most of these hierarchical arrangements are completely arbitrary. It is rarely necessary to have had an introductory course in sociology or psychology or political science or history or literature or anthropology to understand the "advanced" courses in these subjects. One might in fact learn a great deal more freed from the stultifying effect of each field's hoary preconceptions and unexamined conventions. Introductory courses are notoriously tedious, save on those rare occasions when some eager assistant professor, unacquainted with the rules for getting ahead in a university, goes out of his or her way to make it exciting.

There are dedicated teachers in every university—trying in every possible way to arouse, enhance, or facilitate the desire to learn—but they have a hard time of it. Their popularity, the excitement they create, is looked upon with suspicion by their more traditional colleagues. They have trouble getting tenure because they are more interested in teaching than in writing and research; and universities, like all bureaucracies, tend to reward those activities that can be quantified and will enhance their image. Hence those who write a great deal and regard teaching as an unpleasant ancillary chore (and I must admit I was one of these) find their path to tenure smooth, while the dedicated teachers are scorned and cast out. Their very success with students is held against them. They are accused of either entertaining or being manipulated by the students and of "lowering academic standards."

The assumption underlying these accusations is that learning should be arduous, tedious, and unpleasant, and that if students enjoy it and are excited by it something underhanded is going on and should be squelched as quickly as possible. Knowledge must be doled out sparingly, lest the wrong people get hold of it and use it in the wrong way. Authoritarians love to say that "a little knowledge is a dangerous thing." But *no* knowledge is the most dangerous thing of all.

THE IVORY FORTRESS

By virtue of their transience, students tend to have little power in the system that is supposed to serve them. In the university they constitute an inferior subject class, and they are approved of by the society as a whole only if they are inconspicuous or very far away. Americans feel deeply for students who march and demonstrate in China and Prague, but are extremely critical of those who do it in the United States or Latin America, although they are, of course, exactly the same breed of troublesome idealists saying exactly the same things. Some of the people who were horrified by the events in Beijing in 1989 were cheering when riot troops and helicopters attacked, clubbed, gassed, and shot American students during the sixties.

Even some liberal academics—ardent supporters of democracy in Mississippi and self-determination in Southeast Asia—found these notions reprehensible when students in the sixties began to apply them to their immediate environment. They were irate when they saw their carefully controlled environment unraveling—when students flocked to marathon teach-ins on world events, deserting their tidy classes.

Academia seems to act as a kind of insect trap for obsessive-compulsive personalities—it attracts them in larger numbers than other institutions and they tend to accumulate there. They prefer a tightly ordered environment over which they have complete control. They like to design things on paper and hate to see them altered. A faculty debate on the issue of whether a science requirement should consist of six credits or eight can go on for months, with the bulk of Western civilization brought in to justify positions on either side.

LICENSE FOR MEDIOCRITY

Many of those concerned about the decline of democracy in America have singled out the professions for particular attention. James Fallows comments on the trend toward a kind of Mandarin order— based on educational tracking and credentialing—in place of the free-ranging, unbounded, self-defining democratic initiative that created the promising society America once was.

It is always tempting to attribute wisdom to people who claim it—especially when they have banded together and agreed to attribute it to each other. This is the problem with professional licensing—it tells us that our own criteria for evaluating competence are of no consequence, that we should rely exclusively on the criteria the professionals themselves have set up. One becomes an expert by taking certain courses and/or being approved by other experts. A profession is a kind of union against the consumer—a device for ensuring that the consumer cannot choose a healer or legal adviser simply on the basis of past performance at a price established in a free and open market.

As Fallows points out, there is often very little relationship between the skills required to obtain credentials and those required to practice effectively in the field. Professional licensing systems make it possible for many individuals too incompetent to practice in a free and open democratic market to make a good living simply by going to school and passing examinations.

Fallows observes that once a professional passes the initiation tests demanded by his particular sodality, his or her competence may never again be subject to review. Once having entered the hallowed fold, the licensed tend to be immune from later scrutiny.

Not only may they diminish in skill, knowledge, and morality without fear—some professionals are inclined to believe that their certification entitles them to exercise their "expert" status in areas in which they have no particular experience or competence. Doctors, for example, are viewed by many naive people, including themselves, as competent to speak with authority on virtually any subject; and even a Ph.D. has a range of credibility far beyond whatever particular assemblage of meticulous details gave rise to it.

What is dangerous is the claim made by professionals that they know better than we do what is good for us. And this is dangerous only if we believe it. Many people, for example, will consult a doctor or a lawyer on the recommendation of a colleague—though such recommendations are usually made on the basis of personal friendship, obligation, or hearsay. Unless the referring professional has actually been treated or represented by this colleague, the recommendation is usually worthless.

Can one trust the recommendation of a doctor, for example, when doctors will not criticize a colleague to "outsiders" even when he or she is guilty of gross negligence or lethal incompetence? A demented gynecologist was recently slapped on the wrist for performing crippling and grotesque operations on the vaginas of women without their consent—supposedly to enhance their sexual response, but actually creating incapacitating pain. Despite the fact that surgeons for miles around not only knew what he was doing but were kept busy (and well-paid) trying to undo the damage he had wreaked, he was able to mutilate hundreds of women over a twenty-two year period without ever being challenged by another doctor. This demonstrates the limits of "medical ethics," or the ethics of any group placed beyond the reach of democratic controls.

Intelligent people select a professional on the only reasonable basis on which one can make such judgments: the reports of satisfied customers combined with one's own experience. It is the wearer, not the shoemaker, who is the best judge of whether or not the shoe fits—a fundamental democratic principle that the medical profession seems to have forgotten.

I place particular stress on medicine because it is the most powerful stronghold of authoritarianism in the United States today, outside of the military. Where else can one find such rigid insistence on titles and deference? Doctors complain about the high cost of malpractice insurance, but a Harvard study found recently that only one out of ten patients injured by medical negligence ever files suit, so successfully has the industry managed to overawe the nation with its authority. American doctors have established a monopoly over the healing art that is unparalleled in the Western world—to the point where competitors can actually be jailed for "practicing without a license."

Fallows is particularly concerned with the way educational tracking has begun to create a special Mandarin class in our society. He points out that the IQ test is the most common device used to *class*-ify individuals in this way. Since the test is largely one of familiarity and comfort with middle-class urban culture, it is primarily a measure of social standing—immigrants and people from rural areas do poorly until they become acclimated, for example, whereupon their scores shoot up dramatically.

Tests—IQ or otherwise—measure the ability to take tests and often very little else. Fallows points out that people who have been determined by IQ test scores to be morons or imbeciles have subsequently become successful managers and professionals. A fundamental principle of democratic education is that people develop uniquely, unevenly, erratically, and continually. Only in an authoritarian society are a priori decisions made about a child's future. In a true democracy, competence is demonstrated, not scored. Fallows observes that "America was built by people who broke out of categories, defied probabilities, and changed their fate." Has this democratic potentiality been permanently stifled in our society today?

CHAPTER 7

Walls against Womanhood

Have we forgotten all those old legends...about dragons that transform themselves into princesses at the last moment? Is it possible that all the dragons in our lives are just princesses—waiting for us to act, this once, with grace and courage?

—Rainer Maria Rilke

One of the more astonishing achievements of the authoritarian era was that it created social structures in which the most important social functions were performed by the people with the lowest status.

Raising food and raising children—two activities essential for human survival—were the responsibility of two groups that stood at the very bottom of authoritarian society: peasants and women. Peasants raised the food that fed the society, women bore and raised the children that perpetuated it. Without their activities life would have ended, yet so discredited, so inglorious, so degraded was their status that those with more exalted positions took the most excruciating pains to avoid having themselves identified with either group.

As we have seen, peasants were so devalued that the nourishing and fertile earth, on which all humans depend for their existence, came to be considered impure by association. The "upper" strata had clean hands—no dirt under the nails—and the ultimate sign of social elevation was never to touch the earth at all—to be carried or to have carpets continually beneath one's feet. Dirt became "dirty," soil became "soiled," and the once holy earth—the mother of all life—rejected and despised.

Efforts by authoritarian men to avoid being identified as women have been even more extreme. Just as words for peasant became terms of abuse, so did words for femaleness: *effeminate, soft, womanish, weak sister, sob sister, sissy, Mary, nervous Nellie, pussy,* and so forth. To call a man a woman has for several thousand years been the deepest possible insult. As a result, maleness has come to be defined the world over in largely negative terms— as an *absence* of femaleness: *not* to show emotion, *not* to be demonstrative, *not* to be "soft," and so on.

THE DEEPEST PREJUDICE

When democracy started to make its first tentative challenges to the global sway of authoritarianism, the terror of getting one's hands calloused began to decline, and in modern society there is a sturdy tradition of working-class chic. But the terror of sexual misidentification seems as violent as ever in authoritarian societies. This suggests that the subjugation of women is even more deeply rooted in authoritarianism than the class system itself. Or to put it another way, that *sexism is the greatest obstacle to the achievement of full democracy in any society.*

This is apparent in the fact that while slavery was abolished in 1863, and an amendment extending to blacks the right to vote passed a few years later, a similar amendment extending the same right to women was not passed for another half-century, while the Equal Rights Amendment, giving women the same rights accorded recently freed slaves a hundred and twenty-five years ago, has still not been passed.

Some of the most exclusive clubs in the country have opened their doors to blacks, hispanics, and other minorities in recent years, but have fought bitterly to keep women out. While many "avant-garde" male writers, artists, poets, radical activists, and scholars, who pride themselves on their sensitivity to the most subtle nuances of racial and class bias, become vehemently obtuse where sexual prejudice is concerned. Revolutions have occurred all over the globe in this century—each one casting out the wealthy classes and proclaiming a new order—without any notable improvement in the position of women. This is one of the main reasons, in fact, why such revolutions tend to lapse back into authoritarianism and class privilege.

The depth of this prejudice is an extraordinary phenomenon. Familiarity has dulled our reaction to it, but it cries out for explanation. Why is the need to exclude and oppress women so deep-seated in authoritarian culture?

When the Nazi party held its first general membership meeting in 1921, one of its very first acts was to pass a resolution that women could never be admitted to positions of leadership or even sit on the executive committee of the party—an example of the indissoluble link between authoritarianism and sexism and the extreme nervousness that authoritarian men feel in the presence of feminine power. Once this feminine menace was removed, the party felt free, a few months later, to abolish all democratic and parliamentary practices, elect Adolf Hitler chairman with dictatorial powers, and begin recruiting storm troopers.

AUTHORITARIANISM AND GENDER

Authoritarianism is a male creation, founded in war. Hence the position of women underwent a sharp decline in the transition from the hunter-gatherer megaculture to authoritarianism, as Eisler and others have pointed out. Since women play such a small part in warfare, they tend to be viewed by the ruling males as unimportant—objects to be fought over, the prizes of conquest. They were at the "bottom" of society—even the "lowest" male could be a dictator in his own home.

But as we have argued (chapter 3), this debased position of women is not a mere by-product of authoritarian culture. It is the foundation on which the entire edifice rests. The warrior is created by shutting down a part of himself—by losing contact with the feelingful part of his being, the spontaneous, playful, "soft" part, the "feminine" part. He must have periods where women are excluded from his presence, lest he forget he is a block of wood, a weapon—lest their "softness" become contagious. Yet at the same time, since he has made himself only half of a full human being, he is utterly dependent on women to fill the void his self-hobbling has created. Just as the knight in shining armor would starve to death without the labor of the peasants he grinds underfoot, so would authoritarian society as a whole crumble without the integrative functions performed by women. Since the warrior cannot do without women altogether, he must mask his dependency with social disparagement.

A society can survive without violence. It can survive without domination, sadism, and exploitation. It can survive without bureaucracy, compulsive competitiveness, and runaway egoism. It can survive, in short, without any of the things authoritarianism offers, with the single exception of protection from external attack. This is why authoritarians are so addicted to finding enemies. Without enemies there is no reason for the system to exist, no justification for the oppressive social burden under which humanity has groaned for the past five thousand years.

A society can *not* survive without integration, without regeneration, without the management of human emotion. In authoritarian societies it is left almost entirely to women to perform these functions—to keep the peace, to mediate, to nurture, to bolster, to placate, to reassure—while men play the surface game of giving and taking orders.

Authoritarianism is a total system—if one piece is altered the system starts to unravel. You cannot have a fully authoritarian culture without belligerent, egocentric, macho men. You cannot have a fully democratic culture *with* them. Similarly, a fully authoritarian culture will not function without women who have been trained to be submissive and placating, and a fully democratic culture will not function *with* them. Authoritarianism depends on rigid separations and specializations. Democracy depends on full human beings having the potential to perform all functions at any given moment.

Recent studies of psychological development stress the fact that women tend to be more empathic than men and more attuned to their connections with others—more aware of the complex web of relationships in which all human beings are embedded. How much of this gender difference is innate and how much is an artifact of authoritarian socialization is impossible to determine, but it seems fair to say that in a fully democratic society the difference would be sharply reduced.

Some years ago I suggested (and other writers have since developed the notion further) that this gender difference derives from the fact that while young girls can *identify* with their mothers (still the principal caretaker in most families) as part of their maturation, boys are expected to *separate* themselves from their mothers while retaining an interest in the opposite sex—leading to a lifelong proneness to compartmentalization. But how much of this masculine need to separate and differentiate is derived from the residues of authoritarian culture—from the warrior's need to make himself into a block of wood? If there was no longer any *cultural* demand for men to deaden themselves to "softer" feelings—if they were no longer pushed by the demands of macho tradition to deny their own vulnerability—how much of this rigid abnegation of the mother would be necessary?

Obviously this question cannot be answered until the democratic megaculture is more fully developed, but in view of the distinctions made above between democratic and authoritarian ways of viewing the world, the conclusion of psychologist Carol Gilligan—that boys tend to see relationships in terms of *hierarchical* images, while girls use images of a *network* or *web*—suggests the close tie between democracy and feminism.

"A MAN'S GOTTA *NOT* DO"

Even in today's society, women tend to assume more responsibility for social integration. It is usually women who are the caretakers of relationships, although some have begun to complain about this. Men, they say, are emotionally unavailable to their partners, ignore them, don't listen to them, never try to draw them out or show interest in what concerns them. Men tend to abdicate responsibility, in other words, for the maintenance of the relationship. They often seem unable or unwilling to express feelings directly (except for anger, the one permissible emotion for authoritarians) and to depend heavily on their partners to interpret their emotional states and anticipate their emotional needs.

Women are also given responsibility in most families for the maintenance of external personal relationships—mediating, interpreting, arranging gift exchanges, trading services, and organizing get-togethers (even with relatives of their male partners). And it tends to be women who oversee the ritual life of the household, keeping track of holiday observances, birthdays, and so forth.

In pre-authoritarian societies these integrative activities tended to absorb much of *everyone's* time and energy. Nothing was felt to be of greater importance than the maintenance of strong relationships. It isn't too surprising that we Americans suffer today from widespread social decay and disintegration when most of our population considers human integration less important than competitive striving.

One reason authoritarian men have difficulty attending to integrative matters is that they are so deeply involved in vertical positioning. Since women are less committed to this system, they are more often able to attend to other issues.

A study by Philip Blumstein and Pepper Schwartz bears out this difference. They examined relationships among various kinds of couples—straight, gay, married, and unmarried, and found that gender differences overwhelmed all others. Men, gay or straight, were more competitive with their partners, found it difficult to enjoy a partner's success for its own sake, and tended to see money and physical beauty as increasing power in the relationship. One of the reasons many men seem to have difficulty giving themselves to a relationship may be that they are always compulsively measuring themselves against others.

Under these circumstances it isn't too surprising that men are healthier and happier when they are married, and women when they are not; the women, after all, seem to be doing all the work.

BLAMING THE UNDERLING

The survival of any authoritarian system depends on directing blame "downwards" when anything goes wrong. This protects the ruler's image from being tarnished. Underlings are supposed to anticipate the boss's less savory wishes and to take the blame if caught redhanded. (This is the famous principle of deniability.)

Any failures within a traditional family system will similarly be blamed on the adult with the lower status—the mother—by virtue of her having been constantly on the scene. By absenting himself so much of the time, the father not only increases his status and prestige, he also escapes most of the blame for problems that arise.

A study reported in *Psychology Today* found that professional therapists, faced with any kind of psychological disturbance, almost universally blame the subject's mother for it. In a sample of 125 professional papers, 72 different disorders were attributed almost exclusively to maternal malefaction. It seems to be safer to blame the "possessive," "nagging" mother than the male-dominated system that created this behavior.

One difficulty mothers have in our society is that they are too often expected to curb their natural socializing instincts in raising male children—to give sons more latitude so as not to interfere with their becoming "real boys" (that is, insensitive, selfish, destructive, violent, and incapable of caring for themselves). Yet at the same time the boy is to be obedient to his father and outside authorities. Much has been made in the psychological literature about mothers placing their children in double binds, but much of this behavior can be traced to the double bind in which the mother herself is placed in the authoritarian family system. Perhaps the thing mothers have done that has caused the most damage to the delicate psyches of their sons has been to follow the advice of male "experts" who tell them to ignore their own needs at all times to cater to those of the growing boy. This advice, which is simply the familiar male dream of the ideal mother-slave, has caused generations of mothers to behave in unnatural and distorted ways.

Not only is the mother held responsible for relational difficulties within the family, she often is also expected to cover up for the father when he fails to give emotional support to his children. One of the more popular characters today in films and TV is the crusty, ungiving, authoritarian father who "really loves" his children but for some reason is not only incapable of expressing this love, but seems bent on trying to disprove it. He may be spiteful, rejecting, competitive, punitive, and mean, but in the end we are to understand that he really has everyone's best interests at heart. These stories are commercials for authoritarianism. They assert that it is the duty of the family to make allowances for the authoritarian father—to understand that his emotional cowardice is in the service of some higher good.

DOUBLE STANDARDS

The more absolute the power of a position in an authoritarian system, the more likely it is that virtue will automatically be attached to it. If the king is kind, he is admired for his generosity. If he is cruel, he is admired for his manliness. We may, in the light of history, say a king was good or bad, but in the moment the most important thing is that he is king, and therefore in some way admirable. There are always limits to this, because there are limits to power, but in the ideal case of an omnipotent king, morality would not apply at all. We do not say, "our God is a bad God." The God of the Old Testament is unjust, spiteful, jealous, and vain when judged in human terms, but since He makes the rules, none of this applies.

This is the reason for what has come to be called, with some indignation, the double standard. It is usually applied to sexual mores—to the fact that women have often been condemned for doing things that men were not censured for doing. In fact, when we examine sexual customs the world over and throughout history, we find that restraints on heterosexual behavior are almost all restraints on women. The rules of sexual behavior, by and large, are made by men for women, and apply to men scarcely at all.

But rules about sex are only the tip of the iceberg. The double standard applies to virtually every aspect of female behavior. Terms of superficial disapproval are often used about men in such a way as to convey overt or covert admiration: "He's a rogue, a sly dog, a handsome devil, tough sonovabitch, mean old bird, tricky devil." But this is much less frequent with women; "rogue" becomes "whore," "tough sonovabitch" becomes "nasty bitch," and so on, with no admiring smile attached. This may change as women become more equal in the society—we can see it already in the emergence of richer character roles for women in the media—but it is still very pronounced. There are very few likeable villains of the female persuasion in fiction. If women aren't "good" they tend to be viewed with humorless horror and brought to a bad end.

The amount of hatred and fear an aggressive female villain can arouse in male movie audiences is astonishing. Men's voices scream out, "Kill her! Kill her!" as if they were afraid she would jump right off the screen and attack them. (I have never heard this response to a male villain, perhaps because the camera so often looks through the eyes of the killer.)

The Good Woman in an authoritarian film is much seen and little heard. She "understands." She is the permissive mother to the male hero—undemanding, adoring, giving. A yes-woman. The Bad Woman, on the other hand, is heard a lot but never really "seen." She is alien, *other*. She may act just like an admired male hero (stubborn, pugnacious, fickle, bad-tempered, tormented, or whatever), but she is rarely admired for it.

An exception is the spirited heroine who is "tamed" by the hero. Once he kisses her she becomes an utter simp and plays no part in the rest of the action, except perhaps to get into a helpless jam and have to be rescued. This, too, is beginning to change—active heroines are appearing more and more often on the screen—but the authoritarian form is still the most common, especially in films directed toward a juvenile audience (like *The Princess Bride* and *The Little Mermaid*).

In authoritarian systems, men are continually jockeying for position and measuring themselves against each other. In order for them to keep on doing this, women have to mind the store—to smooth ruffled feathers and pour large quantities of oil on troubled waters. In other words, they must be *reactive*, focusing all their attention on mending the social fabric that men are tearing holes in with their competitive narcissism. For women to take initiative—to act in response to their own motives—is to threaten the whole system with collapse. Hence in authoritarian societies a woman who takes initiative is a Bad Woman.

Much has been written about the "whore-madonna complex" found in authoritarian societies with heavy sexual taboos—men splitting women into the mutually exclusive categories of sex object and mother. But a far more widespread form of psychological splitting is the division between the evil, mature woman who initiates things and the innocent, passive, accommodating virgin who does not. This split is not even considered pathological, at least not by males.

Women in an authoritarian society are there to do what men want, and to the extent they do this they are defined by this society as Good Women. To the extent they do what they themselves want, they are Bad Women. Men, on the other hand, are expected to do what they want and will be admired—openly or secretly—no matter how much arrogance, childishness, treachery, selfishness, dishonesty, and cruelty they display in the process. They will be admired for their energy and singlemindedness in the pursuit of their goals. Artists, writers, intellectuals, revolutionaries, performers, and entrepreneurs are especially appreciated for this; but women who approximate this singlemindedness are objects of hatred and fear, unless their achievements are performed in the service of a man—a widow carrying on a husband's business, for example, or a married woman trying to rescue her husband from danger or imprisonment.

NERVOUS LAUGHTER

Ridicule is a powerful weapon for maintaining social dominance, and women tend to be mocked particularly for traits that are in fact more characteristic of men. Women have been stereotyped, for example, as bad drivers and inveterate talkers, although in fact men have always had many more traffic accidents, and studies have shown that they tend to dominate discussions when both sexes are present, interrupting frequently, overtalking, and revealing an inability to listen. But the use of these inverted stereotypes helps men "keep the floor" and stay "in the driver's seat."

Another example is the stereotype of the Jewish American Princess—subject of countless jokes over the last decade or two. Again, the stereotype is ironic, since in perhaps no other culture are male children so elaborately enthroned. WASP culture provides an even more outrageous example, the venerable saw that Hell hath no Fury like a woman scorned. One cannot help wondering what it is these scorned women do that strikes such terror in male bosoms. Do they cry? Do they scowl? For it is *men* who tend to get violent at such times; almost every week we read about some high school boy who murders a girl for not reciprocating his affections, or a discarded lover who blows away his ex-girlfriend, or a jealous ex-husband who hacks up his wife. In many of these cases even the word *scorned* would be an exaggeration—there just doesn't seem to be any way to let these men down easily enough.

All these projective stereotypes serve to maintain the status quo. The more women are exploited and constrained, the more they will become "the other," and be feared. It is in traditional Islamic societies, for example, that we find the most vicious, tyrannical, faithless, and vengeful women in mythology and folklore.

EMOTION AND POWER

From time to time some man will remark that a woman should not be president because we would not want to have a woman's finger on the nuclear trigger while she was experiencing premenstrual stress. This, too, is projective, for women seem to be more competent than men at discharging their feelings in normal ways. It is men who bottle things up until they explode in violence. Are we really safer in the male hands of a Hitler or a Stalin? Or even in the hands of a John Kennedy playing nuclear chicken to prove to Khrushchev that he was tough? And would anyone claim that security is to be found in the emotionally alienated rationalism of an Eichmann or a Pol Pot?

Behind-the-scenes descriptions of the workings of our own government are hardly reassuring on this score. The Vietnam War, with all its useless slaughter and destruction, might have ended with no loss of American life if Johnson and Nixon had not been so caught up in street-gang values. At every point that a decision was to be made—despite all the factual input and intelligent advice—locker-room mores rose up and obliterated judgment and foresight. When the invasion of Cambodia was being discussed in the White House, Alexander Haig leapt to his feet and shouted, "The basic substance of all this is that we have to be tough." Despite all the sophisticated data gathering and analysis that went on throughout the war, the final choices were based on the mental and emotional assumptions of nine-year-old boys.

MACHO PAWNS

Men in authoritarian cultures define their masculinity negatively, by stressing that they are not women. They do this by being emotionally constipated, making their bodies stiff and rigid, looking grim and tough, and being insensitive and incapable of empathy. But it is just this rigidity, this tendency to define oneself by limiting one's options, that makes authoritarian men so easy to manipulate. Their leaders can get them to fight and kill each other merely by suggesting that they are women if they do not.

Corporations also find it easy to exploit macho workers. Their ads will sometimes actually boast of dangerous working conditions, as do the workers themselves. Many men would rather brag about how many people are killed on the job than unite to improve conditions. How many millions of men have given up their lives rather than admit they were less willing to take unnecessary risks than some fellow worker or soldier?

It is sometimes argued that we should be indulgent toward the oppression of women in certain third-world societies "because it is part of their indigenous culture," and "because men need to feel pride"—the assumption apparently being that women do not. Yet many other aspects of these cultures are being dropped without a backward glance. Why should the exploitation of women be placed in a different category from illiteracy and disease? The answer is that the exploitation of women is the keystone of any authoritarian system, and the desire to preserve it is simply the desire to preserve that system. This exploitation does not serve the male workers of such a society, it serves their authoritarian rulers. For no society can ever become fully democratic within the framework of a macho tradition.

It is no accident that the empowerment of women has begun to occur at this point in history, when the democratic megaculture is beginning to arise throughout the world. As pointed out in chapter 1, when social change occurs those who benefit least from the status quo are naturally most highly motivated to embrace the new order. Since women are far less committed to authoritarianism than men are—less beholden to it, more oppressed by it—they are perhaps in the best position to assert the values of democracy, the values of cooperation, integration, negotiation, openness, and equality.

This perhaps accounts for the increasing gender gap appearing in modern opinion polls. On most issues more women than men support democratic opinions and oppose authoritarian ones. Gilligan points out that women, accustomed to swimming in the troubled waters of emotional relationships, tend to see order where men can see only chaos. Women are more comfortable with the ambiguities, complexities, and confusions of interdependence. It is their element, their medium, and they can more easily find their place in it. Men, on the other hand, tend to be frightened by situations they cannot easily control, and are more prone to escape fantasies—fantasies of driving off on some empty highway to some controllable never-never-land. This is another reason why women should—initially at least—feel more at home in the democratic megaculture that is to come.

CHAPTER 8

The Rectangular Mind

Perhaps the only limits to the human mind are those we believe in.

—Willis Harman, *Global Mind Change*

Democracy is the art of thinking independently together.

—Alexander Meiklejohn

People throughout the world are calling for democratic reforms, yet resisting the accompanying mental changes that alone will ensure the longevity of these reforms. This is only natural. A cultural change of the magnitude envisioned here will take many generations to complete. It is difficult to open our minds to new realities when they are still cluttered with the mental baggage left there by the previous tenant.

In the United States, for example, we have never had a military coup or battles to decide conflicting claims to the "throne." We have had a partial democracy for two centuries and have presumably left all that authoritarian nonsense behind us. But in our language it persists. An attempt to garner votes is called a *campaign*, and there are *battles, strategies, camps, forces, offensives,* and so on. Military language is so much a part of our thinking that few people even laughed a few years ago when a headline announced that President Reagan had declared war on violence.

DUALISM

Dividing life into eithers and ors can be useful at times, but our authoritarian heritage sometimes makes it difficult for us to see beyond these dualities to the totality that embraces them. The authoritarian universe is permanently and inalterably split into warring elements—good versus evil, black versus white, higher versus lower—a world founded on irreconcilable strife. This obsession with warfare often prevents us from seeing the larger unity that embraces light and dark, female and male, capitalism and communism.

Authoritarians also have trouble seeing *more* than two sides to anything, and our own two-party system is a hangover from this archaic dualism. The range and variety of opinion on any issue must somehow be squeezed into the corset of paired opposition, to be decided in the "battle" of the ballot box.

Our approach to social issues reflects this residual militarism. We *fight* disease rather than healing people; *declare war* on poverty, crime, and drugs, rather than addressing their causes; and boast about *conquering* inflation, *wiping out* pollution, and so on (which is perhaps one reason why these problems continually worsen). Corporations *invade* new markets, doctors *attack* infection with *magic bullets*, lawyers have courtroom *battles*. Attempts to balance, integrate, resolve, or heal seem to produce yawns in this bloodthirsty society we inhabit.

It is this same authoritarian mental baggage that makes us rely so heavily on banning things that create problems. We seem to believe that if we forbid something to exist, it will go away. The Prohibition Amendment was our most massive experiment with this approach, and although today we smile at its naiveté, we are engaged in a full-scale repetition of that disaster with our "war on drugs." This preference for repressive force also governs our approach to ecological problems—J.E. Lovelock argues that we should be finding *uses* for toxic waste, as nature does: "The negative, unconstructive response of prohibition by law seems as idiotic as legislating against the emission of dung by cows."

The idea of "making war" on a problem assumes that it can be "conquered" once and for all—that some sort of "all-out assault" will result in an ultimate "victory" over the problem, a "final solution" that will put an end to it. But social problems do not end. They may be dealt with more or less creatively and successfully, but they do not go away. Disease, poverty, crime, pollution, alcoholism, and so on, have been the object of many "wars," but they have not disappeared. The problems of being human beings—living together, having conflicting aims and desires, suffering discontents and inequities—are always present. Problems are not "over" merely because we are currently managing successfully to keep them in bounds. This belief that problems are best dealt with by some sort of coercive action is another reason why authoritarian systems deal so poorly with change.

VERTICALITY

We discussed in chapter 3 how the idea of physical elevation came to be associated with social value. In most written languages *higher* holds the meaning of "closer to the rulers," and an obsession with hierarchy lies at the core of authoritarian thinking—everything is seen as owing allegiance to something "higher." This bureaucratic vision is even applied to the human organism: the body must obey the mind, the feelings must obey the will, and so on.

The same vision proclaims that nature must obey man. Nature becomes not an entity of which we are participating segments, but something "below" us, a "lower element," something to be subjugated, enslaved, manipulated, controlled. The result of this odd vision is not that we will destroy the planet—this is merely another expression of the same authoritarian view of nature as subjugated and helpless—but only that we will destroy ourselves. As Lovelock points out, the planet is quite capable of taking care of itself, and will with or without us.

THE MASK OF OBJECTIVITY

Scientists as a group have generally placed themselves firmly on the side of democracy, quite rightly regarding the authoritarian addiction to secrecy and rigid control as lethal to scientific progress. They have often spoken out for the open exchange of ideas, opposing bureaucratic constraints on the free flow of information.

Scientists also like to claim that science helps immunize democratic populations against the irrational appeals of authoritarianism, but this claim is far less convincing. Germany boasted one of the world's most prestigious scientific communities before World War II—one that nonetheless (with some exceptions) served Hitler enthusiastically—and many scientists in both the United States and the USSR became willing servants of Cold Warriors. Science as it has traditionally been practiced has many points of incompatibility with the democratic ethos.

In the first place, the vaunted rationalism of science is often merely a guise for the zealous suppression of feeling which authoritarianism has always demanded. This bias against emotion is certainly not scientific in any real sense, but it has always been an important convention in the field. Modern science originated in a world that saw itself as a hierarchy with God at the top and the poorest classes toward the bottom, just above the animals and even "lower" forms of life. Emotion was felt to reside down at the bottom of the ladder, while abstract thought popped right up to the top. Much of this particular warp survives in scientific thought today.

But rationality does not exist in a vacuum. It cannot generate motives. Rationality has to do with means, not ends. It tells us the most reasonable way to achieve our goals, but it cannot tell us what those goals are. Einstein and Eichmann were equally "rational," but they had very different goals. The most irrational of all beliefs is the belief in rationalism—that is, the belief that ends can be selected through a consideration of means—and the most subjective of all delusions is the belief that objectivity is possible. Reason is the tool we use to carry out our motives. To pretend that we are *governed* by it is merely to blind ourselves to our own motivation. When we persuade ourselves that not only our means but our *motives* are rational we are averting our eyes from our own needs, desires, feelings, impulses, and purposes—and from this internal secrecy, as we all know, no end of mischief can arise.

In recent years several writers, notably Evelyn Fox Keller and Donna Haraway, have pointed out that far from being neutral, the scientific method itself is governed by motives that can only be described as authoritarian: the need to distance oneself emotionally from the rest of life, to control it, to dominate it rather than participate *with* it. The goal of the traditional scientist is not merely to understand, but to *predict*—not merely to comprehend nature but to enslave it, to "harness" it to his own power drive, to force it to do his bidding, to make it work for him as an involuntary servant.

The obsession with "objectivity" has another motive: the desire to maintain the status quo. For any approach that anchors itself firmly at the center of general opinion, and looks briefly to either side before returning to its safe haven, will tend to be regarded as objective. It is easier for those who are satisfied with things as they are to appear neutral, unemotional, and unmotivated. The motivational impetus of those who seek change is more visible. They are more likely to be seen as "shrill" or "strident." They wear their purposes on their sleeve. Those who seek change—those who attempt to challenge the powers that be—must speak louder in order to be heard at all, and the demand for a quieter, "more objective" voice is an effective way to silence them. If official government sources were to saturate the media with the insistent claim that a current White House incumbent was the reincarnation of Abraham Lincoln, and some private citizen were to protest that on the contrary he was a fraud and a charlatan, you could count on the media to assert piously that this lone dissenter should have presented a more "objective" and "balanced" view, showing "both sides of the question."

When dissenting voices grow in number, authoritarian leaders will often stave off change by calling for further study. This has such a sensible ring to it that to object seems like mere impatience, even when delay might be more hazardous than precipitous action. But, as Follett points out, "the accumulation of information does not overcome diversity."

THE BUILDING-BLOCK MODEL

Although modern science has been an important force in bringing about the decline of authoritarianism, its own roots lie deep in the authoritarian age, and it has by no means freed itself from the hierarchical assumptions of the era in which it began.

In the beginning scientists saw themselves as engaged in rearing an edifice. This edifice rested on foundation stones which had to be absolutely firm since they were holding up the rest of the structure. The Bible and Aristotle were the original cornerstones, but as science became more empirical these rather risky underpinnings were gradually replaced by "facts." Science rested, it was argued, on a foundation of fact. They had to be "hard" facts (however this was defined by current fashion), for if a single flaw could be found in one of them, the entire edifice would crumble. Hence inconvenient factual discrepancies have sometimes been stubbornly ignored for long periods in the history of science—an obvious hoax like the Piltdown Man went undiscovered for a half century in our own era, for example. If you view knowledge as a building that will collapse utterly if one of its foundation stones proves faulty, you will be understandably reluctant to see anything wrong with that stone.

Contemporary science employs a more democratic metaphor. It sees itself as a continually evolving, constantly shifting, gravity-free holographic approximation. There are no foundation stones. There are only theories. You have a theory, you test it in practice, if it works you adhere to it until a better one comes along—until knowledge advances so far that the tiny errors you could barely make out, and easily live with, loom large enough to force changes in the theory. There is no "place to stand" in democratic science, only room for improvement.

Yet old habits of mind persist, even among the most sophisticated. Heisenberg, for example, remarked that as a result of quantum theory "the *foundations* of physics have started moving; and . . . this motion has caused the feeling that *the ground would be cut* from science." And Einstein said that "it was as if the *ground had been pulled out from under one*, with *no firm foundation* to be seen anywhere, upon which one could have built."

This feeling of disorientation, this psychological earthquake, comes from the collapse of the erector-set model of science that goes all the way back to Aristotle. It is an image copied, not from nature, but from social history—from the social pyramid in which a king stands on the backs of men with weapons, who in turn stand on the backs of those who produce the necessities of life and keep the whole thing from toppling to the ground. And just as this image has come to seem less and less relevant as a model of our social world, so has it come to seem less and less relevant to science.

But the process has only just begun. Many scientists and most of the lay population still cling, consciously or unconsciously, to the building-block model. Many years ago, for example, a visiting speaker delivered a brilliant lecture on American society at a university to which I was then attached, and after the lecture I asked a colleague what he thought of it. "Well," he said, "early on he said something about Chinese history that didn't sound right to me, so during the break I ran upstairs and looked it up and he was wrong; I didn't listen to anything he said after that."

Space exploration will make the democratic model of science easier to grasp. For people who could never conceive of a gravity-free state, the building-block model made sense in a primitive way. It is no accident that the democratic model began to emerge with the recognition that the seemingly universal human experience of a severe gravitational pull is in fact a local and variable phenomenon, and that *up* and *down* have no meaning outside our little corner of the universe. For "higher" and "lower" are the heart and soul of authoritarianism, and the ability to see beyond these arbitrary categories is the ability to free ourselves forever from their petty, cruel, and stupefying chains.

THE DECLINE OF DUALISM IN SCIENCE

Modern physics has also freed science from the mental constrictions of authoritarian dualism. It is no longer necessary to engage in verbal fisticuffs over whether an event is due to Cause A or Cause B, for single causes are as obsolete as trench warfare and the cavalry charge.

Modern science tends to be integrative rather than divisive. It searches for the relative contribution of many factors. It sees each aspect of the world as part of a larger whole, rather than as an individual warring element. The old walls that barricaded the mind from the body, the spiritual from the material, and science from religion are rapidly dissolving. "An elementary particle," for example, "is not a *thing* but a set of relationships," and the world itself a "complicated tissue of events." The old mental apartheids—the rigid categories and uncrossable boundaries—are being abandoned in science, just as they are being abandoned in the social and political sphere. A particle is at the same time a wave, while matter is just frozen energy. And since it has been demonstrated that things do not have to be physically connected to be part of one another, it has become easier to see the universe as the hunter-gatherers saw it—as a living organism of which we and all living things are component parts.

The traditional scientific obsession with control—with analysis and causation—made it difficult until recently to understand cybernetic systems, which cannot be comprehended causally. It is not accidental that the ability to think beyond causality and control is concurrent with the recent explosion of democratic ideas. They are of a piece. The old notion of a mechanistic universe set in motion by a Higher Authority—a closed system with immutable rules and predictable outcomes—had obvious appeal to the authoritarian mind. Chaos theory was initially resisted by scientists because it attacked this linear vision at its core. All unruly nonlinear data had been treated as noise until chaos theorists pointed out that the noise was in fact the message.

The Second Law of Thermodynamics, for example, reflects the authoritarian vision of social and psychological existence as a set of delicate structures fighting a strong gravitational pull toward disorder. Human beings were viewed as incorrigibly entropic: only a strong hand could keep the mind from sinking lethargically into emotion, the will into pleasure, the ego into the id, the spirit into the flesh, the state into anarchy. The Second Law echoed the familiar sense of hanging on to a linear mental and social order in the face of an unruly mob of barely governable impulses.

By contrast, the implicit worldview of chaos theory is creative: it sees complex order as bubbling up out of simple processes. When chaos scientist Doyne Farmer talks of "the spontaneous emergence of self-organization," he is defining democracy. Even the language that chaos theorists employ is suffused with democratic metaphors: they talk of "choice," "variety," "opportunity"; of "dynamics freed . . . from the shackles of . . . predictability"; of "systems liberated to randomly explore their every dynamical possibility." Their methodology reflects decentralizing forces as well, with its preference for modest computer terminals that "allow for flexible interaction."

Science is beginning to turn away from the examination of component parts in a mechanistic universe, looking instead at the processes that govern the whole. Bell's theorem and the Einstein-Podolsky-Rosen experiment—demonstrating that the universe cannot be understood as a collection of separate entities linked by physical and local communication, but only as an inseparable totality—brought science back into agreement with what Willis Harman calls "perennial wisdom," the vision that enlightened men and women of every age have shared.

The timing of this is not happenstance. Science has stumbled onto the oneness of the universe just as the peoples of the world are being forced to confront the fact that they constitute a single organic community. Old customs take time to die out, and it will be generations before we have shed the mental habits of authoritarianism, but change is taking place today in every aspect of human thought.

CHAPTER 9

The Myths of Slavery

In the end, the machinery of repression is more likely to vanish, not with war or revolution, but with a puff, or the voice of falling leaves.

—Bruce Chatwin, *Utz*

The stories that people like to hear and tell are a good index of their cultural preoccupations. The themes that appear over and over again in a particular culture reveal that culture's major tensions, stresses, and fault lines. European dramas of the seventeenth and eighteenth centuries, for example, tended to revolve around conflicts between love and masculine honor (especially in Latin countries), while Victorian dramas tended to focus more on conflicts between love and social convention; modern American films seem obsessed with crime and violence, and so on. But beyond these local differences are megacultural themes that dominate storytelling at all levels, from children's fairy tales and cartoons to sitcoms and murder mysteries. An examination of these themes will suggest how much of our collective consciousness is still in the grip of authoritarian anxieties and concerns.

We can barely conceive, for example, of a world in which no one tells stories about men slaying monsters and rescuing women. Many people assume that tales of conquering heroes, helpful and accommodating maidens, and wars between Good and Evil forces have all somehow wormed their way into our unconscious via the DNA.

Conservatives have always sought to portray the status quo as a natural and/or God-given condition. The divine right of kings, slavery, the oppression of women, child labor—there is scarcely any human folly that has never enjoyed this elevated status at one time or another. And myths are no exception. Hearing the favorite morality tales of authoritarianism, people tend to speak in hushed tones of universal myths and archetypes.

Yet many of what we consider to be universal themes are not found in surviving hunter-gatherer tribes and seem to be the exclusive property of authoritarian cultures.

Authoritarian myths deal with the social and emotional problems that arise in societies that are—or have been—primarily devoted to war and conquest. There are three such problems that all authoritarian societies must solve:

(1) They must convince themselves that it is a good idea to kill and enslave strangers. This leads to the myth of the Triumph of Good over Evil.

(2) They must convince themselves that they will get along best by obediently subjecting themselves to the commands of a single leader, chief, or king. This leads to the myth of the Heroic Leader—the One Who Overcomes the Many.

(3) Males must convince themselves that it is necessary to renounce any emotional vulnerability that might interfere with their

performance as killers. This vulnerability—the son's need for the mother—and its renunciation are expressed (in projective form) as the myth of the Slaying of the Needy Mother (often appearing in the guise of a large messy dragon).

But while these myths offer ideals that are both gripping and inspiring, they also raise problems. If Good is always triumphant, why bother to fight? If our Heroic Leader is so perfect, what do we do when he dies? And if the Needy Mother has been slain, what do we do for love? Each of the three myths requires a qualifier to answer these questions.

How can we maintain a belligerent spirit, for example, if a final victory of Good over Evil is inevitable? To solve this dilemma it is necessary to invoke the myth of the Immortal Evil Adversary, who is always overcome but always rises again to provide fresh martial motivation.

And what do we do with our obedience when our perfect Heroic Leader weakens, sickens, grows old, or falls prey to the corrupting influence of power? To cope with this dilemma, it is necessary to invoke the myth of the Pure Son Who Overthrows the Bad Father. This takes many familiar forms—the cruel king challenged by the brave knight, the cruel cattle baron challenged by the lone cowboy, the cruel mobster challenged by the honest private eye, the cruel megalomaniac multinational corporate tycoon challenged by James Bond.

And finally, if the authoritarian male has renounced vulnerability—renounced tenderness, gentleness, empathy, and affection—how can his need for love be met? This problem gives rise to the myth of the Unmotivated Female Puppet-Ideal. She springs like a phoenix from the ashes of the Needy Mother-Monster just in time to be rescued by the hero. She desires nothing except the hero's welfare and has no needs of her own—no purpose in life except to make him happy and bear his children, no power except the power to give him an erection. She is nurturing but stripped of all control, bleached of all humanity, shorn of all agency. She is merely the envelope for the hero's letter to the world. Whether placed high on a pedestal or sprawled in a *Playboy* centerfold, she is pure object.

HEROES À LA MODE

These myths and their qualifiers are usually combined in various ways. The same heroic leader may overcome the many, kill the female monster, rescue the fair bimbo, overthrow the corrupt father, and have a run-in with the immortal evil adversary before living happily ever after.

What is common to all these myths is that they involve battle. Someone must be conquered, slaughtered, overthrown. It is difficult for us even to conceive of an interesting story that doesn't involve an enemy to be beaten. We tend to assume that fighting and conquering are an inherent part of storytelling. But in hunter-gatherer mythology conquest plays an insignificant role. People quarrel, of course—conflict of some kind, internal or external, is the basis of myth—but they do not carry on wars or take slaves. Heroes and heroines wander, hunt, meet strangers, outwit them, are fooled by them, have affairs, steal things, get in trouble, are trapped, escape, undergo transformations, make friends, quarrel, lose things, find things, get lost, find their way home again. Their problems are *not* finally and permanently solved by the destruction of an adversary. (Perhaps this is why many people today find them uninteresting.)

Why, then, are tales of battle and conquest so much a part of our lives today—from children's cartoons to TV crime shows to *Rambo*? We no longer live in warrior societies and no longer have serfs. Yet the old myths persist, although they now share the stage with the more democratic themes of personal growth and conflict resolution that are the basis of most of the better TV sitcoms and non-crime dramas, many films, and most plays and novels. There will always be survivals, of course, but conquest myths show few signs of diminishing in appeal; blockbuster films are almost always of this genre.

Conquest myths served three purposes: they kept alive the spirit of battle, justified the suppression of slaves and serfs, and reinforced each male's renunciation of emotional vulnerability. And while war is rapidly losing its glamor today, and domination is not highly valued, our competitive economic system still seems to depend heavily on masculine self-suppression. The psychic cost of this stance is so high that it must be continually buttressed by stories in which male heroes conquer "the forces of darkness"—softness, femininity, emotionality, and so on. One part of the personality—the ego—must suppress the rest. There is no resolution or integration. The only "resolution" in an authoritarian myth is destruction. You have to crush something—part of yourself, part of the world, part of life. Some aspect of humanity must be trampled underfoot, even if it is your own.

ONE AGAINST MANY

Reinforcing the class system has always been an important part of authoritarian mythology. The Triumph of Good over Evil is in many cases a thinly disguised rendering of "how we came to rule over our peasants." Since Good and Evil are represented by "higher" and "lower" it was easy to see the warrior aristocracy as good and the peasant class as evil. As noted above, *villain* was originally just a term for peasant, and in the popular fiction of past centuries the villains were usually of the lower class—city hoods, country yokels, ethnic minorities, foreigners. If they were rich and powerful, they were upstarts, nouveaux riches, while the heroes were well-born with aristocratic-sounding names. Villains were also ugly and often physically handicapped.

Today we are somewhat more sophisticated and ethnic groups more resistant to negative stereotyping, but these patterns have by no means disappeared. The ethnic image problem is often circumvented in TV dramas by having the ethnic villain savagely victimize a sympathetic ethnic character at the beginning of the show, thus permitting the white male hero to administer a brutal beating in revenge later on.

In a classic authoritarian drama the hero single-handedly holds an enemy throng at bay by virtue of his nobility, courage, and superior weaponry (whether sword, armor, and horse, or automatic weapon, napalm, and helicopter). This theme of the One Who Overcomes the Many is sometimes mistakenly viewed as implying identification with the underdog, but if being outnumbered is all it takes to be an underdog, most slaveowners are underdogs. The myth of the One Who Overcomes the Many serves as an apology for the rich and powerful—a celebration of their victory over the disadvantaged. Generations of Hollywood writers and producers have become rich and powerful themselves by catering to these traditional sentiments.

We no longer think of villains as peasants, but the ancient equation lives on in a new garment. Until recently the favorite modern enemy was "the Communist," which in practice meant poor and primitively armed peasants in third-world countries like Vietnam. Today it is the drug dealer—almost always a member of an ethnic minority.

From samurai to Rambo, the myth of the One Who Overcomes the Many expresses our covert admiration of the privileged few who hold the underprivileged many at bay and persuade them to keep toiling—of the ruthless dictator who is able to hold an entire population hostage. The persistent appeal of this myth perhaps reflects the frustration we feel as individuals today, confronting the faceless impersonality of the forces that seem to control our lives.

Authoritarian Survivals in American Society

HARMLESS REBELLIONS

Myths express not only the dominant goals and values of a society but also the stress they create—the conflict between these cultural goals and the feelings they inevitably violate. In authoritarian myths this conflict leads to some sort of battle, ending usually in a victory for repression—will over impulse, honor over love.

War is the failure to deal creatively with conflict—the inability to live with the stimulation of difference or to invent new syntheses. War is a futile attempt to eliminate difference through suppression or homicide; when the battle is over the conflict still exists, since it is within everyone.

The myth of the Slaying of the Needy Mother, for example, expresses not only the rejection of all things feminine but also the longing to give into them. The rejection is symbolized directly by the slaying, while the longing is expressed indirectly by the hunger and power of the monster.

In real life the detachment of the boy from the mother is made easier by the fact that the mother in traditional families is assigned the task of maintaining domestic order and safety. Young boys are inducted into male fellowship by joining in a pleasurable rebellion against these feminine demands for order (an order the males themselves have often insisted upon). Male solidarity is to a large extent based on this anti-maternal conspiracy, this rebellion against feminine constraint.

This is a favorite theme of male-created plays, films, sitcoms, and cartoons: the young boy sneaking off with a favorite uncle or grandfather to indulge in some harmless but forbidden activity in order to avoid chores or escape some stuffy social function, or several boys together defying some prudish old busybody, or two grown men getting drunk and conspiring to evade their angry wives waiting at home with rolling pins.

This rebellion is entirely harmless to the established order. No male authority is being challenged—no tyrants confronted or overthrown. Far from threatening the status quo, it actually helps to maintain it, by deflecting and draining off rebellious impulses and blaming women—the primary victims of the system—for its constraints.

Movies that celebrate personal independence, for example—that express rebellion against convention and freedom from social constraint—rarely direct their barbs toward the males who actually hold power in the system. Even when a film threatens to make a serious attack on some aspect of the authoritarian order, a female character is often brought in to represent the establishment, so that we can be reassured that it is only "Mom" and domesticity that are being assailed, not the real powers that be. An extreme example is *One Flew Over the Cuckoo's Nest*, where the nurse who carries out the orders is the major villain, instead of the doctors that issue them. Even recent films like *Stand and Deliver* and *Pump Up the Volume* find it necessary to make a female the spokesperson for authoritarian male traditions.

The target of many of these rebellions is the neurotic, overpowering, destructive mother who makes her little son mixed up. Usually Jewish or Southern, she is alternately a figure of fun and an object of terror. She is portrayed as (a) living in a fantasy world and (b) too wrapped up in her children. It never seems to be noticed that in this respect she is merely carrying out the wishes of males, for in traditional authoritarian society men are in charge of the "real world," while women are expected to stifle their active interests and compress them into motherhood—that is, to be (a) unrealistic and (b) possessive. It seems to be a defect in the human imagination that we always bite at the stick that hits us instead of at the hand that holds it.

Many boys are still trained in the warrior tradition of emotional cowardice. They are taught, for example—not consciously but nonetheless systematically—that affection is to be expressed only by being playfully aggressive (lightly punching the objects of their affections, or throwing them in water); and that the appropriate response to feelings of emotional vulnerability is to become *seriously* aggressive. This is the core of authoritarian gender training for men.

THE SWORD IN THE BEDROOM

During most of the authoritarian era the legendary heroes—from Achilles and Samson to D'Artagnan and Rambo—have been successful warriors—men who have killed a lot of people. But as the system began its gradual decline in the seventeenth and eighteenth centuries, the favorite heroes began increasingly to be men who had "conquered" a lot of women. The prototypical hero for authoritarianism in decline is Don Juan. A rather ordinary aristocratic bully, Don Juan preys on those physically or socially weaker than himself—women, old men, servants, peasants—until he is finally undone by the stone statue of one of his victims. Why should a man with almost nothing unusual or admirable about him so capture the imagination of authoritarian men?

First, by his predatory approach to women he has "solved" the problem that is so acute in the authoritarian system—how to be a "real man" without loving women. The myth of Don Juan was pleasing because he managed to prove his virility without ever having to deal with a woman on an equal footing.

The second appeal has to do with his demise. Don Juan is dragged down to Hell by the statue of an old commander he has killed—in other words, by a male authority. The essence of authoritarian mythology is that authority always wins in the end. Don Juan is a tragedy only because in killing an authority figure he "went too far."

THE USES OF TRAGEDY

Tragedy itself is an authoritarian invention. It is an unknown art form in hunter-gatherer societies. For the message of tragedy is that no matter how exalted the hero may be, sooner or later he will fall because in an authoritarian society there is always someone above you to whom you must submit—even a king must bow to the power of an authoritarian god. Tragedy teaches that there is a strict, hierarchical order in life that must not be violated.

Hunter-gatherers were certainly aware of the dangers of ignoring nature's guidelines. But tragedy added a punitive, parental element not present in pre-authoritarian tales. Hunter-gatherer mythology is full of protagonists who make mistakes and thereby cause trouble for themselves and others, but this trouble is not seen as punishment. It is simply reality. You disturb a tiger and it bites you. You annoy a deity and it will also bite you. Next time you'll watch where you're stepping.

Tragedy redefines these missteps as divine retribution. The pratfall becomes a whipping. In tragedy the emphasis is on the suffering and/or death of the hero. He has been "brought down." Most likely he will indulge in a lot of breast beating and self-justification while falling, for tragedy is a kind of plea for understanding—an appeal to authority which is ultimately rejected.

In most tragedies the hero has somehow risen above his station, either in his family or in society. He challenges authority, in the person of fathers, uncles, kings (Oedipus, Hamlet, Macbeth, Prometheus), and/or the rules that maintain and preserve that authority and its orderly transfer (Lear, Richard III, Coriolanus). These upstart tragic heroes are forced to acknowledge a greater power in the end, so the authoritarian male gets to enjoy both the vicarious thrill of the hero's self-assertion and the pleasure of seeing him get his comeuppance.

THE VICTORY SHAM

Authoritarian myths assume that difficulties vanish when the dragon or enemy is killed. This is the governing delusion of the authoritarian mentality—that you can destroy a conflict. But since we are all connected, a part of us dies when the dragon or enemy dies, while the conflict merely resurfaces inside the killer. And whatever impulse inspired the dragon or enemy will inspire others.

Resolution never comes from destroying. Resolution comes from integrating, from inventing creative ways to accommodate conflicting needs and goals. This is what democracy is—the peaceful accommodation of conflicting needs and desires. It is far less appealing to the authoritarian mentality than a nice bloody battle, but the victories of combat are always illusory in the long run. The map of Europe has been altered dozens of times by war in the last few centuries. Many have tried to unify it through conquest—empires have grown and collapsed, small nations have been born, swallowed up, and born again, boundaries have flown back and forth like the vicissitudes of hemlines—but it is only now, after years of peaceful negotiation, that Europe is beginning to settle into an integrated unity.

NEW MYTHS

Myths are about conflicting desires and goals, both between and within individuals. Even in myths, however, these conflicts do not necessarily culminate in battle; we get deeply involved in stories of people who struggle to overcome personal handicaps, ambivalent desires, lack of recognition, unrequited love, social injustice, and so on. War and combat comprise only a part of our fantasy life.

Even when democracy has taken a firmer hold on us these older themes will not necessarily disappear. They will simply become progressively less popular—of interest primarily to the folklorist, just as hunter-gatherer myths seem quaint and somewhat irrelevant to the average person today. It seems impossible now to imagine a time when mass homicide would not attract huge audiences in America, but cultural change seldom gives advance warning (witness the explosions of the sixties after the quiescent fifties, or the upheavals in Eastern Europe today). Fifty years ago it would have been impossible to imagine the movies without westerns, yet they attract few people today.

Each megaculture generates myths in keeping with its central preoccupations. Hunter-gatherer myths were *exploratory*, and the valued traits were mobility and adaptability. The protagonists encountered numinous beings, places, and objects, and were transformed by these encounters. Authoritarian myths deal primarily with *combat*. The ultimate goal is power and status and the valued trait is physical courage. The hero is someone who beats up someone else. Democratic myths are *creative*, and deal with the integration of disparate elements. The valued traits are imagination and vision.

But the transition from one ethos to another is never absolute. Old themes are appropriated and twisted into new shapes. The exploratory wanderings of the hunter-gatherer myths develop a more focused, conquistadorial aspect in the authoritarian age and lose the sense of integration with nature. In the same way, the dreary bashing of aliens that characterizes authoritarian mythology tends, in our more democratic age, to become a vehicle for the examination of the internal conflicts of both the winners and losers.

Battle may also be used to set up the reconciliation and integration that will form the core of the new myths—a reversal of what happened under authoritarianism. In the past we waited in suspense for the final battle. In the future we will wait in suspense for the reconciliation.

We can see the beginnings of this transition already. After World War I, when it first struck large portions of the male population that fighting in a war might not be the fun-filled adventure they had always been led to expect, a relatively new plot began to appear in popular fiction and film with some frequency. This plot expressed the old militaristic values, but in a somewhat camouflaged form: the hero, for some reason (usually hidden from everyone else in the story and thus leading to accusations of cowardice), must avoid fighting at all costs, and does so despite great provocation until the climax, when the ban is lifted or the provocation becomes too great and he is finally allowed to bash the villains into insensibility or fill them full of lead. By the beginning of World War II the entire nation was playing out this scenario of uncomfortable pacifism and constrained eagerness for battle. Films like *The Quiet Man* and *Shane* are examples of this genre.

In this plot, the hero's pacificism creates the tension leading up to the climactic battle. But in the next phase, represented by many films of the past few years, we find this plot being stood on its head. Instead of pacifism providing the tension that is released by the fight, we find chronic antagonism providing the tension that is released by a climactic reconciliation. Will these traditional enemies ever become friends? Can their differences ever be transcended?

This type of story, which I call the Reconciliation Plot, is by no means new. But it began to be increasingly popular in the late fifties and early sixties with films like *Me and the Colonel, The Defiant Ones*, and *In the Heat of the Night*—films centered on racial and ethnic prejudice. Then, after a lull, the popularity of reconciliation films began to reach flood proportions in the late eighties—with films like *Midnight Run, Outrageous Fortune, 48 Hours, Kiss of the Spider Woman, Alien Nation, Baghdad Cafe, Ruthless People, Orphans, Russkies, Mona Lisa, Enemy Mine, The Mission, Throw Momma from the Train, Running Scared, Driving Miss Daisy*, and many more.

In these films the hero or heroine is thrown together either with someone from a different (usually disliked) ethnic group, or with some traditional enemy, or with a rival—someone with antagonistic goals. Initially there is hostility between them, but ultimately they come to mutually appreciate their differences. Often the one with less status proves to have unexpected strengths—as if these stories were expressly designed to illustrate Follett's remark about opponents having something to give us.

The drive toward democratic integration expresses itself in other ways. The late eighties also saw a rash of films in which people exchanged positions—in some cases through an actual exchange of physical bodies, thus enabling them to see the world from an entirely new perspective. Although designed as comic vehicles and played for laughs, films like *Trading Places, All of Me, Vice Versa, Big, Like Father Like Son* (not to mention transvestite films like *Tootsie, La Cage Aux Folles, Victor, Victoria*, and others) suggest a new flexibility, a hunger to understand the experience of others, an empathic questing that anticipates the democratic future.

Despite the fact that most blockbuster films are old-fashioned celebrations of violence and conquest, the increasing popularity of these newer themes suggests that changes in the mythic consciousness of Americans may have already begun. Whether they can survive the continual onslaught of reactionary images from Hollywood remains to be seen.

CHAPTER 10

The Changing Face of God

At the core of democracy, finally, is the religious element.

—Walt Whitman, *Democratic Vistas*

Our concepts of deity, like everything else, are shaped by the cultures we inhabit. For hunter-gatherers, God tends to be localized and particularized. Every rock, river, mountain, spring, animal, plant, bird, and insect has its own deity. Hunter-gatherers are interested in what is unique about an object or being. Each divinity has its particular place in the universe. They are not ranked. One is not "higher" than another. They are simply tied to the landscape as the hunter-gatherer is tied to it.

Authoritarian ideas of God, on the other hand, are hierarchical. When one bellicose tribe conquers another, the particular names the conqueror uses for his deities are accorded preferred status. To the authoritarian, God resides not in the landscape, but *above*. God is perceived as a kind of landholder, with stewards and overseers and slaves; a masculine tyrant with absolute power over his subjects, demanding unquestioning obedience, and subject to petty tantrums when disobeyed or insufficiently flattered. He is detached from nature—nature becomes an even lower form of slave—a slave of slaves.

This has led to many misunderstandings about so-called primitive religion. We used to believe that pre-literate peoples, in their ignorance, "worshipped" stones and trees, in the sense of worshipping an idol—bowing down, expressing subservience. But this was not the spirit in which hunter-gatherer peoples expressed their religious sentiments. They simply saw sanctity in everything. Their "ignorance" was merely an ignorance of slavery, of bowing before ruthless power to avoid annihilation. But it is difficult for us—the descendants of slaves and slaveowners—even to conceive of worship that is separate from notions of submission, obeisance, and sacrifice.

Genuine religious feeling is not dependent on these authoritarian forms. They are the garb in which we are used to seeing religion cloaked, since most current religious traditions were born in the authoritarian era. But these forms are not the substance of religion, not what keeps otherwise democratic people worshipping in what appears to be inappropriately authoritarian modes. The substance requires neither a rock, nor a statue, nor a cross, nor humanoid figures in the sky. The substance of religion is the joy and awe that comes from recognizing that we are each a breathing part of something much greater than ourselves.

What confuses people is that the feeling of awe and self-abandonment produced by this awareness is conveniently expressed through the authoritarian symbols of prostration, kneeling, supplication, and so on. But it need not be so. Religious devotion is a part of the everyday lives of hunters-gatherers, but they do not bow, scrape, or abase themselves.

Many people today find traditional religion irrelevant for just this reason—the fact that it is so deeply mired in authoritarian language and ritual. There is an increasing need to find ways of expressing religious feeling that are free of these forms. The explosion of alternative religious practices in the United States today is a manifestation of this need.

THE SLAVEOWNER GOD

Authoritarian religion transformed the chaotic concreteness of the hunter-gatherer religious landscape into the rigid tidiness of the organization chart. Religion became a matter of placating remote absentee landlords who wielded absolute power over their earthly slaves. And since we clothe our deities in the familiar fashions of our own culture, God began to take on the mundane qualities of human despots. We find the gods of the Greeks, Romans, Israelites, Hindus, and so on behaving as humans have always behaved when given too much power—becoming capricious, self-indulgent, narcissistic, petty, irascible, vindictive, impatient, arrogant, petulant, and infantile.

The God of the Old Testament is so vain, for example, that he can be manipulated by Satan into cruelly torturing his most devoted follower merely to win an argument. The Book of Job is the ultimate slaveowner's morality tale—asserting that no matter how much the Master beats and tortures you it's for your own ultimate good, since he has the power to enforce his every whim, including the whim to annihilate you. When God answers Job at the end of the book, it is to point this out in an orgy of boastfulness. Sneering at Job's powerlessness, he rants dyspeptically at his hapless servant, whose only crime was to wonder why his faithfulness had been rewarded with torture.

God is portrayed here not as an enlightened entity, but as a tyrant so insecure emotionally that he has to subject his most devoted slave to an itemized list of his achievements and possessions. Even after Job apologizes and abases himself, God is too wrought up to end his diatribe. To anyone except poor downtrodden Job it might seem that the heavenly slaveowner "doth protest too much." Is he perhaps feeling guilty over his persecution of a faithful servant? Or foolish that Satan could so easily trick him into doing it in the first place?

God's clinching argument to Job is the claim of property ownership—"whatever is under the whole heaven is mine," like some old Hollywood cattle baron boasting of owning land "as far as the eye can see." It is understandable that farmers and shepherds three thousand years ago would have to rely on this familiar model, but it is a tribute to the strength of human habit that so many people still cling to this crude image today.

One of the favorite metaphors of authoritarian religion is that of the shepherd and his sheep. But, as I.F. Stone points out, the aim of the shepherd is not merely to care for the sheep, but also to fleece and slaughter them. Authoritarianism is not designed for the benefit of the slave, but for the slaveowner. Any stray bit of mercy or kindness that enters into the relationship is merely one of those engaging little corruptions that human beings manage to introduce into all formal systems to make them more bearable.

Taking God out of the world and putting him/her in the sky as a slaveowner had some unfortunate effects. It made people lose touch not only with the sanctity of the world around them, but also with the sanctity within themselves, with the sense that they belong to some larger entity. This has left humanity with a pervasive feeling of aloneness from which it has never fully recovered—a sense of incompleteness which, in an authoritarian environment, is easily converted to feelings of unworthiness and self-hatred. People try to recapture the sense of belonging through various forms of self-abasement but, like a drug, they provide only temporary relief.

Authoritarian religion also contributed the idea of *punishment* to religious thought. Hunter-gatherers were familiar with the idea of bad consequences—break a taboo and something bad will happen to you, just as it will if you annoy a bear. But the notion of a personal punishment by a heavenly ruler could only come into the human mind when there was a great deal of that sort of thing going on on earth—when large communities were full of slaves who could only be kept in line by beatings and the promise of future rewards and punishments.

In time this vision of a heavenly master led to the concept of Hell. Many cultures have had some notion of an afterlife—a locale where departed spirits assemble—but the idea of making this locale the repository of rewards and retributions was fully developed under Christianity. In the East we find the more impersonal idea of karmic reincarnation (the more obedient you are in your present life, the more you will rise in the social structure next time around, and vice versa); what the West added was the personal touch of the slavemaster with the whip.

In order to keep God from assuming the unflattering image of a sadistic torturer, it was necessary to create Satan, who acts as a kind of assistant principal in the high school of life. This follows standard authoritarian procedure—to blame all unpleasantness on the hatchetman who carries out orders rather than on the one who issues them (who must retain a benign image in order to encourage obedience).

But it wouldn't do to have the source of all evil represented as an agent of God, so an alternative idea was required—that Satan was a rebel angel. This was highly satisfying in some ways—there could hardly be any greater sin in authoritarian thinking than disobedience. It also fit beautifully into the dualism that is so attractive to warlike cultures, providing the militaristically inclined with a permanent enemy.

But the invention of Satan—while it furnished a scourge and a convenient explanation for the unpleasantness of life under authoritarianism—led to other difficulties. What kind of rebel leader, for example, would torture his own followers? How could he hope to gain converts that way? And if God was omnipotent how could anyone rebel against him? These problems have plagued theologians for centuries, and although they have demonstrated great ingenuity in finding verbal solutions, the tensions inherent in defining God as an authoritarian dictator have persisted.

CHRISTIANITY: THE REVOLUTION THAT FAILED

The teachings of Jesus were an attempt to sweep away this rigidity and the problems attending it, but his efforts were ultimately co-opted and subverted. Jesus was a reform rabbi who sought to democratize Judaism. Since he opposed warfare and the amassing of wealth, his challenge to the authoritarianism he found everywhere around him was far more radical than the democracy of the Athenians, although no more enduring.

Jesus advocated reducing all the finicky dos and don'ts of Judaic law to two general principles: to love God and to love one's neighbor. This approach was significant because it delegated the details of ethical behavior to the individual. It is the essence of authoritarian leadership to give only specific orders and withhold the overall purpose to which they are directed. Jesus was revealing that purpose and delegating to all human beings the authority and initiative to decide just how it could best be implemented. This is the soul of democratic leadership.

Yet the net result of this radical movement was a religious system even more authoritarian than the Judaism that Jesus found around him. For while the Judaic God is prototypically authoritarian, the commitment of Judaism to the written word allowed for a unique degree of decentralization during the height of the authoritarian era. How was the democratic radicalism of Jesus turned on its head? How did a religion that preached peace, poverty, and democracy become one that condoned grotesque wealth, slavish authoritarianism, and unending slaughter?

Unfortunately, the democratic revolution that Jesus attempted came before authoritarianism had peaked, and the prevailing rigidities of the era simply closed around his teachings like the tide enveloping a rock. It was a long and gradual process that began with Paul and is maintained by so-called fundamentalists today.

The spread of Christianity was due in large part to the fact that its leading proselytizer was both a Jew and a Roman—at home in two dissimilar cultures. Paul was a man who knew his audience—knew that the radical democracy of Jesus would never sell in its original form. Yet he was committed to it and ultimately died for it. His solution was to focus on the *death* of Jesus—on the idea of Jesus as a sacrificial lamb, a notion that appealed to the authoritarian consciousness of his day. The radical ideas Jesus had preached were de-emphasized—the important thing was that he had died to save all believers from punishment. This was the "Good News" Paul used to spread his message, and it worked. Paul was unaware of the fact that this sugar-coating was the only thing that would survive, while the medicine itself—the teachings of Jesus—would be largely ignored and rejected by the majority of Christians within a few centuries, as authoritarians took over the religion and twisted it to suit their own purposes.

The first twist was to reassign the blame for Jesus' death. As we have seen, authoritarian populations like to shift blame from the highest authority to a subordinate. The highest authority in this case, the Roman governor, Pontius Pilate, must have "clean hands" (an early form of "deniability") so he can be touted as a basically nice guy who doesn't know what his naughty subordinates are doing.

There was considerable advantage in shifting the blame from the Romans to the Jews, for there were fewer Jews, and the Romans, who had a weak and decadent religious tradition, were easier to convert. But it was also extremely important to the authoritarian mind that the highest earthly authority should not be to blame. This desire enabled later generations to ignore the obvious fact that crucifixion was a Roman, not a Jewish, punishment.

In June of 1988 the Kennedy family expressed displeasure at a plan to make a museum out of the building in Dallas from which John F. Kennedy was shot. "To focus on that instead of a person's life just seems to me disgusting," a former aide said.

Yet this was precisely what was done with Jesus. A "museum" was created out of his death, while his life and teachings have been of remarkably little interest in the authoritarian era. His crucifixion by the Romans was only momentary compared to the crucifixion he has suffered from Christians themselves, who have kept him nailed to the cross for two thousand years. By making Jesus' death more important than his teachings, Paul opened the door for authoritarian church fathers to substantially negate those teachings.

Jesus the pacifist became Jesus the soldier, at war with Satan; and Jesus the healer and forgiver of sins became Jesus the harsh judge, herding sinners into Hell just like Satan himself. His message of peace and love became one of blood, torture, and sacrifice. Instead of being worshipped as a wise and saintly teacher, he was worshipped only as a victim.

Hierarchs and fundamentalists alike are hostile to Jesus the preacher—they are interested only in Jesus the man who died and was resurrected. Fundamentalists view his message of poverty and peace as communistic, and use quotations from the Old Testament to negate that message. It is no accident that fundamentalism is strongest in the South—that part of the United States with the most recent experience of slavery—but Jesus' pacifism is threatening to all authoritarians, who cannot function without an enemy.

In focusing so much attention on Jesus' suffering and death, authoritarians have insulted a lifetime that was devoted to the spread of democratic religious ideas. A truly fundamental Christianity would demand that we finally take Jesus down off the cross and revere him as the prophet who taught peace, nonviolence, cooperation, and the vanity of competition and wealth. It would insist that instead of worshipping his pain and suffering, we put an end to it and focus attention on his teachings.

RELIGIOUS EVOLUTION

Religious beliefs have never been static. Within every religious system they are continually evolving, in spite of the authoritarian longing for some fixed point in the universe—some despotic mental "given" to which all other thoughts will bow down.

Contrary to the belief of some leftists, religion is not inherently authoritarian. The early Christians were radically democratic, as recent historians have pointed out, and it took centuries of oppression by the Church "fathers" to stamp out this radical Christianity and substitute the peculiar brand of repressive, misogynistic, prudish authoritarianism that still dominates much of organized religion in America. Yet there are many Christian sects that preserve the original democratic orientation, and liberation theology is one of the most vital forces in Christianity today. The struggle between democracy's effort to reach full maturity and authoritarianism's determination to squelch it is nowhere more apparent than in the field of religion.

Within the Catholic Church this struggle has involved challenges to the Church's historical misogyny and to its irrelevant obsession with sexuality. It has pitted papal officials, who tend to identify with men of wealth and power everywhere, against individual priests and bishops, who often identify with their poor parishioners. The efforts of men and women in the field to respond to the changing needs and concerns of parishioners has been met with the rigidity and traditionalism that so often characterizes officials insulated from the real world by their hierarchical elevation.

A Vatican letter in 1989 warned of the "dangers" of people seeking their own avenues to spiritual fulfillment through yoga, meditation, and other forms of New Age spirituality—revealing an anxiety approaching panic that parishioners might find God on their own without going through the proper channels. It would be a deathblow to authoritarian religion if too many people came to the conclusion that God was accessible everywhere and to everyone without having to pass through an array of receptionists, security guards, and aides-de-camp.

In contrast, nuns and priests in Latin America have sacrificed their lives to protest right-wing tyranny and oppression. In the United States the popular Dominican priest, Matthew Fox, has called for a return to the life-affirming Christianity of Jesus and an end to the "sadomasochistic obsessions" of the Church patriarchs who corrupted that message.

Among Protestants the struggle is largely between Christian pacificists and militarists—the former trying to create a peaceful community of nations, the latter eagerly anticipating World War III. Some fundamentalists have been trying desperately, as the Cold War has thawed, to whip up anticommunist sentiment by talking about Armageddon. In the fall of 1988, for example, Mormon leader Ezra Taft Benson told his flock that all humanity would soon have to "choose up sides" for the coming battle between God and the Devil. Authoritarians *must* have war—the idea of synthesis is beyond them.

Opposed to these bloodthirsty traditionalists are liberal religions with long and untainted democratic traditions, like the Quakers and the Unitarians, who have consistently been in the forefront of movements for peace and democracy. And black church leaders like Martin Luther King, Jr. were responsible for both the nonviolent character and the success of the civil rights movement.

THE RELIGION OF DEMOCRACY

What is a democratic concept of God? In biblical times religious leaders were unable to imagine anything more awesome than some sort of super-aristocrat, "Lord of lords," "King of kings," with all the nasty human traits pertaining thereto. Hopefully modern imaginations can reach beyond the puny pinnacles of earthly power to find more inspiring symbols. Just as our country is something too vast and inclusive to be symbolized by any mere president, so is creation too profound to be captured in the image of a well-preserved old white man with a beard. The Old Testament vision of God as some sort of cosmic sheep rancher falls short of what many modern Americans can worship.

Yet we are human, and we have a hard time relating to concepts like infinity and oneness. We look for images that have a concreteness and a specificity that fits the tactile realities of our everyday lives. People are forever trying to create new symbols and rituals to replace the old, but these substitutes lack the fullness of meaning that centuries of usage have attached to the old—like the richness of marble worn smooth by many footsteps. We are in a kind of limbo—the old symbols don't fit, the new ones haven't arrived yet. Perhaps this is why so many people today feel lost and at sea—why they seem to feel a need to clutter their lives with material junk. It is as if somewhere in that chronic yard sale of American life will be found the homely symbols—star, cross, bread, book, or cup—that were meaningful and comforting to people in the past, symbols both personal and universal, particular and general, ordinary and transcendant.

A truly democratic people will envision God in a variety of ways, since tolerance is central to democracy. But it will be a participatory vision. In democratic theology, God is seen as an entity of which we are all a part. Just as the individual members of a truly democratic society partake of the total power of that society, so in democratic theology do all partake of the power of God. And just as in democratic societies some do not acknowledge, exert, or take responsibility for the power that belongs to them, so some individuals fail to acknowledge, exert, or take responsibility for the spiritual power within themselves.

CHAPTER 11

Secrets

The first casualty of war is truth.

—Hiram Johnson

For the authoritarian, democracy is a disease, and the most common prescription against this disease is secrecy. A foolproof test of authoritarianism is the strength of an official's anxiety to have information withheld from the public. The official may be public or private, the pretexts used may be eminently plausible or patently ridiculous—it is the desire that counts.

Official secrecy betrays a mistrust of the people's ability to make sound judgments, yet authoritarian officials continually strive to weaken that ability. They are unremitting in their attempts to mislead and "disinform" the public in order to manipulate it for their own convenience. As noted above, the alleged poor judgment of democracies is usually based on inadequate and doctored information previously served up by authoritarian leaders.

THE SECRETS OF MEN

Secrecy seems to have a special fascination for men. They love to create secret societies and secret languages and secret passwords and secret handshakes. They pass effortlessly from the code rings and secret words of childhood to the arcane initiations and rituals of fraternities and lodges—from Ob and pig latin to the codebooks and clandestine signals of covert operations—without any visible interruption from maturity.

Bruno Bettelheim saw in this fascination with secrecy an envy of women, of the mysteries of gestation and birth, but any such propensities have certainly been enhanced by authoritarian culture, in which status is maintained by the hoarding of information from those further down the ladder. To form a secret society of any kind automatically gives you a higher position than someone else, at least in your own mind.

Secret languages, handshakes, and rituals, codes and secret names, and all the silly paraphernalia of covert operations may be harmless enough in private play, but in the public sphere we expect to find grown men and women working together to solve the needs of the peoples of the world—not playing childhood games. The posturing of a Gordon Liddy or an Oliver North may seem laughable, but it is no laughing matter to have our nation's policies subject to the influence of people operating at this level of emotional development.

CLASSIFIED INCOMPETENCE

If you create dark places, all kinds of vermin tend to gather there. C.P. Snow argues that secrecy breeds insanity, and this is certainly suggested by much of what goes on in less accessible corners of our federal government. The bizarre behavior of Lyndon Johnson during the Vietnam War era provides some chilling examples, as do the Nixon-Kissinger years, with government officials bugging each other's offices in an orgy of interdepartmental paranoia.

The primary purpose of secrecy in government is to hide incompetence, corruption, and malfeasance from the public. The declassification of government documents invariably produces a rich harvest of egregious waste, antidemocratic abuses, calamitous errors in judgment, and major crimes. Military procurement scandals, the Iran-Contra affair, illegal spying on American citizens opposed to administration policies, unethical and grossly unscientific experiments with brainwashing and harmful chemicals, drug running, assassinations, the violent overthrow of popularly elected governments in other nations—these are only a few of the fatuities that governmental secrecy has engendered.

In the late 1950s, for example, the CIA recruited a prominent Canadian psychiatrist (and former head of the American Psychiatric Association), Ewen Cameron, to experiment with brainwashing techniques. The CIA was looking for a way to program an individual to kill someone and then erase the deed from his memory—part of the infamous MK-ULTRA project. To assist them in this harebrained scheme (a result perhaps of an oversupply of comic books in CIA lounges), Cameron subjected a total of fifty-three unsuspecting clients to a battery of mind-annihilating techniques, including massive electroshock, round-the-clock taped messages, sensory deprivation, and drugs. Most of the subjects were reduced to near-vegetable status by this effort and some never regained full sanity. The CIA, under Richard Helms, later tried to cover up this incident—one of 130 such experiments carried out in the late fifties and early sixties—but some ten thousand documents survived the shredding, and led to a large lawsuit. The CIA tried to have the case thrown out of court on the predictable grounds that intelligence sources and methods would be compromised. When this device failed the CIA settled out of court. The settlement was the largest ever paid by the United States government to a foreign national, and the largest ever paid by the CIA to anyone.

Documents acquired through the Freedom of Information Act (since sharply curtailed for "security reasons," that is, because of the long list of felonies and foolishness it has already revealed) give a startling account of CIA malfeasance. American citizens died or were rendered psychotic from surreptitiously administered drug injections, for example, and in one experiment a man was given a local anesthetic and a hallucinogen and asked to describe his visual experiences while parts of his brain were being surgically removed. Virtually all the illegal new drugs that entered the U.S. during the sixties were introduced by the CIA in its search for chemical agents that could be used against the public "in the event of a civilian insurrection." Drugs rejected by the FDA as having harmful side effects were routinely acquired by the CIA and used experimentally on unsuspecting subjects. Nothing of value came out of these experiments.

The record of such foolishly conceived and inanely executed schemes by intelligence agencies would fill volumes. In any well-run business a cost-benefit analysis of covert operations over the last forty years would result in their prompt termination. The Vietnam War, the Iran hostage crisis, the Iraq invasion, our problems in Central and South America—all can be traced in part to short-sighted secret actions taken in the past. And who knows how many similar actions are being carried out today whose consequences will bedevil our children and grandchildren?

Many of these operations were instituted in the face of contrary intelligence gathered by the very same agencies. Unlike covert operations, intelligence *gathering* is a necessary and valuable function, and has for the most part been accurate enough to make one wish that decision makers had paid more attention to it. During the Vietnam War, for example, a CIA analyst discovered that according to official statistics the Vietcong had already been eliminated, but when he tried to get the Pentagon to accept more realistic estimates of enemy strength he was disciplined. To speak such truths during the Vietnam War was considered treasonable—figures had to be juggled "in order to maintain public support."

This is the very same public that has "poor judgment," it should be noted. It is ironic that officials whose goal is ostensibly to further the cause of democracy should explain their deceptions by saying that "there would be protests if the public knew." It never seems to occur to such officials that the public has a stake in these lunatic adventures, which they are paying for at present and for which they may have to pay even more in the future. We are still paying for the Vietnam War, and so will our great-grandchildren. Yet each escalation of that war was based on a deliberate deception, most notably the Tonkin Gulf incident, on the basis of which a hood-winked and submissive Congress yielded to the president its constitutional powers—powers which it has never regained.

In the Iran-Contra hearings the same anxiety about public protest was evident. The two principal issues that were not allowed to be discussed in open hearings, "for reasons of national security," were (a) the CIA's heavy involvement in drug trafficking, and (b) secret plans to create a police state "in the case of national emergency." These are both issues in which the public has a heavy stake, to say the least.

"National security" also requires keeping secret the callous willingness of government bureaucrats to endanger the health and lives of American civilians. The Soviet Union was roundly criticized for delaying news of the Chernobyl disaster for a day or two, yet the United States, a supposedly "open" society, for *four decades* covered up a series of radioactive emissions from the Hanford weapons facility in Washington that were many times higher than the radiation from Chernobyl and were estimated to have exposed twenty thousand babies to milk from radioactive cows. The government was aware as early as 1946 that there was a severe risk to the health of residents in the area, but took no steps even to warn them. And when a manager recommended that workers leaving the Hanford and Oak Ridge facilities be told that they had been exposed to excessive radiation and be given medical assistance, he was overruled by an AEC committee, which instead advised that departing employees be assured of the great care that AEC facilities took in "protecting each employee."

Early in 1990 Warren I. Cohen, chairman of the State Department's Advisory Commission on Historical Diplomatic Documentation, resigned in protest over the department's unwillingness to release thirty-year-old documents that would have helped correct the "grossly misrepresented" picture of U.S. activities in the Middle East in the 1950s. "At a time when the Soviet Union and its former satellites are revealing their most terrible secrets," Cohen observes, "the U.S. government continues to publish blatantly fraudulent accounts of its own activities in Guatemala, Iran, and Southeast Asia in the 1950s."

At one time, Cohen notes, the Foreign Relations series published by the department had "an extraordinary reputation for its thoroughness and integrity," but since the 1950s this reputation has been badly tarnished by the bureaucratic self-serving of Cold Warriors. Ronald Reagan dealt democracy a further blow by extending from twenty to thirty years the period during which the truth could not be told, and the Bush administration has now decided that even *thirty* years after the fact is too soon to let the American people know what its public servants have been up to. The Cold War is over, the information being withheld is old news everywhere else in the world, but it is still considered too strong to be served to the American people. This illustrates the utter contempt in which democracy is held by the authoritarians who dominate American foreign policy today.

REVEALING REASONS

Government bureaucrats usually attempt to justify their demands for secrecy on the grounds that "the enemy" will otherwise learn our secrets. The hollowness of this claim was exposed in 1988 when, after the conclusion of arms talks with the Soviet Union, the Russians were made privy to military information that was still classified "top secret" for the American people. Baritz observes that during the highly secretive Nixon-Kissinger regime in the early seventies, "the most important secrets were kept from the American public and Congress, not from the North Vietnamese, Chinese, or Russians."

Authoritarians argue that only the president and his advisers are competent to deal with foreign policy, but the history of the last four decades suggests that these may be the *least* qualified people to deal responsibly with such questions. We heard a great deal during the eighties, for example, about "the Reagan foreign policy" and "the Reagan doctrine," and certainly public involvement in the development of these policies was at an all-time low. As Hedrick Smith points out, there have been few administrations in American history as fanatically obsessed with secrecy as the Reagan White House, with its incessant internal "loyalty" probes, investigations of leaks to the press, and even a presidential veto of a bill that would have protected whistleblowers from retaliation. Considerations of efficiency, budget reduction, and morale all took a back seat to this obsession with keeping the public misinformed. The rationale was that the well-informed president could then make policy in peace, uninterrupted by uninformed noise from the ignorant populace. Washington bureaucrats were apparently content that our foreign policy was being formulated by a president who praised the South African government for having "eliminated the segregation that we once had in our own country."

The problem with secrecy is that no one can be well informed about everything, and a secretive president not only creates an ignorant public, he increases his own ignorance as well. A president who demands the kind of unquestioning "loyalty" on which

Johnson, Nixon, and Reagan insisted eventually *becomes* uninformed, since those close to him are afraid to share information that might cast doubt on the wisdom of his policies.

There is a famous story about a military efficiency expert trying to understand why motorized artillery battalions always paused for a few moments just before firing. He was enlightened by an old soldier who had been a cavalry officer: "They are holding the horses."

This kind of mindless persistence in routine is the inevitable result of the automatic obedience authoritarians love so well. It could never happen in a completely democratic society—there would always be someone to say, what's *this* for?

The function of secrecy is to prevent anyone from being able to ask, what's *this* for? People finally said it about the Vietnam War, but too late to prevent fifty thousand Americans from dying. People are beginning to say it about Reaganomics, but too late to save millions from poverty. People are finally saying it about environmental destruction, but too late to save us from a host of ecological calamities. The primary function of secrecy is to permit a chosen policy—no matter how short-sighted and destructive—to continue unchecked and unchallenged.

KEEPING THEM IGNORANT

H.A. Overstreet is quoted as having said that democracy was unique in its willingness to put up with a long period of confusion in order to give people "a chance to grow up" in understanding and responsibility. This is what the Cold Warriors of the last forty years have been entirely unwilling to do, and that unwillingness renders them ineligible to speak as representatives of democracy.

It is not because these officials have made mistakes. To act is to make mistakes. It is because of their unwillingness to allow the American people to make their *own* mistakes, rather than be forced to blindly endorse those of their leaders. To protect anyone from making mistakes is to forbid learning, and authoritarians are extremely reluctant to permit Americans ever to hear any point of view other than the official one. Ronald Reagan, for example, justified his unwillingness to allow foreign thinkers, writers, and scientists into the country on the grounds that the American people would be "exposed to propaganda." But if it is dangerous for Americans to hear another viewpoint, then democracy is already dead and doesn't need to be defended any more.

In May of 1988, Cuba gave a group of American citizens "virtually unrestricted access to six Cuban prisons of their own choosing," while the U.S. State Department refused visas to a comparable group of Cubans who had arranged a similar visit to prisons in this country. Yet we are continually told that Cuba is a "closed" society while ours is an "open" one.

Just how far from open it actually is was made clear in a report by the Association of American Universities in 1988, which complained that the Reagan administration's efforts to restrict the flow of scientific information could soon become "irreparably damaging" to our position in the world—inhibiting scientific progress, jeopardizing our competitiveness in the world economy, and weakening national security.

Not only has the White House attempted to suppress the flow of scientific information to and from other countries—it has also tried to suppress the flow of information from Americans *to* Americans. Early in 1989 a study by James E. Hansen (director of NASA's Goddard Institute for Space Studies), suggesting that the continued use of fossil fuels was having a severe impact on global climate, was censored by the White House Office of Management and Budget, which rewrote Hansen's paper to delete his conclusion.

To these authoritarian officials the public is an animal to be kept at bay—preferably in a starved and weakened condition. Information is the food that strengthens it the most, and information revealing its own strength and power is the most dangerous food of all. This is why officials tend to downplay protest rallies, consistently giving estimates of their size that are far below those of neutral observers. During the Vietnam War, for example, the government released an aerial photograph to the newspapers purporting to show how small the crowds around the Washington Monument were at the height of an antiwar rally. James Yorke, the mathematician who later gave the science of chaos its name, analyzed the shadow of the monument and demonstrated that the photo had actually been taken late in the day, when the rally was breaking up.

The reason officials hide information from the public is that if the public had that information it would object. Why else do people lie? It is our prerogative, of course, to blind ourselves to anything we don't want to look at. But how many of us want others to make that decision for us? When is it ever for our benefit that information affecting our welfare is withheld from us? How can we make intelligent choices about our future without such information? Have we forgotten what democracy is about?

GRUDGING ADMISSIONS

When exposure of an official lie does occur, confession is gradual and incomplete. Official reaction is drawn out into three discrete and reluctant phases.

Authoritarian Survivals in American Society

The first response is outright denial. The American public—conditioned by advertising—does not expect anyone to tell the truth when it is unflattering, and this particular lie is considered a kind of free throw, and is seldom held against the liar. Washington and his cherry tree notwithstanding, every president is allowed one cover story, and the same generosity is extended to cabinet members, other high-level federal bureaucrats, governors, corporate executives, and any other official who appears frequently in the media.

When this stance becomes untenable the fallback position is amnesia. The official doesn't remember, didn't know anything about it "that he recalls." When it happened, he was out of the room, out of the loop, or out of his head. A person so busy and important can't be expected to remember everything that happens.

Failure of this device leads to the final confession, which is always made in the passive voice: "Mistakes were made." Not, "I made a mistake." The implication is that some group of flunkeys on the official's staff somehow managed to mess things up in such a way as to produce exactly the result the official wanted but would never, never have sought, knowing the public was against it.

By these gradual steps, the official can minuet out of the shadows without ever once telling the truth or admitting personal guilt. The public meanwhile has gotten used to his or her crimes and misdemeanors and come to accept them as "part of the game" of politics, business, or professional ambition.

PRIVATE MATTERS

Secrecy in the so-called private sector is easier to achieve, since what a corporation does is felt to be none of the public's business in the first place. But the public has never looked with favor on having large sums of money transferred from its own hands into the hands of the few who already possess a disproportionate share of the nation's assets, and since a great deal of this sort of thing is going on at all times there is a need to see it done as unobtrusively as possible.

It is felt to be particularly important that when the public is placed in physical jeopardy through the incompetence and/or greed of corporate officials, it should be kept unaware of the fact as long as possible, lest the corporate image be damaged. Consumers exposed to toxic products, neighbors exposed to toxic waste, and workers exposed to toxic materials, for example, are usually the last to know about it. Whenever some industrial disaster occurs one can predict with confidence that the first public statement of the corporation in question will end with the words, "there is no danger to the public"—an excellent indication that there probably is.

A 1988 report found that in a single year there were 104,000 incidents in the United States in which nuclear workers were exposed to radiation, and that "lax oversight of nuclear safety and *deliberate withholding of information* characterize both the DOE's handling of the nation's nuclear weapons reactors and the NRC's regulation of commercial nuclear power plants."

BLAMING THE VICTIM

This knee-jerk mendacity is responsible for the regularity with which industrial and transportation accidents are blamed on human error. Before Ralph Nader came on the scene, it should be remembered, human error was seen as the *sole* cause of automobile fatalities.

This claim has a specious plausibility that has given it a long and undeserved life. "Human error"—we can all identify with that, can't we? Recalling our own mistakes we shrug sheepishly and sigh at the incorrigible carelessness of the species. But it is the very universality of human error that makes the claim an evasion. Since to err is human, any corporate decision that fails to take this into account is irresponsible and—where human lives are at stake—felonious. Any industrial design that depends for its safety on a perfect human being is a homicidal design—a fatal accident waiting to happen.

Yet the technique works—perhaps because individuals are more newsworthy than corporate negligence. The main focus in Exxon's *Valdez* disaster was on the ship's captain, although massive oil spills have become a commonplace of shipping accidents and could be prevented if—and *only* if—the companies involved were willing to spend the money to retrofit their tankers. Ships run aground all the time, whether their captains drink or not.

Blaming the victim is not merely a corporate practice. The U.S. Navy, plagued throughout 1989 by accusations of mismanagement, tried to blame an accident on one of its victims, calling it an act of "suicidal sabotage"—a bit of alliterative slander that was resented by the dead sailor's family and ultimately shot down by the GAO.

COMMUNICATION AND EFFICIENCY

People in management positions talk a great deal about communication. They complain about the difficulty of "communicat-

Authoritarian Survivals in American Society

ing" to particular groups who don't seem to want to be "communicated" to. Lectures, seminars, and workshops are given and books are written about "how to communicate more effectively." At first this seemed puzzling to me. What was the problem? Later I came to realize that what these people really wanted to know was how to "communicate effectively" without telling the truth, and this, I have had to admit, is a difficult undertaking, and merits all the workshops and books that have been devoted to it.

Secrecy is a wasteful and inefficient use of human resources. What secretive managers and officials are saying in effect is, "Look, we have this problem we're trying to deal with here, and although we're not doing very well with it we don't want any help, because someone's bound to come up here and tell us we're going about it the wrong way, and we certainly don't need that, because we *like* doing it this way and we want to keep *on* doing it, even if it doesn't work."

Tom Peters, outlining the directions American corporate leaders must take in order to maintain their adaptability in today's world, insists that virtually *all* information should be shared throughout the organization: "All the tools to induce and support action-taking," he argues, "must be available at the front line."

To authoritarians this strategy seems utterly impractical. But Peters is not some woolly idealist in search of a straight-talking utopia—he is discussing ways to make American corporations more competitive. His argument is that *secrecy is impractical.* And it is—impractical and inefficient in industry, and impractical and inefficient in government. The Russians, who have a thousand-year tradition of authoritarian secrecy behind them, have finally begun to realize this.

The inefficiency of secrecy lies in its poor use of resources. Sharing information about any problem maximizes the possibilities for solution, since people have different skills, different ways of looking at the world, different contexts in which to place the information. It is no accident that prophets are more honored in foreign lands; that great insights and breakthroughs in knowledge so often come from mavericks or people "outside the field"; or that inventions have come so disproportionately from people working outside corporate R&D departments. The farther you go up any pyramid the more people you find who are locked into the status quo—into obsolete agendas and strategies.

The advantage of democracy is that it increases the pool of human resources—that it maximizes the availability of new ideas and perceptions, bringing to bear the insights of people who have very little stake in perpetuating the useless or self-defeating habits of the day. Secrecy is a curse not just because it is a mask for corruption and incompetence. Secrecy is a problem because it strangles growth and development—because it *shrinks the pool of possible adaptive responses to any situation.* Authoritarian leaders would rather have an ineffective policy controlled by themselves than an effective one shared with others.

CHAPTER 12

The Muffled Voice of Freedom

Americans were told not about a President who harbored
an apparently pathological disregard for truth, but about
a well-meaning Everyman who at times got his figures
wrong.

—Mark Hertsgaard, *On Bended Knee*

The media are the fuel pumps of democracy: democracy feeds on information and withers without it. By the same token, authoritarianism cannot survive in the presence of truly independent media. The independence of our media today is therefore of vital importance to the progress of American democracy.

The media must hold the attention of their audience in order to exist. They must avoid boredom at all costs. So even if they were governed solely by the desire to entertain and titillate, that same desire will produce exposés of government malpractice. The baring of secrets is interesting to the public, and authoritarianism is built on secrecy. No matter how lethargic and cowardly the media may have become, their need to interest the public puts them into automatic conflict with authoritarian officials.

Today the media are under attack from all sides—from officials who feel indignant when they are unable to behave in a dictatorial fashion without criticism, and from media critics who complain that the media are failing to do their job of informing the public.

The most serious criticism is that news reporters in recent years have tended increasingly to repeat dutifully whatever distorted version of reality government spokespersons have seen fit to dole out, with no attempt to corroborate or verify it—a trend that has disturbed journalists themselves although they seem helpless to reverse it. It is probably fair to say, in fact—given the new freedom and diversity appearing in the Soviet press under Gorbachev—that our mainstream news media today are scarcely more independent of the government line than *Pravda*.

Despite this fact, the media are under continual assault from right-wing authoritarians for not being subservient enough. These attacks are a form of intimidation. They reached an all-time high during the extraordinarily secretive Reagan administration, which went as far as having the FBI and CIA infiltrate news organizations.

The power of public officials to give, withhold, and above all "manage" the news is the most serious threat to democracy in the United States today. The Reagan administration, for example, used to spend much of its time manufacturing what was called the "line of the day"—a catchy ad-like slogan reflecting in some positive way on the president and his programs. These were then given out to the press, who submissively passed them on to the public unchallenged—a process indistinguishable from the handling of news in totalitarian countries.

News management is certainly not new. In the early days of TV, when news programs had small budgets and staffs, they were entirely dependent for international news on handouts from the then secretary of state, John Foster Dulles, whose paranoid fanaticism was to become the cornerstone of American foreign policy for the next third of a century.

Dulles was the first secretary of state to hire a PR man to manage the news, and all foreign newscasts went through his office. Newsreels were subsidized by the CIA, along with a network of ostensibly private radio and TV stations. Dulles orchestrated travel shots of himself in various parts of the world, as a backdrop to predigested "news." He was filmed from below to give him an "American eagle look," and encouraged to retain his rural pronunciation of the Evil Enemy—"Commonism"—to provide a folksy touch. He insisted on final approval of all news films dealing with foreign policy, and reporters who were sufficiently subservient obtained private briefings from a "high government source." Under the code name "Kingfish," the CIA infiltrated film companies, magazines, newspapers, and book publishers. It is little wonder that Dulles's peculiarly demented approach to foreign affairs became so entrenched. For years the American people saw world events only through his distorted vision, and knew only as much as he was willing to tell them.

Dulles was not unaware of the impact he was having, but argued that the United States was "still at war," and that therefore civil liberties no longer mattered. He took the familiar position that the Soviets were immoral and ruthless, and that we could only best them by throwing all our democratic institutions out the window and hence becoming just like them.

Dulles's ability to manage the news stood him in good stead during the Arbenz affair. In 1953 Jacobo Arbenz, a popular socialist, won a major electoral victory in Guatemala. At a time when a handful of individuals owned 90 percent of the land (much like today), Arbenz had promised to expropriate some reserve lands held by the United Fruit Company, paying the company off in low-yield government bonds. Dulles (whose brother Allen, head of the CIA, was on the board of United Fruit) promptly told reporters that a Moscow-directed conspiracy was taking over a country in our own back yard, and that a "reign of terror" was in progress to kill all anticommunists. He then reported a "spontaneous patriotic uprising," in the form of a military force organized by the CIA in Honduras and Nicaragua, with U.S. air cover and led by a U.S.-trained right-wing Guatemalan colonel. U.S. planes bombed Guatemala City, Arbenz fled, the colonel was installed—along with U.S. military and economic aid—and United Fruit kept its unused land. It was decades before most Americans had any idea what had really happened, and by then nobody cared.

As news gathering became more efficient with technological improvements, it became more difficult for government officials to achieve the kind of stranglehold over foreign news achieved by the Dulles brothers, but it was not from want of trying. Lyndon Johnson attempted to suppress news stories about Vietnam, and verbal controversy about the war was kept off the TV screens long after the newspapers were full of it. Nixon tried to disguise his own escalation by showing pictures of returning troops and refusing to allow pictures of their replacements. When there were leaks about incursions into Laos and bombings in Cambodia, he attacked the networks and put pressure on affiliates to reject "negative" network programming if they wanted their licenses renewed. Newsmen who seemed "too independent" were investigated by the FBI, and he managed to make CBS so nervous that it dropped its "instant analysis" of presidential addresses.

Eventually news management tends to sow the seeds of its own destruction. Official reports are boring, and with all the glitz in the world, the "line of the day" will get tiresome when the same stale minds are producing it year after year. What isn't being said eventually becomes more interesting than the manufactured verbiage, and a leak becomes irresistible.

It is the illusion of invulnerability that helps bring this about. Officials begin to believe their own rhetoric—seeing their values and those of the people as one and the same. They become overconfident and careless. The CIA, for example, might have gone on overthrowing Latin American governments indefinitely without protest if Allen Dulles had not been so anxious to advertise its "successes." When he started taking bows for the overthrow of Mossadegh in Iran and Arbenz in Guatemala, it began to open at least a few American eyes. Those who still believed in democracy were somewhat appalled that the CIA had overthrown democratically elected leaders and substituted clones of the dictators we had just defeated in World War II. And although these actions have continued, the level of public protest has increased each time.

Three decades and a dozen dictators later, the covert operations of the CIA are a lot better known and are subject to considerable debate. The collapse of one dubious protegé after another—Chiang Kai-Shek, Batista, Thieu, the Shah, Marcos, Somoza, and so on—has activated a serious examination of the whole futile enterprise.

WILLING SLAVES

But with each passing decade official manipulation of public opinion becomes more sophisticated and is made much easier than it should be by the media themselves, who collude in the suppression of dissident opinion and critical facts. Under the Reagan administration they became content to regurgitate government handouts that were little more than propaganda, and even today most newspeople simply parrot what officials tell them, even when a simple check of sources would identify the story as a deliberate falsehood. "Investigative reporting" since the eighties has come to mean interviewing friends about their shopping habits.

Media sloth at its worst is exemplified in the practice of airing pre-made videos that have been spoon-fed to network news staffs by interested parties. These are little more than commercials being passed off as news simply because they save the news staff the trouble of gathering their own data. But even when TV reporters do their own filming, the scene they shoot has often been carefully arranged to create a desired impression. One TV newsman remarked that during the Reagan era "Michael Deaver should have been listed as Executive Producer on all our newscasts," so faithfully did the news media reproduce scenes that were staged and orchestrated by the Reagan administration.

There is a built-in problem in reporting honestly about government affairs: newspeople tend to be dependent on officials for information and therefore need to stay on good terms with them. They cannot expect to write critical or revealing articles one day and get a juicy item from "a government source" the next. Gossip columnists and interviewers can sometimes get away with this sort of thing with movie stars, who are interested only in notoriety. But people in government are in a position to punish newspeople who are critical or challenging in any way and rarely hesitate to do so. Reporters who probe too deeply may find themselves writing society news.

Most journalistic censorship is self-censorship. Reporters whose material is edited out by their bosses learn what to avoid in their copy. As long as the media are competing for information the government holds, they will be easy to manipulate, and the concept of a private, independent press will be little more than a pleasing illusion.

But this *assumes* the very authoritarian system that the media are supposed to protect us against. It is true that the government has tremendous news resources, and that by virtue of being a center of power and decision making has interesting things to report. But if the news media are relying on governmental resources alone for their information, they are not doing their job, and if they are spending all their time hanging on every word that drops from the mouths of people in power they are simply victims of their own obsequiousness. One of the Reagan administration's techniques, for example, was called "manipulation by inundation." Reporters were deluged with so much predigested pap that they had little time to dig up anything on their own. Michael Deaver worried only about Fridays, because they were slow news days and, as he once remarked, reporters might have time to go out and *find* a story.

Calling Reagan "the teflon president" was a way for the media to excuse the fact that they never challenged him with enough conviction to make an impression on the public. If the child in Anderson's fable had said, "It is the opinion of certain opposition politicians that there might be fewer threads in the emperor's new garments than were reported in the official announcement," would anyone have paid any attention?

The Benneke case is a good example of media reluctance to deal with news that reflects badly on authority. Richard Benneke, a former CIA agent, testified during an Iran-Contra trial that he had personally travelled to Paris in 1980 with George Bush and William Casey to work out a deal with the Iranians, the substance of which was that the Iranians would continue to hold the American hostages until Reagan was inaugurated (which was, in fact, when they were released), in return for which Reagan would supply them with arms. As a result of this testimony, Benneke himself was immediately brought to trial by the government on charges of making false declarations. The jury, after hearing the testimony and reviewing the documents, took only five hours to decide that Benneke was telling the truth. Yet this story, suggesting that Reagan and Bush captured the election by fraud (since the hostages were a major campaign issue), violated an act of Congress (by making deals with the Iranians), and callously forced several hundred Americans to remain an extra five months in captivity (there were expectations of imminent release)—a story that would have been headline news in any real democracy—was virtually ignored by the media, or reported marginally and without comment.

This unwillingness to challenge authority is also due in part to the establishment bias of today's media representatives—a bias that arises quite naturally from an identity of class and interest. As media analyst Mark Hertsgaard points out, the most influential news organizations in America are owned by a handful of Fortune 500 corporations, and the members of the press are overwhelmingly white, middle-aged men in the top two percent of the population by income. They are traditional and conservative in outlook and have very little idea of how most people in America live. They are out of touch with the needs and problems of the average American. They want to preserve their advantages and comforts and are reluctant to think ill of their associates in power. C.L. Sulzberger of the *New York Times* was "indignant" when Allen Ginsberg told him the CIA was heavily involved in the heroin trade and bore considerable responsibility for introducing it into urban ghettos in the early sixties. He later apologized to Ginsberg when the evidence became impossible to ignore.

Newscasters who want someone to interpret the news naturally look to like-minded individuals who will reflect their own perceptions and assumptions about the world. A recent study by Marc Cooper and Lawrence C. Soley revealed that the "experts" who appear most frequently on evening newscasts to interpret current events are almost always white males with a pronounced conservative bias. One-fifth of these analysts account for one-half of all appearances, and some of them seem to have no credentials except having appeared often in the past. Republican spokesmen tend to be billed with neutral, "objective" titles, while the occasional Democrat is always labeled as such—as if only Democrats were partisan. Similar results were found in a study of "Nightline," where the most frequently invited guests were members of the Reagan team.

Authoritarians are nonetheless dissatisfied with this built-in establishment bias among journalists, and have attacked it unremittingly for the small shards of independence that occasionally manage to make themselves visible. The press and the electronic media are accused of being too critical of authority and of having a liberal bias. These attempts at intimidation, furthermore, have been all too successful. They receive far more attention than repeated opinion polls showing that the *public* feels the media are *not critical enough* of establishment policies. Unfortunately the public does not pay journalistic salaries.

But the establishment bias in the media is much more serious than mere conservative like-mindedness. As Ben Bagdikian points out in his book, *The Media Monopoly*, it is due to two major factors—monopolistic control and censorship by advertisers.

Virtually all of the media in America—newspapers, magazines, television, radio, movies, and book publishers—are owned by two dozen corporate conglomerates, and some predict that this last number will be halved within a decade. This means, in effect, that in a very few years a dozen individuals will be able to decide what the American people can see, hear, or read—a situation comparable to conditions in the Soviet Union during the Brezhnev era.

The comparison is not extreme considering the amount of censorship that already exists. Bagdikian gives several examples of books, thought by editors to be important and worthy of publication, which were vetoed by conglomerate executives who thought they were too critical of corporations, advertising, or American foreign policy. In one case the book had already been printed and advertised when all copies were ordered destroyed.

Censorship by advertisers is far more frequent. Most media depend on advertising for survival, and the threat of an advertiser's withdrawal constitutes a powerful censorship weapon. When the *New York Times* ran a series of articles on medical malpractice, drug companies threatened to withdraw advertising from a medical magazine it owned, and the *Times* sold it. The threat of advertising withdrawals kept the link between cancer, heart disease, and cigarette smoking out of the media for decades, while millions of Americans died and millions more became addicted. Even after the link was definitively established and made public in 1953, programs and articles about the lethal impact of smoking were taboo (and in many places still are), for tobacco is the most heavily advertised product in America.

But censorship by advertisers goes far beyond suppressing news pertaining to their own product. They frequently demand that critical comment on corporations in general be suppressed and frown on any type of muckraking or too ardent an expression of democratic values. TV advertisers like Procter and Gamble have insisted not only that corporations and businessmen be given a positive image in TV news and entertainment programs, but that authority figures be cast in a positive light and establishment values emphasized. Programs must be light and escapist to "assure a good environment for our advertising."

Popular taste is often blamed for the poor quality of TV programming and the fluff that fills newspapers and TV news shows. Yet the dramatic shows of the fifties—"Studio One," "Robert Montgomery Presents," "Playhouse 90," and others—which were serious and often uncompromisingly realistic, were also extremely popular with the public. It was the *advertisers* who hated them and withdrew support. And as for news, Bagdikian writes, "*Every serious survey, including those by the newspaper industry itself, makes it clear that readers want more hard news.*" But today's monopolistic publishers seem to be concerned not with the taste buds of the public but with the noses of advertisers.

VIRGIN BIRTHS

Words (or pieces of videotape or film) do not in and of themselves convey information. They must be structured in a certain way in order to convey meaning. This is what makes the notion of objectivity nonsensical: from the confusing flood of data before us, we must select and arrange in order to find meaning. Watching a bulldozer knock down a building, we will probably ignore the blinks and scratches of the driver, or the fact that an ant is crawling over his shoe or that the sun has moved a fraction. But this selection is never neutral—it is based on what is important to us—what we *want* to perceive and what we want others to perceive. Meaning and bias are therefore inseparable.

One of the ways in which we create meaning is through *context*. A human figure lying on the ground conveys very different things depending on whether the ground is a sunny hillside meadow, a dirty alley in the city, or the middle of a highway. *Historical* context is also important. Cases of alleged police brutality are often decided on the basis of whether or not the policeman in question had good reason to believe he was about to be shot.

It is in the area of historical context that the news media seem most pitifully inadequate; events seem to pop up like gophers out of a hole, as if nothing had led up to them. And while it is not the responsibility of the media to be history teachers, it *is* their responsibility to provide context. If they are going to present "background segments," it seems reasonable to ask them to come up with something other than prepackaged government handouts.

When Nicaragua was so much in the news, for example, it was the responsibility of the media to give at least minimal attention to our past relations with that country. Was it not more than a little relevant to know that in 1928 U.S. Marines were sent to that country to ensure that a right-wing general was elected rather than a popular democratic candidate (a result achieved by intimidating the populace and destroying thousands of ballots)? Or that the family of the U.S.-backed Somoza, who for decades headed one of the most brutal regimes in Latin American history, owned 40 percent of all the land in that critically impoverished country by the time he was overthrown by the Sandinistas? Only a minority of

Americans supported our funding of the Contras—would there have been any support at all had they been adequately informed of the history of Somoza's infamous National Guardsmen, who made up the bulk of the Contras?

We cannot expect the media to do what our schools have failed to do, but neither should we expect them to present each event as if it had just dropped out of the sky. Since the cost of a series of thirty-second TV commercials is equal to the annual budget of many American schools (which says something about our priorities as a nation), we can certainly expect more than we get from TV. When Soviet media are beginning to reveal some of their government's more unsavory past actions, it would be humiliating to think that in a supposedly free country like ours, our media are too obsequious to do the same.

THE ONE WHO OVERCOMES THE MANY STRIKES AGAIN

A president seems to be admired by the media to the degree that he can present himself as someone who is a despot at heart with an unusual amount of self-restraint. They heap scorn on Congress when it attempts to struggle with the complex issues dumped in its lap, and tend to fawn on anyone who promises to sweep these difficulties under the rug. When candidates gather to discuss the issues of our time, columnists, cartoonists, and commentators never tire of calling them mice or dwarves—thus exposing their own longing for some general on horseback before whom they could comfortably prostrate themselves. If modern journalists had been in charge of the news in the eighteenth century, we would still be part of England.

The media talk a great deal about charisma, as if it were a quality essential for leadership. They criticize presidential candidates for not having enough of it, and dismiss as "not interesting" those who discuss issues. But charisma, after all, is what Hitler had in such large quantities: the ability to mislead the public. It is an ability that media people admire to the point of envy—they wish *they* could come up with such good copy every day.

The media are above all a vehicle for advertising, and advertising is a matter of surfaces and appearances, of packaging and images. Who cares what the product is or does as long as it looks nice and sells? Hence people who work in the media often tend themselves to be on the superficial side—if not by temperament, then as a result of training and experience. The reason media people talk about political campaigns in such amazingly trivial terms is not because "that's what the people want to hear about," but because that's what *media* people like to *talk* about. It's the way they think. It's their job to think that way. Presented with a complex, intricate, and layered stimulus, most will see only its surface. That, after all, is what they are trained and paid to see.

Much moaning and gnashing of teeth took place after the 1988 election because of the omission of any real issues from the campaign. As usual, this omission was blamed on the candidates, who, after all, were mere "politicians." But it was the media who defined the campaign in terms of image and charisma. As one campaign worker commented, "The candidates responded in policy proposals to what the media asked about. And if we talked about something *the reporters weren't interested in*, it didn't get covered."

The result of this lack of interest by reporters was not only one of the most boring presidential campaigns in history but one that never dealt with the horrendously serious issues threatening our future. I would argue that it was precisely *because* the campaign was so superficial—*because* it centered on matters of interest only to media people—that it was so tedious for the rest of us.

Americans are not as stupid as the media would have us believe. Every day, Americans attend meetings and fight for things they care about. They are aware of as many issues as they have access to. Most of us would like to survive, live in peace, have enough to eat and a roof over our heads, and extend those privileges to other humans. We are as lazy and frivolous as people everywhere, but not more so.

Democracy is not about charisma, debating skills, or standing tall, firm, or pat; it is about finding ways to accommodate the conflicting needs and desires of various groups of constituents. The worst politician does this better than the most charismatic image-package around.

Media authoritarianism also reveals itself in the tendency to turn everything into combat. Ellen Goodman argues that the media are only interested in people who have rigid, simplistic, one-sided views, who are then thrown into a kind of gladiatorial combat with each other—the idea being less to decide what makes sense than to decide who's winning. As David Riesman once remarked, a debate makes the absurd assumption that there are only two sides to every question.

Debating skills have minimal relevance for a job requiring the integration of conflicting points of view and the discovery of creative syntheses. When societies spent most of their time killing and enslaving their neighbors it made a kind of sense to choose leaders who could beat everybody else up. In a modern democracy it makes as much sense as choosing a plumber by how well his or her shoes are shined.

THE MASS COMMUNITY

Providing the public with information is an important media function but not the only one. The most vital function the media perform is integrative—weaving together what is already there, rather than merely adding to the heap of thread. The media do this, as people everywhere have always done it, through storytelling and ritual. Most air time and column space—in TV, radio, newspapers, magazines, and books—is devoted to storytelling in one form or another.

Some people feel there is no comparison between ancient myths and the stories we tell each other today. But in fact the soap operas, films, and sitcoms of today perform the very same ritual and integrative functions as the legends and folktales of the past. We forget that the myths that have come down to us are a distillation—that for every ancient legend or tale that we know there are thousands that have been happily forgotten.

The media are an attempt, however inane and fumbling, to recreate the small community on a large scale. The fabled triviality of TV today is the triviality of a small town newspaper or an organization newsletter. Gossip columns and magazines like *People* are a pale echo of the intimate familiarity with other people's lives that characterizes village life, leaving a gap to be filled by the fictional gossiping of the soap opera, the sitcom, and the crime drama. For gossip is the lifeblood of a community, knitting people together in a recognizable common destiny. We talk about each other to establish and rearrange our connections and preferences, and to share our humanity or the lack of it. We laugh at each other's foibles in recognition of our common absurdity and the hazards of being an awkward species in an unpredictable world.

TV is accused alternately of giving undue attention to extremist elements in our society and of homogenizing the nation into a bland, mediocre pudding. To an extent both are true. All media are attracted to the unusual and all media try to appeal to the center (and are forever in search of it). But in doing these things, they are serving the integrative and synthesizing function for which they are designed: exposing all members of the society to its most variant facets in order that all possibilities may be made apparent to everyone, and all members may be linked in some way. Whether they are the radicals, hippies, and communards of the sixties, or the fundamentalists, antiabortionists, and skinheads of the eighties, the statistical exaggeration given them by the media helps focus attention on the continually shifting boundaries and edges of the society and adjusts them. Racial, ethnic, religious, and sexual minorities are suddenly incorporated into sitcoms and soaps (in token form, of course) and the divisive issues and conflicts of the day are alluded to in a comic setting. The issues are trivialized, but problem solving is not the province of TV. Its function is merely to *familiarize*—in the most literal sense of that interesting verb.

It is easy to sneer when every show suddenly has a token black or gay or whatever group is currently being drawn into Beaverville, but TV's impact on cultural change should not be underestimated. We have become accustomed to, and impatient with, a rate of social change which would have been unthinkable even fifty years ago, when you could expect the most trivial shift in public acceptance to take three generations. The gains won by blacks, women, and other groups in recent decades—however minimal relative to the inequities still present—have been accelerated in a major way by the familiarizing effect of television. For all its faults, TV performs this integrative and reconciling function far more effectively than any medium has ever done in the past.

The importance of that function makes it imperative that it not be distorted in the service of authoritarian goals. Somebody has to pay for what comes through the media, and those who pay like to have some influence over what they pay for. Democracy will prosper to the degree that the source of this payment, and this influence, is as widely dispersed as possible.

CHAPTER 13

The Dictator Within

We have met the enemy and they is us.

—Walt Kelly, *Pogo*

To the average American—indoctrinated by decades of exposure to TV, films, and rock lyrics—the antidote to authoritarianism is what we have come to call *individualism*. An individualist is a person who believes, as David Riesman puts it, that "no ideology, however noble, can justify the sacrifice of an individual to the needs of a group." This stubborn assertion of individual rights ought, in theory, to be a great encouragement to democracy, but in practice the individuals who benefit most from individualism are authoritarian rulers.

It is hard to disagree with Riesman's statement, given the phrasing: the individual is "sacrificed," evoking images of Aztec altars and cannibal feasts; and not to "his group" or to "her group," but to a "*a* group," which gives it a sinister, alien ring. What is this group that suddenly demands our sacrifice, we wonder with a slight shudder, and what are these needs that it has? The definition seems to suggest something more serious than being asked to contribute to an office birthday gift or pay your income tax—more like being asked by a bunch of complete strangers to throw yourself on a grenade.

On the surface the individualist seems impeccably anti-authoritarian—appropriately contemptuous of red tape, of convention, of "the system"; singing of freedom and the wide open spaces, and not about to be ordered around by anyone. And through it all, entirely unaware of having been indoctrinated since birth to think this way.

THE OLDEST STRATEGY

Individualism may be the greatest boon to authoritarianism since the whip, and has helped prolong it well beyond its natural lifespan. Its message is: "Yes, fight the system by all means—we all hate it, don't we? But you must fight it alone. That's what a real warrior does. Groups just stifle your creativity. You *must* stand alone!" It reflects the oldest authoritarian strategy—divide and conquer.

The dissolution of a tyrannical system is possible only by a cooperative effort. Therefore an ideology that sneers at cooperation, instills an allergic reaction to groups, and idealizes the lonely hero tilting at "the system" serves to preserve that system, since it attaches our antiauthoritarian impulses to an approach that holds no possibility of success.

Individualism as it is usually understood contains two built-in flaws: first, it fails to make any distinction between authoritarian structures and groups of equals; and second, it assumes a static, mechanistic conception of both the individual and society.

In individualistic thinking giant bureaucracies and one's own friends, neighbors, and colleagues are all lumped together as "the system" against which the lonely individual struggles. Communities can of course be stifling and oppressive, but we should not confuse the difficulties we may have in asserting ourselves in a group of peers with the problem of maintaining our own *or* the group's integrity in the face of the authoritarian structures that still govern so much of our lives.

The irony is that the regimentation we complain about so much comes not from too much connectedness but from too little—not from the active "we" of community but from the passive, withdrawn "I" of individualism. It is the inability to cooperate, to negotiate actively about the things that concern us, that leaves room for—and makes necessary—the vast impersonal systems against which we rail, and upon which the individualist heaps so much impotent scorn.

There is little threat to an authoritarian system from the random rebellions of isolated and uncoordinated individuals, and if these rebellions are confused with, and/or joined with, acts of enmity and defiance against the individual's neighbors, the head that wears the crown will rest easy.

Yet the Individual versus Society—the rebel who stands alone against "the system" *and* his neighbors—is one of the most popular themes in our culture. This myth helps to preserve the authoritarian status quo because it encourages feeble gestures and disparages democratic cooperation. It persuades us to vent our discontent by railing ineffectually at a system we deny our participation in, and hence never organize ourselves to change.

THE HIDDEN AGENDA

The Individual-versus-Society myth certainly makes good theatre. We all feel alone against the world at times and are rarely allowed to indulge these worm-eating proclivities in public. But there is a more sinister side to the myth: in the lonely hero rebelling against "society" we can recognize our old friend, the One Who Overcomes the Many.

The individualist, in other words, is not rebelling in order to bring democracy to the people. After all, he feels as oppressed by "the people" as he does by the tyrannical forces that control him. He is rebelling in order to become a dictator himself. The individualistic adventurer of today is the dictator and colonialist of tomorrow.

The underlying dream in individualism is not merely freedom from oppressive authority, or freedom from arbitrary mechanical rules and senseless bureaucratic regulations; it is the dream of being able to act unilaterally throughout one's life—never having to deal with the maze of human relationships. Being able to be arbitrary, capricious, disconnected, all-powerful. Riding down the highway of life in a powerful, irresistible car, completely detached. Never having to deal with anyone.

EVERYONE A DICTATOR

But people do not live in a vacuum, and the aggressive assertion of one person's freedom usually curtails someone else's. This interdependence is hard for some people to accept. It used to bother Howard Hughes, the deranged billionaire, that undergound reservoirs of oil and water refused to respect property boundary lines—flowing promiscuously under the land of many different owners. Hughes felt he had a right to anything he could pay for and was very aggrieved when he found he couldn't control everything around him. He ended his days in a dark room—a prison of his own making—the one place where he could exercise complete control over his environment.

Extreme individualists like Hughes want to deny kinship with the rest of life—to find a refuge inside their own egos. Our dense bureaucracies, our mass of confusing and contradictory laws, our endless lawsuits and court battles, our strangulating technology—all result in part from this dream of sailing through the sea of community without meeting anyone. They are Frankenstein monsters constructed from our own discarded community skills. Our scorn for politicians and lawyers is a case of shooting the messenger who brings bad news—the news that our individualistic dreams cannot be fulfilled.

THE GREAT FALLACY

Everybody wants to "beat the system," but individualism makes it impossible to grasp what the system is, for it assumes that an individual exists *apart* from the family, group, community, or nation of which he or she is a member. You can speak of self and system separately, just as you can speak of finger and hand separately, or hand and body. But when that finger or hand has been permanently severed and lies on the floor, it has for all practical purposes ceased to exist as anything but a prop in a horror movie. It is no longer a functioning unit.

The same is true of the human individual. We do not exist apart from the society in which we live. It is a part of us. No matter where we run, it will be there, inside us. We can no more escape our society than we can escape our bodies (and the two desires are often paired). *The very wish to escape our culture is itself a product of cultural conditioning.*

A society in which people teach themselves this wish is a society full of illusion, of confusion, of unanticipated and startling frustrations, of invisible and impersonal dangers, and of mushrooming authoritarian institutions. We are the nerve endings of that society, and as long as we blind ourselves to our role in creating it—and withhold our pain from it—it will continue to function as it does.

US AND THEM

The second flaw in popular individualistic thinking is a static, mechanistic conception of the individual-society relation. It visualizes society as a kind of gigantic machine, and the individual as a smaller machine which has the choice of plugging itself into the big machine, doing battle with it à la David and Goliath, or withdrawing from it. But as Follett observes, images like "cog" and "niche" are irrelevant to dynamic organic processes, for the whole of which we are a part is constantly being recreated by the relationships that comprise it—that is, the individual is continually creating what he or she is a part of.

Individualism sets up a phony opposition between self-assertion and conformity, as if one had to choose between imposing one's will on the group and surrendering to it in an orgy of altruistic self-sacrifice—between being a solipsistic boor and a compliant wimp. But in a true democracy self-assertion and cooperation go hand in hand, since both are necessary for the creative syntheses that democracy continually seeks. Follett ridicules the idea that individuality must be sacrificed for the benefit of the group. Such sacrifice, she says, merely impoverishes the group. Neither the person who wants to dominate the group nor the person who "has nothing to add" can be said to be truly democratic—rigidity and self-sacrifice are equally inimical to both individual and group growth. Democracy means participation—it is a matter not of sacrifice, but of *contribution*, which is a form of self-assertion. Democracy requires maintaining one's point of view "until it has found its place in the group thought. . . . The only use for my difference is to join it with other differences." For it is the joining of differences, Follett argues, that is creative. Groups that are excessively like-minded tend to die of "non-nutrition," for uniformity is not unity. "We attain unity only through variety."

Follett is even more scornful of compromise, which she calls "temporary and futile," and which "abandons the individual"; conflicts are resolved not through compromise but through *invention*—the creative redefinition of the problem in such a way as to meet the needs of all. She cites the example of a dairy cooperative that was about to splinter over which of two groups had priority at a loading dock, until someone suggested changing the position of the platform so both groups could unload at once. "Never let yourself be bullied by an either-or situation," she argues. "Find a third way."

This requires flexible participants, people able to look beyond the personal agendas they enter the group with, able to develop along with the group. To the rugged individualist, whose fragile ego makes him view cooperativeness as surrender—who fears that if he blended his goals with those of others he would dissolve into a puddle—she asks, "Do we want to preserve that self or grow a bigger self?"

What sacrifice, rigidity, and compromise all fail to recognize is that a conflict between two individuals is inseparable from the internal conflicts of each, so that a creative integration of the relationship between them will help each of them unify the warring tendencies within themselves, and vice versa. "These are not really two processes, but one; the individual would not be integrating his personality if he lived in a world by himself."

THE UPSTART

The term *individualism* is misleading, for it implies that the individualist is an advocate for the whole person. But individualism is actually an assertion of only one *part* of the individual, and at the expense of all the rest.

Every organism contains within itself a voice that speaks for its personal survival—a kind of individual department of defense. From a biological viewpoint the individual's survival is relatively unimportant once the individual has reproduced, for then the species has no further use for it. Still, in order for an organism to reach the age when it *can* reproduce, it must have an impulse to preserve itself—an impulse which in some species vanishes utterly after (or even during) reproduction, but in more complex forms of life lingers on for some time.

This drive to maintain one's personal existence gives rise to a part of the psyche we may reasonably call the *ego*, in keeping with much psychological usage.

The human organism as a whole is an extremely complex and subtle system, capable of responding on many levels at once. The ego, by contrast, has a simpleminded, binary view of life. Everything—no matter how intricate—is reduced to two categories: threat and non-threat.

This oversimplification is extremely useful in crisis situations, like getting out of the way of an oncoming truck, and of little value the rest of the time. How, then, did this useful but rather shallow inner voice achieve the kind of dictatorial control that it has over most human beings today?

Simplification in a crisis situation is what the Romans had in mind when they appointed a temporary dictator: Cincinnatus is called from his farm, given absolute power for a brief period, saves Rome, and goes *back* to his farm. Unfortunately—in psyches and societies alike—the last item in this program is usually omitted— the fact that he fulfilled it is what made Cincinnatus famous. In the more usual case the dictator manages to discover new crises, new dangers requiring his continued presence. The state of siege is continued—martial law becomes a way of life.

Because of our prolonged infant dependency human organisms have a particularly difficult time distinguishing between real and bogus dangers. For the human infant the absence of maternal love is a genuine death threat. Ensuring parental love has become entrenched as a survival technique long before a child can talk, and by then the habit of monitoring and editing one's own responses in anticipation of love has become so well established that we think we're only doing it for ourselves. Our department of defense has become a department of internal security as well.

The ego's criteria of safety, by this time, may have very little to do with maternal love. Safety may mean placating parents, fighting parents, or ignoring parents. It can be summed up as "what I need to do to feel worthy and/or capable of taking care of myself." This might entail being a nice person or an axe murderer, a cleanliness fanatic or a slob, a household word or an anonymous cipher. For many Americans, it means having a lot of money or possessions. But whatever the strategy, the strategist is the same: the dictator who refuses to return to the farm.

For a large portion of every ordinary day—as sages have been telling us for several millennia—the ego prevents us from appreciating the world we inhabit. It is true that the beauty of a truck's grill should not be absorbing our attention when the truck is about to run over us in the street, but many people tend to apply this cautionary rule to *all* situations. Unexpected delays, rain, insects, other human beings—all are seen as runaway trucks bearing down on them. Our working lives in particular are dominated by this crisis mentality. We spend our days dodging trucks—sounding alarms, going into hiding, calling up the reserves, preparing for flight, cancelling leaves—shutting out all "unimportant" stimuli in order to cope with lethal deadlines, mortal interviews, and life-or-death luncheon meetings, in which the only real dangers are from self-induced heart attacks.

The ego's techniques for maintaining control are like those of any despot. The first technique is the definition of a threat to the ego as a threat to the entire organism, just as threats to a despot's regime are defined as assaults on the nation. "L'état, c'est moi." The ego-despot claims that the only alternative to its tyranny is chaos and anarchy, and continually attempts to frighten the organism with terrifying images of psychotic lawlessness to justify its own oppressive rule.

The second technique is massive overcentralization. The organism's other constituents—the body, emotions, moods, impulses, psychic abilities, connections with other individuals, subpersonalities, traits that don't fit with the ego's conception of itself, the "collective unconscious," and so on—are all ruthlessly subordinated to the *will*, that is, the ego's control, and are denied full expression or independent validity. They are hence forced to operate "subconsciously," as a kind of psychological "underground"— these terms echo the "lower than low" status assigned to dissidents by despots.

The third technique is secrecy. Any feedback suggesting that the rule of the ego-despot might not be altogether wholesome is ruthlessly suppressed. Anything reflecting on the ego becomes "classified"—a process we usually refer to as *repression* in recognition of its familiar political nature.

The fourth technique is the manufacture of crises in order to justify the ego's continued tyranny. Just as the political despot shrieks of "commies in our backyard," or an "international Jewish conspiracy," or "the Great Satan," so the ego creates phobias and anxiety attacks. The function of these is exactly the same—a way of saying, "You aren't worried enough; if you knew the danger we're in you'd realize how much you need my direction and control."

Willis Harman points out that there are enormous reservoirs of creativity in the human organism—that we know unconsciously a great deal more than we "know" consciously. We know how to change our brain waves, blood pressure, temperature—how to produce and alleviate painful symptoms. Creative and successful people, he notes, tend to rely a great deal on intuition—to trust, in other words, the less conscious parts of their psyches. Important discoveries are first grasped intuitively—only later does the ego-despot march in and take command, establishing his dominion through laborious linear logic. Why, then, Harman asks, don't we turn over all problems to this creative, intuitive part of our being? "Resistance to this idea is likely to be immediate and violent," he observes. "For to assent to removing the ego-mind from its position of gatekeeper, governing what questions get asked of the creative unconscious, is to threaten its domination."

The ego-ridden personality is chronically at war with itself, as the ego-despot struggles constantly to maintain dominance and control over the richer, subtler, more complex, and more creative elements of the personality. It never succeeds altogether, yet it manages all too often to prevent the individual from achieving emotional, physical, or spiritual fulfillment.

THE EGO MAFIA

To reinforce their dominion, our egos band together to create a binary culture—a crude facsimile of the world, refashioned in simple linear forms. It is a world filled with regularity—with straight lines and geometric shapes, with particles that are clearly separate from one another and can only be joined by conscious manipulation—a world of rigid boundaries and immutable laws and static conditions. In the world of this "ego mafia," all interactions are governed by agendas, and all agendas are rigidly adhered to. It is a mechanical world, in which everything is quantifiable.

Nature's exuberance is an abomination in this ego-mafia world. Fluid boundaries, and all mixing, fusing, interpenetration, ambiguity, and paradox are loathsome to the ego mafia. Our egos want simple, linear, rectangular, immobile environments that lend themselves to maximum control. "Man-made" environments are usually built to ego-mafia specifications. The difference between the way it feels to be in a high-rise air-conditioned building in the center of a city and the way it feels to be in a mountain meadow or on a deserted beach is the difference between being in a world in which the ego feels comfortable and being in one in which the person as a whole feels comfortable.

THE EMPTY VESSEL

One of the effects of the ego's enslavement of the organism is a chronic feeling of incompleteness, of emptiness. It may be only a periodic faint nagging sensation on the edge of awareness, or it may be a constant, burning, devouring need that dominates one's consciousness and motivates every action, but it is to some degree almost universal. We use the word *enlightened* to describe people who seem to be without it—people who seem entirely devoid of *wanting*, and are joyous almost without reference to their external conditions.

We all have times of sadness and loneliness and loss, but they are temporary and specific. We cry, or seek company, or grieve for those we have lost, and the pain diminishes. But the ongoing feeling that we are deficient and must fill ourselves up with something in order to complete ourselves is an illusion created by the ego. It arises simply because the ego has cut off communication to some other part of the individual's being. It is this blockade that creates the feeling of deprivation and emptiness. We are dimly aware that something *ought* to be there, but the ego refuses to allow contact with it.

When we withhold our thoughts and feelings from other people, we feel lonely and disconnected even in their presence. Our loneliness comes from cutting off communication. We feel unable to share what is important to us. The same thing happens *within* the individual. When we withhold these things from *ourselves* we feel an inner void.

SELLING EMPTINESS

This feeling of inner emptiness is severely aggravated by cultural conditioning. It has been estimated that the average American is exposed to over thirty thousand advertising messages a year on TV alone, and while these messages vary in product and style, they all agree in saying one thing: "You are empty, incomplete, inadequate, and unloved as you are—only by buying can you be a fulfilled and happy human being."

Throughout history sages have agreed that happiness comes from wanting less, not from getting more, but Americans are inoculated at birth against this wisdom. It is drummed into us daily that there is a gap in our being—a deficiency, a lack—which can only be remedied by buying or ingesting something, adding to our possessions, increasing our consumption. We are told that we can become whole only by *taking something in*.

In other words, we are taught to be addicts.

"NEW VACCINE HELPS SWINE PIG OUT"

A recent newspaper article announced the discovery of a new vaccine which "blocks the hormone that tells the pig when to say when." "Pigs are not really pigs," a biochemical company spokesman commented with pride. "They stop eating. But if you inject them with an antigen to the hormone, they keep eating. The idea is to get more bang for your buck of feed." The dope peddler's dream vaccine.

The "health" of our economy today seems to depend on injecting a similar antigen into the American consumer, and the inculcation of feelings of psychic incompleteness serves this purpose—blocking the impulse that tells us "when to say when." We have been indoctrinated to think of ourselves as human trash receptacles, ready to be filled with whatever junk corporate America sees fit to deposit there.

It is rather hypocritical, then, for advertisers, media spokespersons, and corporate leaders to deplore drug addiction, since they teach it every day. (Four of the top ten advertisers are drug companies.) Children are bombarded with messages informing them that their limitations and unhappiness will disappear in seconds if they ingest the proper substance or purchase the proper product. They are being groomed, in other words, for addiction, and when in the course of their lives nicotine, alcohol, prescription drugs, or controlled substances are encountered, they will be psychologically prepared for them. They will at last realize the dream of instant fulfillment promised by the thirty-second commercial.

Psychological addiction is simply the feeling that we can only be completed by ingesting something—that only by adding to ourselves some substance, some bit of matter, some experience, can we fill up the hole, close the gap, make everything right. The object of the addiction is unimportant; one can be addicted to anything—drugs, food, sex, money, power, fame, religion, shopping, people, good deeds, misdeeds, winning, losing, helping people, hurting people, and so on. What makes the object addictive is the individual's inability to feel complete without it.

This is not to say that human beings should be, or can be, self-sufficient. (Belief in self-sufficiency and self-mastery is a common failing of alcoholics, as Gregory Bateson once pointed out.) Our emotional, physical, and spiritual interdependence with others is one of the parts of ourselves the ego-despot is most anxious to shut off. A hermit and a party animal may be equally addicted—the first cannot feel whole in the presence of others, the other cannot feel whole without them. The nonaddict will feel the presence of others within herself in either case, and hence will feel whole with or without them, and will move toward or away from them in response to the needs of the moment—hers or theirs.

Today the American economy has become dependent on inculcating in every child born this inability to feel whole. It is little wonder that bulimia has become a common ailment; it is an appropriate response to this constant pressure to consume—an equivalent to the pig's antigen.

It is not through advertising alone that addiction is taught. It has long been a dramatic cliché that whenever a character in a film, play, or TV drama is undergoing any strong emotion he or she will either light a cigarette or pour a drink. And while television role models have become somewhat less addicted to nicotine pacifiers in recent years, alcohol nipples are still very much in use. One study determined that by the time a child reaches the age of eighteen, he or she will have watched someone on TV drink alcohol an average of 100,000 times. Crime shows and sitcoms average a drink every fifteen minutes.

The irony of these addictive responses is that when one feels empty it usually is not because something needs to be taken in, but because something needs to be let out. (As viewers, we are all aware of this at some level, and our awareness provides dramatic tension; we know the hero or heroine is feeling something that is not being released.) An addiction to alcohol or tobacco serves to prevent this release and hence to maintain the unpleasant emotional state, slightly numbed by the drug.

Many people find glamor in addiction through its masochistic, authoritarian imagery. The term *dependency* reveals all: people describe themselves as "slaves" to their habits. They boast about their addictions the way servile people boast about their dictators. Anything to avoid the terror of being free.

THE MEGA-GLUTTONS

Since we are socialized from birth to be junkies of one kind or another, it is not surprising that addictive patterns, imagery, and thinking are so large a part of American life. But one particular addiction outstrips all the rest. An addiction to money is so endemic in America today that it is considered normal.

A supply of money adequate to meet one's personal needs is a very pleasant thing—as is a degree of personal influence, the recognition of one's neighbors, and so on. Healthy people are content with modest amounts of these symbolic goodies. Some people, however, feel so deprived, so empty, so inadequate and incomplete, that they are forced compulsively to gobble up the world's resources in such huge quantities that they have driven millions into abject poverty.

A friend once said of the oil tycoon, H.L. Hunt, at a time when he was arguably the richest man in the world, "No matter how much money he had, Hunt was always poor in his own mind"—a statement that could probably be applied to any billionaire. For how much security does one person need? The income from a billion dollars, invested conservatively, is over one hundred million dollars a year, which is a pretty big sugar-tit.

Many people identify with these neurotically needy individuals, imagining their expensive pleasures, but this is a misunderstanding of the neurosis. Those who devote their lives to the accumulation of money are rarely capable of enjoying it themselves—this falls to their descendants. A need compulsive enough to push the money addict to this extreme is not going to retreat in the face of reality. Hollywood films tend to romanticize such individuals, portraying them as original and fanciful characters, but in real life they tend to be drab, banal, and monotonously single-tracked. Most of them are notorious misers—one does not amass billions by being generous. We naively associate the wealthy with philanthropy on the basis of a few well-publicized donations, but in fact the very rich are the *least* generous of all segments of the population in contributing to charity. Poor and middle-class people donate much higher percentages of their income than do the very rich.

It is unreasonable to expect the neurotically needy to be easily parted from their money. If they were at all willing to share what they had, they would never have become so rich in the first place.

Unfortunately it has become our national policy—almost a religion—to indulge, encourage, and even arouse this neurotic insatiability. The American community pays a high price to support the neurotically needy—cheering their frantic yet always unsuccessful efforts to fill themselves up, as if we could somehow appreciate the terrible emptiness that drives them to grab food from the mouths of those much poorer than themselves. But this is a serious obstacle to the creation of full democracy in America, for the goals of such individuals are usually authoritarian, and we have given them the power to realize these goals. It is impossible for a billionaire to believe fully in democracy, for a feeling of community and human interdependence would make it impossible for him or her to continue to clutch with such tenacity so disproportionate a share of the world's resources.

REMISSIONS

Not all those who get caught up in the endless pursuit of money are incurable. There have always been people who at some point in their lives were able to recognize the futility of it, people who realized that the hectic scurrying of "life in the fast lane" exists for the same reason that our music is served so loud and our beer so cold—to numb our senses so we will fail to notice the mediocrity of what we are experiencing. For the ego-despot frowns on experiencing a thing for its own sake: all experience must be harnessed to self-protective goals—enhancing one's prestige, power, or income. Hence the senses must be dulled, feelings muted. Drugs like nicotine, caffeine, cocaine, and alcohol are popular because they serve this function—the first three to speed one painlessly and unemotionally through the working day, the last to blur and blot out the assault of backed-up feelings that tend to ambush such individuals during rare moments of relaxation.

Sometimes recognition comes too late. A study of Fortune 500 executives found that almost half of them felt their lives were "empty and meaningless," despite the successful achievement of their professional goals. And a recent article on baby boomers found that many were changing careers in mid-life in order to find more meaningful work and reassert their personal values—usually at a considerable reduction in income.

REINTEGRATION

The ego-despot is a metaphor—an attempt to shake us loose from our habit of identifying with this small piece of ourselves as if it were our whole being.

But ultimately the metaphor itself must be abandoned, for it tends to drag us right back into the dualistic combat mode that dominates authoritarian thought. The ego is not our enemy. We cannot "overthrow" it and survive. The attempt—through meditation, fasting, drugs, or whatever—to achieve a state of mind in which the ego will relax its death grip on consciousness succeeds as infrequently as it does precisely because it is so often defined in these militaristic terms, which only serve to mobilize the ego for battle—the very thing it does best.

The ego exists to keep us alive. It is not something to be deposed, but merely something to be *integrated*—to be restored to its proper and limited function of protecting the organism from real dangers. It is neither the essence of our being nor is it some alien presence. It is simply a part of us that is dissociated from the rest. As always, the task is not to destroy or conquer, but to reconcile and synthesize. The democratic individual, in other words, has the same goal as the democratic society—to decentralize, to integrate.

PART III

Creative Chaos

No human relation should serve an anticipatory purpose.
Every relation should be a freeing relation with the 'purpose' evolving.

—Mary Parker Follett, *Creative Experience*

CHAPTER 14

Stumbling toward Democracy

A decent provision for the poor is the true test of civilization.

—Samuel Johnson

They took it asunder I hurd thum sigh. When will they reassemble it?

James Joyce, *Finnegan's Wake*

The demand for greater democracy is mounting in most of the countries of the world, both East and West. Many of these efforts will fail, at least temporarily. Some will become intoxicated with their new freedom—trying to tear down everything at once—and will frighten themselves into reaction when they realize how confusing democracy can be. Some will be, or already have been, ruthlessly suppressed. But the process cannot be stopped, for it is founded on structural imperatives in modern life.

In many of these countries the people have never experienced anything approaching democracy and understand even less than we do what a fully democratic culture would be like. On the other hand, they have a greater appreciation than we do of what it means to have a say in their own destiny. Most of them also have a clearer grasp of human interdependence. Democracy will take many interesting, varied, and unpredictable forms in these countries, for even those who admire the United States will not produce carbon copies of our institutions.

Democracy begins slowly but sinks deep roots. Once well established it is extremely difficult to dislodge, but it takes decades to achieve that state. We tend to think of democracy as something that happens all at once, but our own democratic traditions did not spring full-blown from the Declaration of Independence and the Constitution. They evolved gradually over centuries, both before and after our secession from England, and each victory has been hard won and subject to continual erosion from authoritarian pressures.

In the United States there are four major obstacles to the continued growth and development of democratic institutions:

(1) The widening gap between rich and poor
(2) The persistence of military attitudes
(3) The tenacity of authoritarians in power
(4) Public apathy

GLUTTONS AND BEGGARS

One of the most disturbing trends of the past decade has been the erosion of the American middle class and the widening gap between rich and poor. A large, educated, and alert middle class has always been the backbone of our democracy, and anything that concentrates wealth tends to weaken democratic institutions.

A study by the Corporation for Enterprise Development found that during the past decade forty-seven of the fifty states showed a marked widening of the income gap, and a federal report found that while the wealthiest fifth of the nation's individuals managed to fatten their pocketbooks by an additional 15 percent from 1979 to 1987, the poorest fifth suffered a 10 percent drop in income.

This result was not due to random economic factors, the report found, but resulted from deliberate policies of the Reagan administration. Food stamp programs, aid to dependent children, and other social programs were cut drastically, plunging many families into catastrophe. At the same time, although not mentioned in the report, the emasculation of unions, the deregulation of many industries, the virtual abandonment of any attempt to ferret out or prosecute white-collar criminals, tax breaks for the wealthy, and giveaway programs involving federal land and assets provided an enormous boost for the compulsively greedy. An economist for the committee also reported that many more jobs paid poverty-level wages in 1987 than in 1979. Most serious of all for our nation's future: 80 percent of all working mothers earned less in 1987 than in 1979. Whether their mothers work or stay home and receive welfare, millions of American children are growing up in unaccustomed poverty. A recent study concluded that the nation's *children, one-fifth of whom live in poverty, are "the poorest group in America"* and getting poorer all the time.

The gap between the wealthy nations and the poorer countries of the world is also growing, in a fashion that is Dickensian in its harsh contrasts—international banks vacuuming up money from people whose annual income would not buy the bank directors' lunches. According to a World Bank report, in 1988 the seventeen poorest countries in the world gave the rich countries $31 billion more than they received. Two-thirds of this money went to private banks.

The social cost of such concentration of wealth is incalculable. Consider the price of bailing out the ironically misnamed thrift industry: as one analyst pointed out, this amount—estimated at the time at $157 billion, but much higher now—was enough to pay the college tuition, plus room and board, of every college student in America (at private college prices), and still have more than $20 billion left over. To put it another way, this money, which is ultimately coming in large part out of the pockets of middle-income taxpayers, could have sent almost *fifteen million* additional students to college for a year. What has happened to our values, that we were unwilling to put this money into something that would enrich our democracy for decades to come and yet quite content to squander it fostering the machinations of a small number of neurotically acquisitive individuals? While we have been pouring dollars into already stuffed pockets, illiteracy in what used to be the wealthiest nation in the world has sharply increased: UNESCO now ranks the United States forty-ninth in literacy.

It should be apparent by now that the neurotically needy cannot be satisfied. That no matter how much of the world's resources we give them—how many goods and services they gobble up, how much power and prestige they manage to buy, how much of their environment they manage to control—nothing will ever fill up the inner emptiness that drives them. Yet to appease their greed we have stripped our treasury, our poor, our middle classes, our land, our natural resources, our cities, our infrastructure, and everything that makes us civilized. To fill that inner void we have sacrificed our children's health and education, taken food from their mouths, and thrown them into the street.

Americans are very generous when it comes to giving money to the rich. We are tolerant and forthcoming when it comes to giving away public lands and assets to people who are already overstocked with both. We are generous to corporations—giving them tax breaks and subsidies, paying their bills when they destroy what doesn't belong to them, bailing them out when they go broke through corruption and inefficiency. We are indulgent toward polluters, poisoners, and white-collar thieves. But we turn stingy when it comes to paying the people who protect our homes or educate our children. And we would far rather see our tax dollars pour freely into the pockets of billionaires than allow a welfare mother living in abject poverty to get one more dinner for her children than she is entitled to by law.

Many Americans seem to admire the neurotically needy and strive to be like them. Yet a good carpenter, baker, or schoolteacher is more valuable to our society than a hundred billionaires, who give to the community only the tiniest fraction of what they spend their lives extracting from it.

What concerns us most here is the effect of these habits on democracy, for severe inequality of wealth reduces democratic institutions to a mockery. Can we call it democracy when political campaigns depend as heavily as they do on media advertising that only the wealthy can afford? When the wealthy can fight every piece of legislation they dislike by dragging it endlessly through the courts? When the press is owned and operated by a continually narrowing handful of wealthy individuals?

Publishers today have become increasingly reluctant to print anything critical of corporations or wealthy individuals, for fear of

Creative Chaos

incurring expensive libel suits. A letter to a newspaper editor opposing a condominium development brought a $63 million lawsuit against the League of Women Voters, for example, and a farmer who informed the government that mine operators had polluted a river was sued for $200,000. Win or lose (and most judges tend to identify with people of their own class), these lawsuits—which the rich can afford and the poor cannot—tend effectively to throttle public protest against the depredations of the neurotically needy. Under these conditions the First Amendment is meaningless.

MILITARY DETOURS

Our authoritarian training is still strong enough so that war, or the threat of it, will always tend to divert us from the path of democracy. War always brings relief and comfort to authoritarians: they can escape the confusing realities of democracy and retreat to the illusory simplicities of combat.

The world has become much smaller in the past forty years—as small psychologically and socially as our own nation was a century ago, and as interdependent. There is no room for war any more—no place to swing a sword so that it won't cut the one who wields it. The major powers often find themselves reluctant even to impose economic sanctions because the world's economies have become so interwoven. No matter what we shoot at we wound ourselves as well. But the more democracy takes hold, the more desparately authoritarians will attempt to whip up hatred against some foreign figure, symbol, or nation. It is their best delaying tactic—one more chance to impose their tottering culture on the world.

The efforts of our own administration to wriggle out of demobilizing when the Cold War began to end shows how deeply it was invested in it. The initial reaction was to press even harder for "first strike capability"—the ability to carry out the kind of decisive sneak attack on Russia that Japan attempted at Pearl Harbor. Then a new pretext was found for maintaining our crushing armament burden—the militarization of the "war on drugs." The invasion of Panama, in which virtually the only American casualties were caused by Americans shooting each other, was followed within a year by the invasion of Humboldt County, California, where combat troops and helicopters—mobilized for the "war on drugs"—harassed and attacked American citizens—who must have thought they had been suddenly transported to El Salvador—in their own back yards. One is reminded of the comment of a Costa Rican official, when pressured by our government to create an army, that a standing army always becomes an army of occupation against its own people.

The same motive perhaps explains the alacrity with which the Bush administration leapt at the opportunity to fight a war with Iraq. Hundreds of thousands of troops were immediately committed—once again to protect an unpopular despotic regime—the Saudi monarchy. In a matter of weeks, U.S. policy transformed Saddam Hussein, a petty tyrant no one liked, into a hero to millions of Arabs. It was said we must contain aggression, and the "lesson of Hitler" was trotted out. Yet Saddam Hussein (like Noriega before him) was one of our own protegés—the Reagan administration helped finance his military buildup with subsidies and loans, and pointedly averted its eyes from the atrocities of his regime. Each folly in our authoritarian foreign policy creates a new military crisis, which is then used to justify its continuation—this was how we became mired in Vietnam. A Middle Eastern war could be many times more devastating to our economy, our culture, and our democracy.

THE DEAD HAND OF POWER

Authoritarianism is a dying culture, but cultures don't die easily, and we can expect a long and bitter struggle before the democratic megaculture is firmly rooted. At some point authoritarians usually resort to violence in resisting democratic change—given their psychological and structural rigidity it is usually the only response they have left.

Protests in communist countries always get good press, but they differ little from democratic protests elsewhere. In 1980 a demonstration against the tyranny of the South Korean government—almost identical to the one in Tiananmen Square in Beijing—took place in Seoul, leading to a bloody repression by the South Korean army which took almost a thousand lives. Yet there was little attention given to it by our media—no hand-wringing or pious words about democracy. This was still the era of trying to make feeble distinctions between "their" tyrants and "our" tyrants.

Many world leaders have failed to recognize that limitations on their power are necessary in order to bring about the changes they seek. This was the folly of Deng, in China, who set in motion democratic forces without appreciating their full meaning, that is, that he could no longer maintain the rigid control that had been the prerogative of Chinese leaders for thousands of years. When the confrontation came, he lacked the flexibility to acknowledge the legitimacy of the people's modest desires. He defined it—in classical authoritarian fashion—as a challenge to his authority, an "us versus them" situation, and in classical authoritarian fashion he responded with violence. The same responses were common in this country during the labor battles of the thirties and the civil rights movement and antiwar protests of the sixties.

The free speech movement at Berkeley in 1964—the first major student protest of the sixties—was over the right to distribute political literature on campus, a right school authorities had tried to abrogate. After great upheaval—with riots, beatings, boycotts, and battles with police—this fundamental democratic privilege was won. Yet although today it seems absurd that any major university would try to stifle free speech, many people thought of the students who fought for that basic American freedom as dangerous subversives.

The students who rioted in Beijing were fired with the same democratic ideals as the American students who rioted during the sixties. They borrowed the same nonviolent tactics and used many of the favorite slogans of the sixties protesters. They put flowers in the soldiers' guns, as our students did in the Pentagon antiwar protest. They were provocative and arrogant at times, like their predecessors, and had the same unrealistic expectation that all resistance would evaporate in the face of their overwhelming numerical superiority.

The main difference between the riots in Beijing and similar struggles in our own country—student protests, labor unrest, the civil rights movement, and so on—is that the amount of violent force applied by authoritarians in this country has at times been constrained by the social status of the demonstrators, resulting in fewer deaths. No such constraints limited authorities when it came to lynching blacks, however, or coping with early labor disputes. In 1913, in the mining town of Ludlow, Colorado, militiamen machine-gunned a tent camp set up to protest conditions at one of the John D. Rockefeller, Jr., mines—conditions indistinguishable from slavery—killing over fifty men, women, and children. Those responsible for this and other lethal attacks were never punished.

It takes an intensely felt issue to persuade hundreds of thousands of people to abandon their daily pursuits and take to the streets, and it is only the extreme rigidity of the authoritarian that makes him incapable of acknowledging the impressiveness of the event and offering the handful of concessions needed to make the crowds dwindle away. He sees it as a contest and worries about his macho image, about being seen as weak. The issues mean nothing—it is a test of power, a matter not of solving but of "winning." Yet all that is ever won is a little time—all of it borrowed.

APATHY

An authoritarian who wanted to halt the growth of democracy in the United States would attempt the following:

(1) To increase the power of the executive branch relative to Congress

(2) To increase secrecy in government and reduce public access to information about executive acts

(3) To increase defense spending and maintain a belligerent posture in foreign relations

(4) To increase the gap between rich and poor and disenfranchise as many of the latter as possible

(5) To reduce support for education, child care, and other programs likely to increase public knowledge and understanding

Needless to say, all these goals were advanced by the Reagan administration and are still being pursued at present. But they are by no means the property of any one party. The first item was an objective of the Democrats during most of this century, and perhaps the greatest increases in executive power occurred under Roosevelt and Johnson. The second and third items have also been nonpartisan authoritarian objectives. Only the last two are specifically Republican goals, and even here we should bear in mind that the first serious emasculation of the progressive income tax occurred in 1962 under John Kennedy. Why is democracy losing ground in the United States, even as it makes gains elsewhere?

As a nation—influenced perhaps by our authority-worshipping media—we have in recent years tended to look to the president to solve all our problems and give us a sense of "national pride." But a genuine and satisfying national pride must be built on positive collective achievements—it cannot rest solely on the ability to bully tiny impoverished countries. In the last analysis a president can do very little singlehandedly to change the course of a nation—this requires an active populace.

Yet while people around the world are giving their lives to be able to vote, Americans seem eager to relinquish even this minimal democratic privilege. Americans rank at the very bottom of all major democracies in voter turnout. But a failure to vote is a vote—a vote for authoritarian rule, a vote for corruption, a vote for those wealthy enough to buy the kind of servile government they can control.

Comments on electoral apathy usually evoke the response that (a) politicians are all corrupt and incompetent anyway, so there's no use attempting to exercise any influence over them, and (b) "the candidates are all the same"—two rapidly self-fulfilling prophecies. Some refuse to vote because they "try to avoid politics"—like a toddler who thinks he's invisible when he closes his eyes—but politics will by no means avoid *them*.

And when anyone suggests that the quality of legislators and public servants might be improved by paying them a fraction of what a similar position of responsibility in a private corporation would command, an immediate howl goes up. But what kind of a democracy can we expect when we are unwilling to pay our legislators as much as the sales manager of a soft drink company? When the public servants responsible for administering the tax laws are paid only a fraction of what the lawyers and accountants get who are hired to evade and circumvent those laws—and hence defraud the rest of us, who must make up the difference? When the top three thousand managers in the federal government earn an average salary that is one-fifth that of the average baseball player? When the purchasing power of a public servant's salary has fallen 21 percent in the last two decades? In the top echelon of career civil servants—the best and most experienced we have—*52 percent* left the government between 1978 and 1985 to work in private industry.

It is said that every nation gets the government it deserves. If this is true, then the people of the United States deserve a cheap, cut-rate, secondhand government, since that's all they seem to be willing to pay for. If they assign greater importance to the personnel manager of a plastic bag company or an engineer in a strip mine or the manager of a dog food company than they do to their own representatives and appointees in government, who make decisions governing every aspect of their lives and those of their children, then they certainly have no reason to complain about anything that happens to them as a result.

But to attribute our waning democracy to apathy alone would be a serious error. In European democracies voters are evenly distributed throughout the population, but in the United States the rich are heavily overrepresented. The majority of nonvoters are poor and unregistered, and as a study by Piven and Cloward shows, this is due in part to deliberate policy. Our registration procedures have been called byzantine relative to those of other democracies, who "assume an affirmative obligation to register citizens." Most other democracies, furthermore, hold elections on Sundays to make it easier for working people to vote, and many make voting virtually compulsory.

In 1980 there were *sixty million* eligible but unregistered voters, and *two-thirds* of these were lower-income people. Some analysts say that Ronald Reagan was elected by nonvoters, since polls showed Carter as widely favored among nonvoters as Reagan was among voters.

This disenfranchisement of the poor is not accidental. Not only has our government failed to *facilitate* registration; local election boards have consistently thrown up obstacles to *block* registration of the poor—refusing to deputize volunteers, withholding registration forms, and setting up a host of other bureaucratic impediments. Places where poor people congregate—welfare centers, unemployment offices, public housing projects, community health centers— have been declared off-limits to registration volunteers.

As Piven and Cloward point out, when a class is disenfranchised, political parties will tend to ignore it, and this in turn will increase apathy—voters feeling that no one represents them.

Old habits die hard, as we all know. It is easy to growl at our habitual failings, difficult to change them. We often try new behavior only to discover that through some malign philosopher's stone it has transmuted itself into an old pattern clothed in a shiny new outfit. The struggle to achieve full democracy often founders on three such old patterns: purism, the obsession with product, and the obsession with "winning."

PURISM

Ideological purity has nothing to do with democracy. It is the authoritarian mentality that pursues linear goals and is concerned with avoiding "deviations" and rooting out ideological errors. The element common to all authoritarian thinking is *constriction*—the need to compress all the rich breadth of life into a narrow vertical mold. It is therefore difficult for a fanatic of any stripe to believe fully in democracy, which requires the accommodation of many varied and conflicting needs and sentiments. A fanatic may have a brilliant and correct analysis of any given situation but cannot be trusted because of his innate impatience, mistrust, and contempt for the public, for the less brilliantly articulated viewpoints of others. For people have opposing needs, and hence conflicting perceptions and analyses; and whether one of these is, from some godlike perspective, "better" than another is almost irrelevant, for all of them must be taken into account if the designation "democratic" is to be anything but a sham and a pretense.

Authoritarianism employs a crime-and-punishment model of change: you set up a utopian ideal and then attack and punish all deviations from that ideal. Democracy uses "errors" for information,

Creative Chaos

for the exploration of new possibilities. Authoritarianism constricts, trying to narrow experience to what is the permitted ideal. Democracy expands, trying to provide the widest range of options.

Authoritarianism means either/or. Democracy means both/and. Democracy is not *imposed* from "on high" but springs from the earth, and hence will not conform to any utopian blueprint. It is constantly growing, changing its goals as well as its shape. Although I obviously believe it is useful to identify patterns of thought and behavior that are authoritarian, I also believe that trying to root them out is an authoritarian approach to a democratic goal. We will proceed most quickly not by eliminating old patterns, but by creating new ones. The past will only give way when there is something rich and appealing to replace it.

A new order always incorporates elements of the old. Every culture is full of contradictions, for, as Lewis Mumford once said, it is only the "laxity, corruption, and disorder" in a system that makes it viable. The search for conceptual purity in human affairs is suspect, futile, and usually catastropic. Authoritarianism is part of our heritage—we need to concentrate not on its crimes but on its *limitations*. Our goal is not to expunge but to transcend.

Cultural evolution is full of odd survivals. The sergeant-at-arms at a parliamentary meeting carries a mace, a purely ceremonial symbol of order carried over from the days when some burly goon carried a real mace to bash in the heads of knights who got out of line. Many such survivals get redefined. Authoritarianism redefined hunting as conquest. Democracy tends to redefine conquest as problem solving. We now have "wars" on social problems, and in time, this is what *war* will come to mean. Rather than trying to eliminate words from our vocabulary, we will gradually alter their meanings. *Conquest* will come to mean unraveling relational nexuses—instead of overcoming opponents, it will mean overcoming the barriers that *separate* us from those "opponents." As Mary Parker Follett once said, "I am never fighting you, but always you plus me, or, more accurately, the relation between you and me."

THE OBSESSION WITH PRODUCT

The most persistent fallacy in all political thinking is the idea that by some optimum arrangement of institutions and rules, an orderly, predictable, and satisfying society can be achieved. That if we can just manage to do thus and so, we will achieve a state of permanent harmony and stability, like the "happily ever after" of the fairy tale and the "withering away of the state" in Marxist theory. But about the only thing we can really count on in human affairs is that things change, and in a democracy they change more quickly than in any other condition—rarely in ways that we expect and always in ways that displease somebody.

Living in a truly democratic environment requires a comfort with constant motion and flux, an ability to accept permanent imperfection, chronic development. This, after all, is what life really is. No one is perfectly alive, but everyone will eventually be perfectly dead.

Democracy is an explicit acceptance of this fact of life. It has little use for the static utopias so beloved of the authoritarian mind—everything ordered to suit the controlling fantasies of their creator. Utopias are a denial of nature's restless, exploring energy—a "final solution" to the discomfort caused by the ambiguities of real life.

Democracy is a process, not a product. It is always becoming, never finished; there is no final state in which democracy is achieved. Democracy must perpetually reshape itself to fit the changing demands of the environment and the changing needs of its participants. As Mary Parker Follett said, "Democracy must be conceived as a process, not a goal. We do not want rigid institutions, however good."

It is common for people interested in social change to fritter away their energies arguing about where to start—institutions versus consciousness, education versus protest, within the system versus outside it, and so on. These arguments all rest on the authoritarian assumption that there is one correct procedure, and that all the others are wrong and reveal an "incorrect analysis." Authoritarians like to assign a rank and a status to everything, even tactics. They fail to recognize that change can only be achieved by many people using different—even logically contradictory—approaches. They want to establish a single monolithic strategy, to which everything is subordinate. Someone must be the master and someone the slave.

This is why progressive political groups so often bog down or splinter; authoritarian fanatics try to constrict the process of change so narrowly that no activity can make its way through this sphincter of intellectual rigidity, and in the end they do nothing but argue and issue manifestos. Those who claim there is only one way to change are against change.

Social change does not depend on correct analysis. It depends on motivation. People are reluctant to change because change is uncomfortable and demands a great deal of energy. Therefore, when people ask where to start working toward democracy, the answer is that since change makes heavy demands on motivation and energy, you should start where you *care* the most and do what you like to *do* the most—that will be where you will contribute the most energy and be most effective.

Authoritarians adore "steps"—linear progressions along a narrow and controlled pathway—but there are no preliminary steps to democracy any more than there are preliminary steps to riding a bicycle. You get on, you fall off, you keep trying until you get the hang of it. You cannot wait for the "cessation of hostilities," the "restoration of order," or the "maturity of the people." Any leader—whether in Eastern Europe or in the United States—who claims "people are not ready" is a despot, however benign and selfless his or her motives may seem. Since democracy is a process, it can be created only by being put into practice. And *practice* means just what it implies—a recognition of the importance of trial and error to the learning process.

All the education in the world cannot teach democracy, any more than books will teach a child how to swim. Democracy is learned through practice—through personal involvement in issues of personal concern. People are "ready for democracy" when they say they are. Since democracy is a process, being ready means being ready to learn that process. Democracy is on-the-job training. There is no preparation, no way to avoid mistakes. Democracy *requires* that we make mistakes. *Democracy is the process of learning through trial and error how to engage in the process of learning democracy.*

THE OBSESSION WITH WINNING

The Italian film comedy, *Down And Dirty*, by Ettore Scola, is about an old man who has won a large financial settlement for the loss of his leg. He lives in a poor one-room dwelling with a huge extended family—most of them bent on stealing his nest egg—and sleeps with a shotgun. Various attempts are made on his life by his family, and there are elaborate feuds with outsiders. The outcome of each of these explosions is that everything returns to "normal" except that there are always, for one reason or another, still more people living in the already crowded dwelling. The poor cannot afford the theatrical gestures of the well-to-do, and the realities of poverty always triumph over dramatics.

This film, a metaphor for the vicious cycle of poverty, might also serve as a metaphor for the futility of warfare. For when the fighting is over, people still have to live with each other as neighbors, and the only thing that has changed is that there are a lot of dead bodies and ruined lives and a fearful mess to clean up.

But conflict is essential to life. It is as romantic to imagine that people can live without conflict as it is to imagine that a battle will end it. Without conflict there is only stagnation. The fallacy lies with the notion of *winning* a conflict. "Winning" means narrowing and impoverishing the pool of human resources by half. As Follett says, our opponents are our co-creators—they know what we lack and we know what they lack. The need to win—to dominate others and limit their influence over us—is a self-impoverishing impulse. "To win" is to deprive oneself of necessary input, to narrow one's perspective, to dry oneself up. For conflict is opportunity—a creative synthesis waiting to be recognized.

Democracy is by definition *inclusive*. Not just in the sense of including *people*, but in the sense of including *ideas*. Authoritarianism is *exclusive*, seeking to *limit*—to shut out disruptive ideas and feelings. Hence it is appealing to those with dictatorial egos—egos that are continually struggling to suppress uncomfortable messages from the interior.

The various liberation movements of the past few decades—the struggles of women, blacks, Native Americans, gays, the handicapped, and other groups to break down the authoritarian barriers that have sprung up like tumors on the body politic—exemplify the importance of inclusiveness to the health of democracy. It is not merely a matter of including these individuals within the framework of rights which our Declaration of Independence claims to be inalienable but which have so often been alienated, it is also a matter of reviving our feeling for the rights themselves.

This trend toward inclusiveness is an international one. Despite the many local wars and ethnic battles around the world, global interdependence has become a reality. The tiresome military posturing that still fascinates our media and our presidency is obscuring one of the most profoundly integrative phenomena in history—the accelerating global cross-fertilization as widely different cultures make increased contact. The recent fusions that have occurred in art, music, dance, theatre, film, literature, and so on are only the beginning of a rich and diverse global renaissance.

CHAPTER 15

Self-Creating Coherence

Democracy is based on the conviction that there are extraordinary possibilities in ordinary people.

—Harry Emerson Fosdick

I believe in democracy because it releases the energies of
every human being.

Woodrow Wilson

The incessantly repeated lesson of the twentieth century is that authoritarianism is bankrupt—that power not only corrupts but also constricts the mind. No idealistic purpose, no humane ideology, no benign intent, no personal magnanimity or virtue or genius can alter the unresponsiveness, the rigidity, the inefficiency, and the basic inhumanity of large centralized structures. This is why revolutionaries so often become exactly what they fought against in the first place.

In 1982 John Naisbitt wrote a book called *Megatrends*, describing ten major cultural shifts taking place in our society today. Of these ten shifts, *eight* reflect the replacement, by new democratic patterns, of the forms of authoritarianism discussed in earlier chapters:

(1) From centralization to decentralization
(2) From a national economy to a world economy
(3) From institutional help to self-help
(4) From an industrial economy to an information economy
(5) From hierarchies to networking
(6) From either-or choices to multiple options
(7) From representative to participatory democracy
(8) From forced technology to technology responsive to human needs

If Naisbitt is correct in his forecasting, we are moving toward a cultural democracy far more comprehensive than the token institutions we now enjoy.

The essence of democracy is not taking votes or standing on soapboxes. It is what Follett called "self-creating coherence"—a structure that *emerges* rather than being imposed. Authoritarianism is a wall; democracy is a forest. A wall is created by placing bricks or stones or cinder blocks on top of one another; a forest grows. The structure of a wall is easy to understand; the structure of a forest is more difficult to grasp. Yet it is there, and there is an amazing amount of order in it—an order we are only beginning to appreciate. In the same way, we are just beginning to grasp the fact that there is order in democracy. Not the order left over from our many authoritarian institutions, but the order that comes from our emergent democracy itself—the coherence that is self-created, the product of many different individual inputs interacting.

Our egos are frightened by this kind of imagery—it seems out of control. They look around desperately for a dictator to take charge and put the mess in some kind of geometric order. It seems "unnatural" to the ego, although it is the way nature itself is

Creative Chaos

organized—an order that is continually evolving. The development of chaos theory at this moment in history is exquisitely timed to facilitate the spread of democracy, because it reassures our egos that there is order where before we could only see irregularity, confusion, and randomness.

THE FEAR OF CHANGE

Every cultural change in human history has been resisted with the argument that the change being sought is contrary to human nature—that the ancient cultural habits being challenged are permanently engraved in the DNA of the species. But a glance at the relics of older cultures suggests that the species is more malleable than it wants to admit.

We are beginning to discover how unlimited these possibilities are, and for many it is frightening. Much of the resistance to democracy has to do with its open-endedness. We all know where authoritarianism leads: to the same comfortable and miserable dead end. But none of us know where democracy will lead if allowed to develop to its fullest. It is always evolving—limited only by our lack of commitment to it.

Democracy is in constant movement—confronting ever-emerging contradictions. It thrives on chronic change and unpredictability. Yet this constant change and confrontation, as Follett points out, mirrors life itself:

> We should see life as manifold differings inevitably confronting each other, and we should understand that there is no peace for us except *within* this process. There is no moment when life, the facing of differings, stops for us to enjoy peace in the sense of a cessation of difference.

Democracy, in other words, reflects the real world.

We are a long way from embracing this reality, but closer than anyone could have envisioned a century ago. It is a disorienting moment in history, with so much of what we have assumed about who we are—and the ways we must live—dissolving under us.

There are no models for what we are moving toward. We may gush over hunter-gatherer cultures and their understanding of the balance of nature, but they have not been where we have been and hence their wisdom is of limited usefulness to us. In the last analysis we are on our own and must reinvent ourselves.

AVENUES

There is no formula for democracy, any more than there is a formula for other kinds of creativity. A megaculture affects every aspect of human existence, so it follows that a shift from one megaculture to another involves changes in all of these aspects. And since influences tend to be reciprocal, *a change in any aspect of anyone's existence may facilitate the transition.*

My purpose here is not to provide a "blueprint for democracy"—which is a contradiction in terms—but merely to prepare the ground. Efforts to change any of the traditional patterns discussed in Part II will have a democratizing impact; they can be roughly summarized under the following rubrics:

(1) *Demilitarizing.*

War is an attempt to avoid *dealing* with conflict—to avoid confronting difference. It is a way of postponing the negotiation which is the inevitable outcome of all conflict.

The creative task presented by conflict is to find a way to utilize opposition productively. Lovelock points out that the emergence of oxygen on our planet billions of years ago was a "pollution catastrophe" for life on earth, but that "ingenuity triumphed," and the threat was removed—not in the combative authoritarian way of trying to reestablish the status quo, but in the "flexible Gaian way by adapting to change and converting a murderous intruder into a powerful friend."

The Cold War is over, yet our military buildup continues, and now Iraq has provided a new pretext for Pentagon expansionism. Bureaucracies never contract—they exist only to bloat themselves. There will always be a "reason" to go to war if one is wanted. There will always be "American lives to protect," because Americans are everywhere on the globe. There will always be "American interests at stake," because American corporations do business around the world. These are reasons to *respond* to a crisis, not reasons to make war. We heap scorn on petty despots like Saddam Hussein, forever parading their muscles and bullying their neighbors, but the alacrity and enthusiasm with which recent presidents have elected to descend to the same level—as if only waiting for the opportunity to jump in the sandbox and play war games with live soldiers—is a little depressing. With all the power and resources at our disposal, one might expect a more imaginative response.

But we have the largest war machine in history, and most of the people who maintain it like to see it put to use—that is, after all, why they are there. *No one is motivated to work for peace except the people themselves.* It will take a major grass-roots political movement to convert our society to peacetime democracy.

It could be closer than we think. Early in 1968 Lyndon Johnson was as powerfully entrenched as any president in our history. No one could imagine him losing his grip on the nation—until Eugene McCarthy came out of nowhere with thousands of volunteers to bring him down in only a few months. If we are not dead as a democracy it could, and will, happen again.

(2) *Containing greed.*

Outside of war, the major reason for the continuing overcentralization of American institutions today is our exaggerated commitment to greed as a motivating force. Judging from the media, it has become not merely a legitimate motive but a sanctified one—the only reason anyone would, or *should*, do anything.

It is a mistake—as so many overcentralized socialist societies have discovered—to try to eliminate money as an incentive. Money is one incentive among many, and has its place. But to put no limits on the impulse to accumulate money obsessively is as destructive as to place no limits on the impulse to commit violence. A viable democratic society needs a ceiling and a floor with regard to the distribution of wealth and assets.

Since the Bushmen—one of the most economically marginal hunter-gatherer societies on the planet—managed to feed, shelter, and care for the nonproductive segment of their population (about 40 percent of the total) without complaining about "freeloaders" and "welfare cheats," it seems reasonable to say that any society unable to perform as well as this for its nonproductive members is a very inferior society. Few so-called primitive societies would allow any of their members to starve when food was plentiful. A society that does this is simply not doing its job. Societies exist for the benefit of all. They do not exist for the sole purpose of making a few neurotically needy people very wealthy. Surely we can envision worthier goals than this.

We need a ceiling on wealth because when the few get richer the many get poorer. And we need a floor under poverty in order to stem the narrowing of consciousness that extreme poverty creates, so that those now forced to concentrate their energies on mere survival will be freed to engage in pursuits that are personally rewarding to them and useful to the society as a whole.

Such proposals are often stigmatized as "leveling," which is a very revealing objection. There is apparently a great fear among authoritarians that without enormous disparities in income we would suddenly discover that everyone was exactly alike and we would be living in some sort of homogeneous Orwellian nightmare. This fear of leveling reveals how narrowly the authoritarian looks at the world. In his constricted vision all qualitative differences have been squeezed out—nothing distinguishes one individual from another except his or her financial status. A person's unique charms, talents, personality, skills, and eccentricities mean nothing unless they command different incomes—they are all one color to him.

Moderating our huge disparities in wealth, far from making everyone the same, would permit us to recognize people's differences more vividly—without the distraction of irrelevant monetary status. It would also permit the people themselves to explore a greater variety of useful pursuits, freed from the necessity of performing useless, destructive, or irksome labor just to keep alive.

(3) *Providing a future.*

We often remind ourselves that "you can't take it with you," but the motto of the eighties seems to have been, "let's not leave any behind, either." With what we squander on useless weaponry and corrupt banking adventures we could give every American child a quality education and the kind of supportive infrastructure necessary to take full advantage of that education. This is an expenditure that would pay us back many times over in the future and provide a lasting resource.

But money will not do it all. As education has become an increasingly scarce resource for American children, and as admission to advanced institutions has come to depend more and more on the ability to give prepackaged answers on multiple-choice questionnaires, educational practice has tended to drift in a medieval direction. If our nation is to have a future this trend must be reversed. The verb *to educate* is from a Latin root meaning "to draw out." Education is an interactive process. It means allowing for experimentation and searching. It does not mean stuffing a dead chicken with stale bread. Working toward improvements in educational practice is thus a vital activity, for it is in its treatment of children that a democracy stands or falls.

(4) *Promoting sexual equality.*

Women working to realize their own feminist goals are automatically making a fundamental contribution to democracy, since authoritarianism depends heavily on the oppression and subordination of women. This is one of the few areas in which the United States still leads the rest of the world, and from a democratic viewpoint American feminism is the one bright spot in an otherwise bleak landscape of authoritarian retrogression. But feminism is still in its infancy. There is certainly far more recognition of the issues than there was even twenty years ago, but in practice very little has changed.

Whether the emphasis is on achieving parity in male-defined arenas or on asserting the special value of activities traditionally defined as female—whether the approach is separatist or nonseparatist—any and all efforts (however contradictory they may seem from a strictly linear viewpoint) to redefine traditional gender relationships will have a profoundly democratizing impact on our society.

(5) *Freeing our imaginations.*

The authoritarian worldview is constricted and exclusive. It likes to narrow, to shut out, to rank, and to classify. Whatever adds breadth to our vision, to our field of opportunity—whatever makes our "we" more inclusive, or enables us to greet people and objects on their own terms instead of by category—will move us toward fuller democracy. Visions are created by institutions, but institutions are also created by visions—the two processes are inseparable. Therefore it is crucial that people work toward the transformation of consciousness—to create new images, new myths, new metaphors for experience, so that we can learn to see through and beyond the artificial cosmic pyramid that authoritarianism has constructed in our minds.

As Willis Harman points out:

> Throughout history the really fundamental changes in societies have come about not from the dictates of governments and the results of battles but through vast numbers of people changing their minds—sometimes only a little bit.

(6) *Opening communication.*

Democracy demands the breaching of compartments—the free movement of people, ideas, and feelings. In a true democracy, nothing is "classified." Its governing bodies are truly *public*, not the private property of a handful of ideologues. Ideas are accessible to all and not immediately categorized and bagged for quick disposal. Information belongs to everyone.

A government that has the full support of its people does not need to keep secrets from them. It took only the brief glimpse offered by the Freedom of Information Act, before it was hobbled with amendments, to reveal the incompetence, self-serving, corruption, and crime hidden behind the designations "classified" and "top secret." Whoever withholds information from the people cannot claim to represent them—such a person, whatever his or her office, is sabotaging our democracy. And by the same token, anyone working to expose secrets—government or corporate—is working to advance the cause of democracy. For democracy depends on an informed populace, on free and open communication.

(7) *Freeing ourselves.*

Unlocking our own secret compartments is also an important democratic task. A fully democratic society demands fully democratic individuals. How can we expect to create freely with each other when we have enslaved our own psyches? The democratic individual is able to utilize the resources of all parts of his or her being—those elements that function best without ego interference are allowed to do so. Impulses are recognized, intuitions credited, the unconscious explored, the body heard. The energy of the organism is not sapped by internal wars—all parts are convened in permanent parliamentary session to negotiate their needs and differences for the common good. For the democratic individual, play is not just something one does to pass the time when work is finished. Play is recognized as the creative center of all activity.

Working toward democracy, then, is not a narrow, limited, one-dimensional task. Each of these seven broad categories, furthermore, has many varied and specific facets—each uniquely important. There is something for everyone to do, whatever their interests and tastes, if democracy is a goal they share.

GETTING ON BOARD

Participation is the bottom line of democracy. Every apathetic individual is a brick in a tyrant's throne. When we fail to exercise power ourselves, someone assumes power over us. This is not to say that we cannot delegate power, but that delegation is temporary. As Willis Harman says, "people give legitimacy and they can take it away." One of the basic tenets of democracy is that there is no position of authority or status anywhere on earth that entitles its occupant to automatic respect. In a democracy, respect—beyond the respect owed any living being—must be earned anew each day.

Democracy is fueled by the willingness of individuals to involve themselves in the issues that concern them—to confront them directly. Democracy satisfies one of the strongest needs humans possess—the need to feel useful. For democracy is on a permanent talent search: it finds uses in everyone and *for* everyone.

The challenges facing us today are greater than at any time in our history. We need to enlarge our awareness to include more options than climbing ladders and making money—to realize that meeting those challenges would be personally fulfilling.

Most of us would like to end our lives feeling both that we had a good time and that we left the world a little better than we found it. Few Americans today seem to be enjoying their frantic pursuit of wealth and status, and the tactics they employ in this endeavor seem destined to ensure that the world they leave to their children will be scarcely fit to live in. This is a waste of our talents and abilities. A viable democracy rewards not only its hustlers and swindlers, but also those who contribute something to the society as a whole.

We talk a great deal about "opportunity" in America, but this too often comes to mean the opportunity to enrich oneself at someone else's expense. Redefining our priorities—directing our attention, energies, and resources toward improving the society we live in—would give us the opportunity to build a great civilization instead of merely adding more refuse to our trash heap of greedy dreams.

This is not a matter of duty or responsibility. As Follett says, "We have to create our ideals. . . . 'Following our duty' often means mental and moral atrophy. . . . It is we by our acts who progressively construct the moral universe."

AN AMERICAN RENAISSANCE

Where will Americans be when democracy sweeps the globe? Will we be able to reclaim our original role as pioneers of democracy and champions of the future? Or will we become just another has-been nation—clinging rigidly to the past, lagging behind our imitators, trying frantically to crush the very process we helped set in motion, watching other nations leapfrog past us into the democratic age?

Many Europeans believe the United States is already over the hill—that we have exhausted our innovative spirit and destroyed our economy with our military sclerosis and our obsession with short-term profits. That we have become smug, fat, sluggish, old-fashioned, and unimaginative.

Yet we are still admired for our loose, decentralized system with its great flexibility; and for our ability to include many disparate racial and ethnic groups and divergent points of view. We have come as far as we have not because there is a single "American Way" to which all must conform, but because the true American way is not to *have* a single "American Way"—not to demand that everyone do things as they're done in Waco, or Manhattan, or Mobile, or Malibu, or Omaha, or Sausalito. We have come as far as we have because we are diverse and chaotic, and if in recent years we have lost ground, it is because we have become more centralized and rigid. As Fallows points out, it is our talent for adaptability, irregularity, and constant self-reinvention that has made us successful, not our recent trend toward educational tracking and professional classes.

I believe the United States has more to offer the world than the most efficient way to murder peasants or how to market inferior products with better packaging. The American flag once stood for integration, not division; for acceptance, not exclusion; for diversity, not uniformity; for peace, not war; and for the many, not the few. When right-wing demagogues wrap themselves in that flag, rattle their sabres, and claim the world as the exclusive property of the neurotically needy, they thereby reveal themselves as frauds and imposters.

Media people are fond of talking about "the American Dream," which seems in their view to consist of owning a heavily mortgaged house, a car bought "on time," and various labor-saving appliances. This has always seemed like a tacky dream to me—self-centered, narrow-minded, mean-spirited, and unimaginative. Is this what will usher in a new democratic era? Home ownership? Is this the meaning of freedom? Having a dishwasher? Is this the spirit of American creativity and inventiveness? Owning a Mercedes? I doubt very much that these joys are the beginning and end of American dreaming. Michael Lerner argues that the American people have a deep longing for "a society that supports loyalty to something besides self-interest."

We need a new American Dream. A dream like that of Martin Luther King, Jr. A dream of a brilliant and just society to pass on to our children—a society whose members are not only fed, clothed, and housed, but also healthy, educated, and creative, and living in environments that enhance rather than destroy natural beauty.

We have the ability to do this—to create an American Renaissance. We were once seen by many as the hope of the world, and have become its despair—a dyspeptic old busybody shooting at anyone who comes near our property. It may be naive and optimistic—all societies eventually become ossified and go into decline—but I refuse to believe this is what we truly are. There is still a great reservoir of creative energy, imagination, and originality in this society. We have merely become distracted and preoccupied with our quarrels and fears—stuffing ourselves with material junk to avoid looking at how complex and intricate our world has become.

Complexity can be stressful, but—approached with an open, experimental spirit, without a demand for rigid control—it can also be exhilarating. If democracy is confusing it is also innovative; if it seems chaotic it is also full of opportunities; if it seems scattered it is also constantly sniffing its way toward integration. It may seem like too much work at times, but above all, democracy is playful. It experiments, it blunders, it reinvents itself daily.

Follett consistently reminds us that democracy is not a matter of majority rule or representative government. "The essence of democracy," she says, "is creating."

Notes

Introduction

2   Bennis and I predicted. Philip E. Slater and Warren G. Bennis, "Democracy Is Inevitable," *Harvard Business Review,* March/April 1964. See also Warren G. Bennis and Philip E. Slater, *The Temporary Society* (New York: Harper & Row, 1968).

5   Borders of politics. Walt Whitman saw democracy as a spiritual element permeating every aspect of human culture, and Mary Parker Follett insisted that "democracy is not a form of government. . . . Democracy . . . is a great spiritual force." See Walt Whitman, *Specimen Days, Democratic Vistas, and Other Prose* (Garden City, New York: Doubleday, Doran, 1935), 290–94; Mary Parker Follett, *The New State: Group Organization the Solution of Popular Government* (New York: Longmans, Green, 1923), 160–61.

1: Why Democracy Happens

11   Bavelas. Warren G. Bennis, "Toward a 'Truly' Scientific Management: The Concept of Organizational Health," *General Systems Yearbook,* 1962: 273.

12   "Chose to discount." Douglas Jehl, *San Francisco Chronicle,* 24 September 1990.

12   Wang computers. *Wall Street Journal,* 14 July 1989, 25 January 1990.

13   "Iron law." Loren Baritz, *Backfire: A History of How American Culture Led Us into Vietnam and Made Us Fight the Way We Did* (New York: William Morrow, 1985), 312.

14   Hedrick Smith argues. Smith, *The Power Game: How Washington Works* (New York: Random House, 1988), 712. Smith notes the collapse of checks against executive power, observing that while Congress has not declared war since World War II ended, Americans have been fighting all over the globe ever since.

14 Mary Parker Follett says. Follett, *Creative Experience* (New York: Longmans, Green, 1930), 174. Follett was perhaps the first person to articulate the full meaning of democracy.

14 This tragic fiasco. See Richard N. Goodwin, *Remembering America: A Voice from the Sixties* (Boston: Little, Brown & Co., 1988), 386; Baritz, *Backfire*, 19–54. Ho Chi Minh had always admired the United States (his charter for an independent Vietnam was based on our Declaration of Independence) and sought American support repeatedly. But when the CIA reported that a free election would give this popular leftist hero 80 percent of the Vietnamese vote, the Dulles brothers scrapped the elections, split the nation in two, and set up a Catholic dictator in the southern half of this Buddhist country. Baritz, 59–98, 341. See also Stanley Karnow, *Vietnam: A History* (New York: Viking, 1983).

15 "War was unwinnable." Goodwin, 384–89.

15 Sycophants. Baritz, *Backfire*, 175–78, Goodwin, 383–87.

15 Agency was forced to cave in. Baritz, 138ff., 259–71.

15 Clinically paranoid. Goodwin, *Remembering America*, 392–416. At one point Johnson even cut newspaper deliveries to White House staff so they wouldn't be exposed to contrary opinions. (Goodwin, 386.)

15 (As macho as Kennedy.) Baritz, *Backfire*, 145–46.

15 (Humphrey ... McNamara.) Baritz, *Backfire*, 154, 182.

16 Statistics were invented. James William Gibson, *The Perfect War: The War We Couldn't Lose and How We Did* (New York: Vintage Books, 1988), 156–68.

16 "Dismissed as *unbelievable*." Gibson, 165. (His italics.)

16 Tuesday lunches. Goodwin, *Remembering America*, 386, 390.

16 Establish his credentials. Baritz, *Backfire*, 205–10.

16 A study undertaken. Baritz, 303ff. The ratio of officers to enlisted men in Vietnam was almost double what it was in World War II. (See Baritz, 301ff.)

16 Falsifying records. Baritz, 301–12; Goodwin, *Remembering America*, 125–28; Gibson, *Perfect War*, 155–62. For other examples of military mismanagement in Vietnam, see Baritz, 233ff., 239–50, 253–58; Gibson, 93–224, 319–82. This is not to imply that the war could have been won with better management. No war can be won without the support of the indigenous population unless the invaders are prepared to occupy that country with a large armed force for several generations.

17 "Fearsome lesson." Goodwin, 390.

17 He complained. Goodwin, 366–67.

18   Irrelevant commands. Gibson, *Perfect War*, 105–22. The defolia-
      tion campaign, for example, which in theory was supposed to
      remove the guerrillas' cover, was not only completely ineffectual,
      but left our own troops more exposed to enemy fire. (Gibson,
      123–24.)

18   Responded to immediately. Coordination in centralized structures
      tends to be left to those "at the top," instead of taking place at
      every level. This leaves executives with "the clumsy task of try-
      ing to patch together finished webs." Mary Parker Follett,
      Freedom and Coordination: Lectures in Business Organization
      (London: Management Publications Trust, 1949), 10.

18   "Local discontinuity." E.R. Service, "The Law of Evolutionary
      Potential," in M.D. Sahlins and E.R. Service, *Evolution and
      Culture* (Ann Arbor: University of Michigan Press, 1960).

18   Marshall McLuhan. McLuhan, *Understanding Media* (New York:
      McGraw-Hill, 1964), 251. Hedrick Smith observes that in the
      Soviet Union, "the entire system, top to bottom, resists new in-
      ventions, new products, new ideas." Smith, *The Russians* (New
      York: Quadrangle, 1976), 232ff. Cold Warriors blame communism
      for Russia's backwardness and authoritarianism, which is a lit-
      tle like blaming alcoholism on the invention of the wine cooler.
      As Smith points out, the bureaucratic absurdities Russians suf-
      fer from today differ little from those satirized by Gogol and
      Chekhov. (*The Russians*, 250–72.)

19   Adams and . . . Brock. Walter Adams and James W. Brock, *The
      Bigness Complex: Industry, Labor, and Government in the
      American Economy* (New York: Pantheon, 1986), xi.

19   "In Japanese folk wisdom." William J. Goode, *World Revolution
      and Family Patterns* (Free Press, 1963), 355.

19   Competitive male narcissism. Richard Goodwin tells how Lyn-
      don Johnson, about to make a speech in the UN containing
      "several tangible and far-reaching proposals for nuclear arms con-
      trol," deleted these proposals in a rage when he discovered that
      Robert Kennedy had already made a speech calling for progress
      in nuclear disarmament. (Goodwin, *Remembering America*,
      397–98.)

20   *Democracy is self-creating.* A constitution cannot *create* a
      democracy—it can only *limit* it, to make it more palatable to peo-
      ple raised on authoritarian assumptions. Such limitations make
      it possible for a degree of democracy to take root in authoritarian
      soil.

20   "No conception of democracy." Follett, *Creative Experience*,
      137–38.

2: The Rise and Decline of Authoritariansim

24 A cross-cultural analyst. William N. Stephens, *The Family in Cross-Cultural Perspective* (New York: Holt, Rinehart, and Winston, 1963).

24 No centralized authority. This is true only of tribes that rely entirely on hunting and gathering, of which there are few examples left today. Richard B. Lee and Irven DeVore, eds., *Man the Hunter* (Chicago: Aldine, 1968), 12, 103, 136; Marshall Sahlins, *Stone Age Economics* (Chicago: Aldine, 1972), 186–87; Nancy Makepeace Tanner, *On Becoming Human* (New York: Cambridge University Press, 1981), 87ff.

24 Not warlike. Lee and DeVore, 9, 12, 135, 333–34, 341; Eisler, *The Chalice*, 73; Laurens van der Post, *The Lost World of the Kalahari* (New York: Morrow, 1958) 38; Tanner, 195.

24 Riane Eisler. For a full discussion of the transition to the authoritarian megaculture from various perspectives, see: Riane Eisler, *The Chalice and the Blade: Our History, Our Future* (New York: Harper & Row, 1987); Marilyn French, *Beyond Power: On Women, Men, and Morals* (Summit Books: 1985); Marija Gimbutas, *Goddesses and Gods of Old Europe* (Berkeley: University of California Press, 1974); Merlin Stone, *When God Was a Woman* (New York: Harcourt Brace & Jovanovich, 1976); Charlene Spretnak, *Lost Goddesses of Early Greece: A Collection of Pre-Hellenic Myths* (Boston: Beacon Press, 1981). Since I am concerned here with democracy rather than gender issues per se, I have used *authoritarianism* rather than *patriarchy* or Eisler's *dominator model*, but in most respects these terms are interchangeable.

25 Animal breeding. Biotechnology is a logical, if extreme, extension of this obsession with power over life.

25 Masculine narcissism. See French, *Beyond Power*, 65–76.

25 Motivational tool. For an excellent refutation of the many myths we hold about competition, see Alfie Kohn, *No Contest: The Case Against Competition* (Boston: Houghton Mifflin, 1986). Using empirical data from several disciplines, Kohn demolishes the notion that competition is more natural or pleasurable or motivating than cooperation. (His book is marred somewhat by the gratuitous misogyny of a patronizing chapter on women.)

26 A tiresome egotist. See Lee and DeVore, *Man the Hunter*, 136.

28 Against some foreigners. For an excellent discussion of this technique see Arthur J. Deikman, *The Wrong Way Home: Uncovering the Patterns of Cult Behavior in American Society* (Boston: Beacon Press, 1990), 101–22.

28 A wrong turning. See Eisler, *The Chalice*, xxiii. I am sympathetic to this view—my book *Earthwalk* (New York: Anchor, 1974) was based on it—but wholesale repudiation of the past can lead to the

kind of fanaticism that produced the witch hunts of the Middle Ages, China's Red Guards, and Pol Pot's excesses in Cambodia. We can turn away from the past without trying to erase it.

29   Someone new to fight. This accounts for the popularity of many space fantasies.

3: The Warrior Mentality

32   Gatherer-hunter. Hunting accounts for only about 30 percent of total consumption, except in areas where plants are scarce. Tanner, *On Becoming Human*, 27; Eisler, *The Chalice*, 68; Lee and DeVore, *Man the Hunter*, 7, 41–43.

32   Position of women. Tanner observes that there was little sexual dimorphism among early hunter-gatherers, and that women also hunted. See Tanner, 61, 220–21, 271ff.

33   A dance of gratitude. See Laurens van der Post, *A Mantis Carol* (New York: Morrow, 1976), 61.

33   Not even human. See, for example, Gibson, *Perfect War*, 131–54.

33   Eisler, *The Chalice*, 17–32. Nor are there any kings or slaves in this art, she observes, nor any lavish burials with living retinues.

34   "Untameable." See Sahlins, *Stone Age Economics*, 85–86, Lee and DeVore, *Man the Hunter*, 89; van der Post, *Mantis*, 96ff.

35   *Socially inferior.* These meanings are so deeply ingrained that if you diagram relationships on a blackboard, the person you place highest will tend to be seen as the leader. This kind of positioning is so irrelevant to the way decisions are actually made that Follett argues for getting rid of the terms *over* and *under* in this context. *Freedom and Coordination*, 2, 35.

35   Animals, once so important. The United States Navy has a plan to employ dolphins as a "naval weapons system," i.e., to carry explosives like live torpedos. A Navy spokesman remarked that the dolphin was a natural "marine operational system . . . begging to be exploited." He described the dolphin as "a self-propelled vehicle with an on-board computer, with operational capability." All that remained, he said, was to program it. *San Francisco Chronicle*, 20 November 1988.

36   The harder they work. To shore up their "natural" superiority, only members of the aristocracy were traditionally allowed to carry certain weapons or to wear armor. They alone rode horses into battle, which not only gave them military superiority but also reinforced their height, and thus gave them moral superiority as well. In the same way kings and other authoritarian leaders like to be physically elevated—on a throne, a balcony, or a podium—to enhance their "natural" moral stature.

36 People of the authoritarian persuasion. See T.W. Adorno, Else Frenkel-Brunswik, Daniel J. Levinson, and R. Nevitt Sanford, *The Authoritarian Personality* (New York: Harper, 1950), 148ff., 228, 237ff., 413–14, 800ff. These are extreme cases, however.

37 Object of fear. Hunter-gatherers had no devil, but many tribes did have a trickster—both sly fox and fool, creator and bungler, sacred and obscene—as many-faced as life itself. Some people believe that the idea of the Devil was derived from Trickster; neither good nor evil to begin with, he wound up in the demonic trash compactor to which the gods of losing tribes are usually consigned by their conquerors.

39 Montagu. Ashley Montagu, *The Nature Of Human Aggression* (New York: Oxford University Press, 1976).

39 Commonplace occurrence. Gibson, *Perfect War*, 133–54; Baritz, *Backfire*, 24–25, 293–99.

39 Riane Eisler observes. Eisler, *The Chalice*, 135.

40 Helps make it possible. Sara Ruddick, *Maternal Thinking: Toward a Politics of Peace* (Boston: Beacon Press, 1989).

4: Military Myopia

46 Holdovers. My interest here is in the United States, but many of the points made in these chapters apply with equal or greater force to other industrialized nations.

47 Lowest of the low. Freshmen at West Point are called "plebes"—an echo of the intimate connection between militarism and feudalistic class systems.

49 Killing of officers. Baritz, *Backfire*, 314–15.

49 Will of those ordered. There are people who are too neurotic to take orders even in the context of a workshop or game and justify this inability to relinquish control by citing democratic principles. But democracy merely claims that ultimate authority rests with the people—not that they are incapable of delegating it. Democracy means that if I lend my lawnmower to my neighbor it is still mine to reclaim at will; I have not given it away (a qualification poorly understood in Washington), but that does not mean I am unable to lend it.

49 Its only strategy. Yet this was the thinking of the generals who ordered the pointless slaughter of World War I, and a half-century later General Westmoreland could think of nothing more imaginative in Vietnam. Baritz, *Backfire*, 178ff.

49 Like every other bureaucracy. See Smith, *The Power Game*, 160–215; James Fallows, *National Defense* (New York: Random House, 1981); and A. Ernest Fitzgerald, *The Pentagonists: An Insider's View of Waste, Mismanagement, and Fraud in Defense Spending* (Boston: Houghton Mifflin, 1989).

49   A military attaché. Smith, *The Russians*, 230.

49   Inevitable withering. Early in the Vietnam War the CIA organized a successful guerrilla program called People's Action Teams— lightly armed men in peasant clothes who elected their own leaders. When Westmoreland heard about it he and his staff were appalled that the guerrillas had no uniforms, barracks, or flagpole, and that they operated democratically. They wanted them to "be made to look like soldiers and act like soldiers." They took over the program and "brought it into line," with predictably disastrous results. Baritz, *Backfire*, 250–53.

49   Managed to overturn. John Prados, *Presidents' Secret Wars: CIA and Pentagon Covert Operations Since World War II* (New York: Morrow, 1986); see also David Green, *The Containment of Latin America: A History of the Myths and Realities of the Good Neighbor Policy* (Chicago: Quadrangle Books, 1971); Thomas Powers, *The Man Who Kept the Secrets: Richard Helms and the CIA* (New York: Knopf, 1979); David Atlee Phillips, *The Night Watch* (New York: Atheneum, 1977).

51   Morally bankrupt. The U.S. has even replaced the USSR as the foremost nyet-sayer in the UN. Among the more bizarre positions taken was our unwillingness to ban the use of children in armies. *New York Times*, 11 December 1988.

53   The percentage spent. *San Francisco Chronicle*, 12 November 1990.

54   Recent documents. *San Francisco Chronicle*, 23 June 1990.

55   Nazi war criminals. Christopher Simpson, *Blowback: America's Recruitment of Nazis and Its Effects on the Cold War* (Weidenfeld & Nicolson, 1988), especially xiii, 47ff., 245–63.

55   George Kennan. Simpson, *Blowback*, 289–90.

55   Thucydides, *The Peloponnesian Wars* (New York: Modern Library, 1951), III: 82.

55   As big as Kennedy's. Baritz, *Backfire*, 112–19, 145–46, 187; Goodwin, *Remembering America*, 389. It has been suggested that incoming male presidents have their genitalia examined publicly by a physician so they won't find it necessary to invade some little country to prove they have the proper masculine equipment.

56   A bad night. Bacon's remark about money—that it was like manure, only good if spread around—is another metaphor that could be applied to power.

57   The right sort of person. This delusion was shared by Plato, who wanted things run by groups of learned men. Anyone who has sat through faculty meetings at major universities knows that learned people can generate as many wrong-headed, short-sighted decisions as any group of people pulled in off the street and will come to fewer agreements per hour of disputation than any legislature in the world.

57   "I have worked." Goodwin, *Remembering America*, 390–91.

58   Bursting bombs. It is often suggested that "America the Beautiful" would make a more appropriate national anthem for a democratic society because it celebrates the positive aspects of America—its landscape, its ideals, its promise—rather than the authoritarian fantasy of survival amid bloodshed and gunfire.

5: The Private Sector

60   What is needed. See, for example, Adams and Brock, *The Bigness Complex*; Warren G. Bennis, "Beyond Bureaucracy" in Bennis and Slater, *The Temporary Society*, 53–76; David Halberstam, *The Reckoning* (New York: William Morrow, 1986); Tom Peters, *Thriving on Chaos: Handbook for a Management Revolution* (New York: Knopf, 1988).

60   1 percent of the corporations. Mark Hertsgaard, *On Bended Knee: The Press and the Reagan Presidency* (New York: Farrar, Straus, and Giroux, 1988), 77.

61   Free from taxes. Not only do these absconding corporations get tax breaks from their adopted countries—their multinational status, combined with indulgent U.S. corporate tax laws, often enables them to avoid paying any but the most nominal U.S. taxes as well. See Barry Bluestone and Bennett Harrison, *The Deindustrialization of America: Plant Closings, Community Abandonment, and the Dismantling of Basic Industry* (New York: Basic Books, 1982), 129–33.

61   Financing this competition. Bluestone and Harrison, 145.

61   Power to finance. Diane Alters in the *San Francisco Chronicle*, 10 July 1989.

62   Bedroom windows. As Bluestone and Harrison point out, while the government "regularly pokes into the minutest details of people's private lives . . . [it] makes only the most minimal demands on private companies to report their investment transactions." (*Deindustrialization*, 26.)

62   "Off 'our' backs." A good example of this rhetoric occurred when five Northern California grocery chains pledged to phase out within six years all produce sprayed with toxic pesticides. This mild step toward consumer safety was greeted by the food industry with the kind of outrage usually reserved for the paroling of a serial axe-murderer. A spokesperson for the Food Marketing Institute talked of intimidation, the McCarthy era, and "food police." *San Francisco Chronicle*, 12 September 1989.

62   "Mexico or Taiwan." See Bluestone and Harrison, *Deindustrialization*, 170ff.

63   Thornburgh. Michael Isikoff in the *Washington Post*, 28 April 1990.

63   Defense contractors. Richard W. Stevenson, *San Francisco Chronicle*, 12 November 1990.

64   Donald Regan. *San Francisco Chronicle*, 12 May 1988.

65   A handsome profit. Meanwhile the Bush administration has encouraged this attitude by quietly cutting most of the funds for long-term scientific studies of post-spill ecological impact.

65   Our national addiction. The much-touted "war on drugs" is therefore rather hypocritical. The social damage caused by illegal drugs is infinitesimal compared with the damage caused by alcohol, tobacco, and prescription drugs.

67   Peters's insightful book. Thomas J. Peters, *Thriving on Chaos*, xi, 9–10, 16–22, 27, 504–8; see also Thomas J. Peters and Robert H. Waterman, Jr., *In Search of Excellence: Lessons from America's Best-Run Companies* (New York: Harper & Row, 1982). Some might argue that Japan's success contradicts my argument, since Japan operates from a deeply authoritarian tradition. Yet in many ways Japan's corporations are run more democratically than our own. They pay a great deal more attention to worker input in the decision-making process and have a concept of the leader as responsive to the led in ways that mimic—though they by no means represent—democracy. Americans, on the other hand, have a Hollywood concept of the leader as a fearless warrior who precedes his men into battle and never listens to anyone else's ideas—a responsive leader is a "wimp." The Japanese ideal is the patient conciliator—the American ideal is General Custer. Japan's economic success is due in large part to the absence of a crippling defense budget, and to their concern with smallness and quality in a shrinking world. See O-Young Lee, *Small Is Better: Japan's Mastery of the Miniature* (Kodansha International, 1984). But time will catch up with the Japanese once these advantages are more widely shared. Their large bureaucracies are quite capable of the same sluggish inability to react to change as our own. See, for example, Halberstam, *Reckoning*, 286–300, 419–32.

67   A "flattening" effect. Richard L. Harris, "The Impact of the Microelectronics Revolution on the Basic Structure of Modern Organizations," *Science, Technology, and Human Values* vol. 11, no. 4 (Fall, 1986), 34–36.

68   "Multiple levels of hierarchy." Harris, 34, 36, 37.

68   Humanly fulfilling. Perry Pascarella, *The New Achievers: Creating a Modern Work Ethic* (New York: Free Press, 1984).

69   Gap between rich and poor. *New York Times*, 23 March 1989.

70   Twelve points to the I.Q. *San Francisco Chronicle*, 17 August 1989.

6: Learning the Ropes

72   While opposing its principles. In the same way televangelists parrot the name of Jesus—the man of peace, poverty, and tolerance—while spewing forth a doctrine of war, greed, and bigotry. This analysis also explains the intense hatred directed toward those who criticize authoritarian acts of government: such critics are being *both* disobedient *and* democratic—the worst of both worlds for an authoritarian.

72   Since the Pilgrims. For more detail see Bennis and Slater, *The Temporary Society*, 20–52. Since the invention of writing there has been a vast amount of nonsense written about bringing up children—perhaps because the people writing about it were so rarely the people doing it.

72   Foreign visitors. Bennis and Slater, 33.

72   Adapt to life here. They also held the promise of material improvement: they would be able to "go further" than their parents—an expectation that did not survive the economic policies of the Reagan administration.

73   The goal of education. Follett, *The New State*, 54.

73   We now stand last. *San Francisco Chronicle*, 19 March 1990.

74   "Changes our activity." Follett, *Creative Experience*, 62.

75   SAT scores. Since knowledge is continually being revised, one wonders how many of today's "correct" responses will be incorrect in fifty years.

75   National Assessment of Educational Progress. *San Francisco Chronicle*, 12 December 1988.

75   Packed into classrooms. For a more radical analysis of this question see Ivan Illich, *Deschooling Society* (New York: Harper & Row, 1971).

76   Encourages passivity. See Jerry Mander, *Four Arguments for the Elimination of Television* (New York: Morrow, 1978).

77   Higher education. Baritz, *Backfire*, 328–31.

78   James Gleick, *Chaos: Making a New Science* (New York: Viking, 1987), 31, 37, 83–90, 180ff., 304.

80   Success with students. This attitude is captured in the film *The Dead Poets Society*.

80   Environment unraveling. Allan Bloom calls the sixties "an unmitigated disaster" for the university. Allan Bloom, *The Closing of the American Mind* (New York: Simon & Schuster, 1987), 320.

80   A tightly ordered environment. Hence when academics enter the political sphere, their impact is usually antidemocratic—witness the regimes of Salazar in Portugal, Pol Pot in Cambodia, and our own McGeorge Bundy and Henry Kissinger.

81   James Fallows, *More Like Us: Making America Great Again* (Boston: Houghton Mifflin, 1989); see also Charles Derber, William A. Schwartz, and Yale Magrass, *Power in the Highest Degree: Professionals and the Rise of a New Mandarin Order* (New York: Oxford University Press, 1990). For an earlier essay on the folly of depending on "experts," see Follett, *Creative Experience,* 5–30.

81   Very little relationship. Fallows, 165–68. Some states, for example, will not license psychotherapists who have not demonstrated a proficiency in statistics.

81   Immune from later scrutiny. Fallows, 165–71.

81   Their "expert" status. Becoming a media expert is easier than one might think. In the early seventies I became an "expert" on communal living—although I had done no research on the topic and had never lived in a shared household—on the basis of a single widely quoted paragraph in a book.

82   A demented gynecologist. The mad doctor entertained a theory that women were incorrectly made by nature and was engaged in a one-man crusade to put this to rights. The concentration of power allows privileged people to put their delusionary systems into practice at the expense of others. Dorothy Storck, *San Francisco Chronicle,* 20 December 1988.

82   The medical profession. The most cogent analysis of the role of medicine in society today is still Ivan Illich's *Medical Nemesis: The Expropriation of Health* (New York: Pantheon Books, 1976).

82   Rigid insistence. Medicine is not the only profession in which authoritarian patterns are preserved. Courtroom etiquette has not altered markedly since cases were heard by the lord of the manor, and the likelihood of a working-class person and an individual from the same social set as the judge receiving "equal protection under the law" is not much greater now than it was then.

82   A Harvard study. Jane E. Brody, *San Francisco Chronicle,* 28 April 1990.

82   A special Mandarin class. Fallows, *More Like Us,* 141–51, 164; Derber, Schwartz, and Magrass, *Power,* chap. 7.

83   Morons or imbeciles. Fallows, 157–58, 173.

7: Walls against Womanhood

85   Working-class chic. Yet few people in history have been as detached from the raising of food as the American urban middle class. Much of the food we eat has for decades been planted, tended, and harvested by people who aren't supposed to be here, and who are kicked out when discovered (often just before being paid).

86   Elect Hitler chairman. Charles Bracelen Flood, *Hitler: The Path to Power* (Boston: Houghton Mifflin, 1989), 177ff.

86   A male creation. This is not to say that women cannot practice it. Women who succeed in the male world often tend to be even more authoritarian than the men, in order to convince those around them that they aren't "soft," just as the first blacks to penetrate white middle class establishments had to be 'whiter than white.' But as their numbers increase, the influence of feminine values begins to be felt. Richard Harris believes the process is circular—that the forces that encourage democratization in industrial organization are making it easier for women to enter the work force, and that their entry is speeding the process of democratization. ("Micro-electronics Revolution," 36–37.) See also Elinor Lenz and Barbara Myerhoff, *The Feminization of America: How Women's Values Are Changing Our Public and Private Lives* (New York: St. Martin's Press, 1985); and Kathy Ferguson, *The Feminist Case Against Bureaucracy* (Philadelphia: Temple University Press, 1985). Ferguson notes that the effect of applying feminist values to bureaucracy is to democratize the organization. For more on authoritarianism and gender, see Eisler, *The Chalice*, 179–82.

86   Founded in war. Hence the position of women begins to improve after long periods of peace and to decline following wars.

87   No reason . . . to exist. Authoritarian men can only demonstrate their manhood through destruction. This causes distress for them in settings where creativity is the name of the game in which they are competing. The solution is to mutilate someone else's creation in the guise of improving it, as satirists of Hollywood are fond of pointing out. There are many competitive males to be dealt with in the complex process of financing, producing, and distributing a film, and by the time each one has lifted his leg on it, the final product is so lopped, humped, and mangled that the audience is left wondering how so much money and talent could have been expended to produce so little of substance.

88   This gender difference. Slater, *Earthwalk*, 125–29. See also Nancy Chodorow, *The Reproduction of Mothering* (Berkeley: University of California Press, 1978), 150; Carol Gilligan, *In a Different Voice: Psychological Theory of Women's Development* (Cambridge: Harvard University Press, 1982), 8ff.

88   Gilligan's conclusion. Gilligan, 33ff., 62–63.

88   Begun to complain. Shere Hite, *Women and Love* (New York: Knopf, 1987).

89   A study. Philip Blumstein and Pepper Schwartz, *American Couples: Money, Work, Sex* (New York: Morrow, 1983), 53–77, 159–64, 245–50.

89   When they are not. Schwartz, 37. Yet single women still *desire* marriage more than single men do—another triumph of illusion over reality.

90   Maternal malefaction. Paula J. Caplan, "Take the Blame off Mother," *Psychology Today*, October 1986, 70–71. In the 125 papers analyzed, not one professional ever described a mother as emotionally healthy, although the fathers were often so described. The bias is perhaps due to the fact that traditional therapists employ the same power technique in their practice as traditional fathers do in the home: emotional distance. A similar bias is found in modern literature and drama.

90   Some higher good. *The Great Santini* and *On Golden Pond* are examples of this theme, but plays and films about father-child (usually father-son) estrangement are common. At the end of these the father is usually forgiven for his derelictions, which is no doubt human and divine on the part of father and child respectively, but it seems a little repetitive. Democracy would perhaps take firmer root if men would abandon this tiresome quest for a good father and start trying to *be* one.

91   Restraints on women. See J.D. Unwin, *Sex and Culture* (London: Oxford University Press, 1934).

93   Islamic societies. See Slater, *The Glory of Hera* (Boston: Beacon Press, 1968), 240–55.

93   The nuclear trigger. The authoritarian always assumes that the most important function of a leader is to make war.

94   Street-gang values. Baritz, *Backfire*, 159, 195–97, 209–10.

94   Incapable of empathy. This makes it difficult for many men to identify with female protagonists. It's fun trying to guess which reason a male film reviewer will select to justify his disparagement of a film that doesn't have a male protagonist.

94   Limiting one's options. Thus the fascination with fantasies of brutal, bandit-ridden, precivilized or post-apocalypse worlds, in which all issues are decided by violence (*Mad Max*). In such worlds, there is renewed justification for authoritarianism and male dominance.

95   Gilligan points out. Gilligan, *Different Voice*, 167–74. Follett's ethical system (*New State*, 52ff.) provides an excellent illustration of Gilligan's views on feminine ethical reasoning.

95   Women ... feel more at home. See Lenz and Myerhoff, *Feminization*.

8: The Rectangular Mind

97   Two-party system. Multiparty systems are intermediate between what Jane J. Mansbridge calls the "adversary democracy" we now have and "unitary democracy"—found only in small communities and informal organizations. See Jane J. Mansbridge, *Beyond Adversary Democracy* (New York: Basic Books, 1980), 8–35.

98   Lovelock argues. J.E. Lovelock, *Gaia: A New Look at Life on Earth* (New York: Oxford University Press, 1987), 27.

98   "All-out assault." The Revolutionary War supposedly meant that we were finished with monarchy, yet we pay almost as much attention to the dull doings of British royalty as do the English themselves. And as recently as 1989 it was believed that sending warships to Colombia would put an end to Americans wanting to take drugs.

99   No end of mischief. Such "objective" and "rationally motivated" giants as Newton, Galileo, Kepler, and Mendel are now believed to have fudged their data in order to help overcome the resistance of their contemporaries. William J. Broad, *New York Times*, 23 January 1990.

99   Several writers. Evelyn Fox Keller, *Reflections on Gender and Science* (New Haven: Yale University Press, 1985); Donna Haraway, *Primate Visions: Gender, Race, and Nature in the World of Modern Science* (New York: Routledge, 1989). These feminist critiques coincide nicely with the emergence of chaos theory, in which the goal of prediction is finally abandoned in favor of understanding.

100   Involuntary servant. The fact that Western medicine was founded on the study of cadavers, for example, helps explain why doctors know so much more about how the body is put together than about how it heals itself. It fostered a concept of the doctor as a manipulater of inert matter—as one who controls rather than one who facilitates healing.

100   "Shrill" or "strident." James Gleick comments that early papers on chaos theory sounded "evangelical." Gleick, *Chaos*, 39.

100   "Accumulation of information." Follett, *Creative Experience*, 5.

101   Contemporary science. For other recent shifts in scientific imagery see Fritjof Capra, *The Turning Point: Science, Society, and the Rising Culture* (New York: Simon and Schuster, 1982). For earlier paradigm shifts see Thomas S. Kuhn, *The Structure of Scientific Revolutions* (Chicago: University of Chicago Press, 1970).

101   Old habits. Heisenberg and Einstein are quoted in Capra, 77. (My italics.)

102   "A set of relationships." Henry Stapp, quoted in Capra, 81. Follett defines the individual in the same way. (*New State*, 75ff.)

103   Noise was . . . the message. Stanislaw Ulam observes that calling chaos theory "nonlinear science" is like calling zoology the "study of non-elephant animals." Gleick, *Chaos*, 68, 83–90, 112–13, 180ff.

103   Defining democracy. In Gleick, 252. Compare Follett's "self-creating coherence."

103   Democratic metaphors. Joseph Ford, in Gleick, 306.

103   "Flexible interaction." Gleick, 38.

103   Bell's theorem. Gleick, 5; Capra, *Turning Point*, 83–85.

103   "Perennial wisdom." Harman, *Global Mind Change*, 106.

103   Mental habits of authoritarianism. *Roget's Thesaurus*, still widely used, organizes the English language in accordance with assumptions so feudalistic as to render it almost useless to anyone operating with a democratic worldview.

9: The Myths of Slavery

106   Large messy dragon. The battle with the Mother-Dragon also expresses a fear of chthonic forces. Slaying the dragon can be seen as an early metaphor for killing the planet, an ambition which fortunately has not yet been achieved.

109   Young boy sneaking off. Although authoritarians never tire of sentimental stories about making up with difficult fathers, conflict with the mother always ends in flight.

109   Rebellion against convention. Consider the fact that the time-honored symbols of youthful rebellion in Hollywood films are smoking, drinking, and driving fast, all of which are highly approved by corporate America and have long figured prominently in advertising imagery. When the word *revolutionary* is applied to films, plays, literature, or the visual arts today, it usually means just what it does in advertising: the most cobwebbed traditions of our culture tricked out in new packaging. Artistic products that feature violence against women and/or the disparagement of minorities are especially likely to be labeled "original" and "controversial."

110   Ordinary aristocratic bully. For an extended analysis of the Don Juan myth see David Winter, *The Power Motive* (New York: Free Press, 1973). Winter stresses the connection between the oppression of women and bellicosity.

111   Acknowledge a greater power. Books and films about ghastly totalitarian societies, while thought to be antiauthoritarian, tend, like all "anti" creations, to have the opposite effect. If you try to create *against* something, the product will either be so unpleasant that no one wants to look at it, or you will end by making your subject subtly attractive. Just as antiwar films tend to make the soldier's suffering (and hence soldiering itself) tragically appealing, so these masochistic tales of totalitarianism tend to make suffering under some futuristic tyranny seem simpler and more romantic than the trials of creating a democratic future.

114   Reconciliation films. To these may be added the romantic couples who begin by disliking each other—in films like *Romancing the Stone, The Sure Thing, Children of a Lesser God, Casual Sex,*

When Harry Met Sally, Someone to Watch Over Me, and so on. This is a genre that was very popular in the comedies of the thirties. Perhaps the ultimate in reconciliation plotting was the comedy *I Love You to Death* in which even the obstacle of an attempted murder was overcome by love.

114   Something to give us. It is interesting that this rash of reconciliation films anticipated the thaw in the Cold War.

114   Empathic questing. This is also seen in the flurry of films of 1988 and 1989 having to do with pairs of brothers, one of whom is not fully functional—*Rain Man, Dominick and Eugene, The Promise*. In these films the more ambitious, "mainstream" brother comes to appreciate the human value of the "less successful" one.

10: The Changing Face of God

118   Stone points out. I.F. Stone, *The Trial of Socrates* (Boston: Little, Brown, 1988), 17–18.

120   Within a few centuries. The democratic, feminist, and equalitarian elements of early Christianity were suppressed by the fourth century. See Elaine Pagels, *The Gnostic Gospels* (New York: Random House, 1979).

120   Jesus' death. This leaves aside the barbaric tradition that an omnipotent God would torture and kill his Son as a sacrifice (to whom?) for humanity.

120   Shifting the blame. Just as in modern times the assassinations of feared radical leaders are always attributed by the authorities to "a rival political faction." There were hundreds of religious sects in Palestine during this period, with all kinds of views and practices; why would one more have bothered the elders? It is far more likely that the Roman governors ordered Jesus' crucifixion for questioning the legitimacy of Roman authority. Given the political threat Christianity consistently posed to pre-Christian Rome, this has all the earmarks of a latter-day whitewash. Consider the "render unto Caesar" incident (Matthew 22:21; Mark 12:17): An effort is made to entrap Jesus in a subversive statement in front of the authorities, and Jesus evades the trap skillfully. The fact that the effort was made implies *awareness* that Jesus and his followers were contemptuous of earthly authority. Is it not then reasonable to assume—given the fact that he was executed soon afterwards in traditional Roman fashion—that the Roman authorities decided to suppress his subversive preaching, which was apparently well known? Why would *Jews* be upset about him telling the populace that they owed allegiance only to the Jewish God and not to the alien conqueror? But this *was* the kind of thing that made the Romans nervous, as it would any colonialist.

121   The Kennedy family. *San Francisco Chronicle*, 2 June 1988.

121   Down off the cross. For many of the ideas about democracy and Christianity, as well as others throughout this chapter, I am indebted to Melita Cowie.

121   His teachings. Thomas Jefferson had similar feelings about Jesus' life, and in 1820 created his own expurgated Bible which emphasized the teachings and left out the miracles. Thomas Jefferson, *The Jefferson Bible: The Life and Morals of Jesus of Nazareth* (Boston: Beacon Press, 1989).

121   The early Christians. Pagels, *Gnostic Gospels*, 41ff.

122   A Vatican letter. Cardinal Joseph Ratzinger, "Letter to the Bishops of the Catholic Church on Some Aspects of Christian Meditation." *San Francisco Chronicle*, 16 December 1989.

122   Fox has called for. Matthew Fox, *The Coming of the Cosmic Christ* (New York: Harper & Row, 1988).

122   Ezra Taft Benson. *San Francisco Chronicle*, 3 October 1988.

123   We are all a part. Lovelock contrasts the authoritarian view that "sees nature as a primitive force to be subdued and conquered" to the Gaia hypothesis which sees humanity as "part of, or partner in, a very democratic entity." Lovelock, *Gaia*, 12, 145.

11: Secrets

126   Bettelheim saw. Bruno Bettelheim, *Symbolic Wounds* (London: Thames and Hudson, 1955).

126   Snow argues. C.P. Snow, quoted in Baritz, *Backfire*, 226–27.

127   Interdepartmental paranoia. Baritz, 196–228.

127   To hide incompetence. The defense establishment is a rich source of examples. The "top secrets' of the Pentagon are expensive planes that won't fly, expensive communications systems that don't function, expensive missiles that can't hit their targets, and expensive rifles so poorly made that Vietcong guerrillas didn't bother to retrieve them from dead American soldiers. Some wags have suggested that giving away all our military secrets to potential enemies would be an act of patriotism. See Smith, *The Power Game*, 160–215.

127   Ewen Cameron. Michael Taylor, *San Francisco Chronicle*, 3 October 1988, 5 October 1988. Cameron may have gotten some of his ideas as a member of the Nuremburg tribunal dealing with Nazi medical atrocities. (The supervisor of these atrocities at Dachau was later given a position at NASA.) See Martin A. Lee and Bruce Shlain, *Acid Dreams: The CIA, LSD, and the Sixties Rebellion* (New York: Grove Press, 1985), xvii–xxi, 5–6, 24.

127   Richard Helms. See Taylor, 3 October 1988.

127   Documents acquired. See Lee and Shlain, xx, 3–12, 19–34, 37–38, 42–43.

128   Short-sighted secret actions. See Prados, *Presidents' Secret Wars.*

128   A CIA analyst. Baritz, *Backfire,* 259ff., 264–70.

128   Each escalation. Goodwin, *Remembering America,* 383–90; Baritz, 156, 202–7.

128   Tonkin Gulf incident. Johnson reported that North Vietnamese PT boats had made an "unprovoked attack" on two U.S. destroyers. In fact the destroyers were there to back up commando raids on North Vietnam, and the shots used to escalate the war may never have been fired at them—Johnson himself thought not. Baritz, *Backfire,* 139–42; Goodwin, 357–61.

129   Many times higher . . . than Chernobyl. *New York Times,* 7 July 1990; Keith Schneider, *New York Times,* 12 July 1990; *San Francisco Chronicle,* 14 July 1990.

129   Warren I. Cohen. *San Francisco Chronicle,* 24 October 1990.

130   "The most important secrets." Baritz, *Backfire,* 227.

130   Reagan White House. Smith, *The Power Game,* 434–46. Smith's book reveals clearly the contempt in which the American people are held by Washington officials.

130   Presidential veto. *San Francisco Chronicle,* 26 October 1988.

130   Well-informed president. Smith, *The Power Game,* 434–46.

131   Blindly endorse. Cabinet members like to carry sealed attaché cases marked "classified" into Congress and wave them about importantly, saying, "If the American people knew what was in here they would support our policies wholeheartedly," which is a little like saying, "If you knew what was in this box you'd give me a dollar for it, but I'm going to let you have it for a quarter."

131   "Six Cuban prisons." Tom Wicker, *San Francisco Chronicle,* 21 June 1988.

132   Scientific information. John Shattuck and Muriel Morisey Spence, "Government Information Controls: Implications for Scholarship, Science, and Technology," presentation to the Association of American Universities, Washington, D.C., 1988.

132   James E. Hansen. Anthony Lewis, *San Francisco Chronicle,* 11 May 1989.

132   James Yorke. Gleick, *Chaos,* 65.

133   These gradual steps. It was Richard Nixon who made this formula famous, but it has been much employed by others in recent years.

134   *"Deliberate withholding." San Francisco Chronicle,* 30 December 1988. (My italics.)

134   Shot down by the GAO. Eric Schmitt in *The New York Times,* 26 May 1990. The Navy also blamed peace activist Brian Wilson

for having his legs cut off by a train going (rather suspiciously) three times its normal speed—after which the engineers who maimed him sued him for "emotional damages."

135   Information should be shared. Peters, *Thriving on Chaos*, 504–8.

12: The Muffled Voice of Freedom

138   Secretive Reagan administration. Smith, *The Power Game*, 434–46; Hertsgaard, *On Bended Knee*, 6, 140–42, 146–47.

138   "Line of the day." Hertsgaard, 5–6, 32–53.

139   Dulles was the first. Erik Barnouw, *The Image Empire: A History of Broadcasting in the United States*, vol. 3 (New York: Oxford University Press, 1970), 92–100.

139   "Still at war." Barnouw, 102–3.

139   Jacobo Arbenz. Barnouw, 97–98.

140   Attempted to suppress. Barnouw, 281–87.

140   Anxious to advertise. Barnouw, 97–99. Vietnam War protests were a result of this same overconfidence. Reporters were welcomed on the scene, and the American people were able to see and hear and read enough about the war to form their own judgments and ignore government propaganda. The lesson was not lost on the Reagan administration—the media were banned altogether from the farcical invasion of Grenada, making it the first time in American history that our government was too ashamed of what it was doing to trust its own people with direct knowledge of a war situation.

141   Pre-made videos. *San Francisco Chronicle*, 4 January 1989.

141   "Michael Deaver." *San Francisco Examiner*, 4 December 1988.

142   "Manipulation by inundation." Hertsgaard, *On Bended Knee*, 32–53.

142   With enough conviction. Hertsgaard, 67–68, 203.

142   The Benneke case. *San Francisco Chronicle*, 1 May 1990. The story had been in the wind for years, but no reporter had had the courage to track it down.

142   Establishment bias. See, for example, Edward S. Herman and Noam Chomsky, *Manufacturing Consent: The Political Economy of the Mass Media* (New York: Pantheon Books, 1988), 37–86. News casting an unfavorable light on administration policies tends to be either ignored or buried in the back pages. For a more recent account, see Martin A. Lee and Norman Solomon, *Unreliable Sources: A Guide to Detecting Bias in News Media* (Carol Publishing Group, 1990).

143   Members of the press. Hertsgaard, *On Bended Knee*, 77–100.

143   Sulzberger. Lee and Shlain, *Acid Dreams*, 262n.

143   A recent study. Marc Cooper and Lawrence C. Soley, "All the Right Sources," *Mother Jones*, February/March 1990. As noted in chapter 6, each "expert" appearance tends to breed—and legitimize—future ones. See also Charles Rothfeld, "Legal Pundits and How They Got That Way," *New York Times*, 4 May 1990.

143   *Not critical enough.* Hertsgaard, *On Bended Knee*, 84–85.

143   Bagdikian points out. Ben H. Bagdikian, *The Media Monopoly*, 3rd ed. (Boston: Beacon Press, 1990).

144   Halved within a decade. Bagdikian, 4–6.

144   Gives several examples. Bagdikian, 27–45, 163.

144   Drug companies threatened. Bagdikian, 162–63.

144   Advertising withdrawals. Bagdikian, 168–73.

144   Their own product. Bagdikian, 167–68.

144   Advertisers . . . frequently demand. Bagdikian, 157–59.

144   Procter & Gamble. Bagdikian, 155–59.

144   Fluff that fills. This is not entirely new. De Tocqueville complained in 1830 about the vacuousness of American newspapers—that they were three-fourths ads and never dealt with the burning issues of the day. Alexis de Tocqueville, *Democracy in America* (New York: Knopf, 1980), vol. 1, 185.

144   Popular with the public. Bagdikian, *Media Monopoly*, 159–60.

145   *"More hard news."* Bagdikian, 137. (Italics mine.)

147   *"Reporters weren't interested."* Randy Shilts, *San Francisco Chronicle*, 23 January 1989. (My italics.)

147   Ellen Goodman. *San Francisco Chronicle*, 14 April 1989.

13: The Dictator Within

151   Riesman puts it. David Riesman, *Individualism Reconsidered* (New York: Doubleday Anchor, 1954), 27. For a fuller discussion of individualism, see Slater, *Earthwalk*, 9–66, 185–212.

153   Howard Hughes. James Phelan, *Howard Hughes: The Hidden Years* (New York: Random House, 1976), 38, 102–4.

154   As Follett observes. Follett, *New State*, 65ff., 75; *Creative Experience*, 101–2.

154   Follett ridicules. Follett, *Creative Experience*, 39; *Freedom & Coordination*, 81–82; *New State*, 27–29, 39. The difference between competition and cooperation, she says, is not a matter of individual vs. social goals, but merely "a difference between a short and a long view."

155   Even more scornful. Follett, *Creative Experience*, 156–63. As she points out, "compromise is still on the same plane as fighting" in that it defines the situation in the same narrow dualistic terms. (*New State*, 26.) She admits, rather reluctantly, that it's better than combat.

155   Creative redefinition. Follett, *Creative Experience*, 117, 163. *Freedom And Coordination*, 65–68. For other examples see *Creative Experience*, 156–78.

155   "Grow a bigger self." Follett, *Creative Experience*, 173. Many people are not interested in jointly creating a new idea, but only in seeing their own will imposed on others. Wherever these old habits persist, committee meetings are stagnant, pugilistic, ego-waving nightmares—another illustration of the fact that full democracy cannot exist until the cultural infrastructure that would support it has gained a stronger grip on human consciousness.

155   "Not really two processes." Henry C. Metcalf and L. Urwick, eds., *Dynamic Administration: The Collected Papers of Mary Parker Follett* (New York: Harper, 1942), 203. In any conflict we are fighting in part with ourselves. "A influences B, and . . . B, made different by A's influence, influences A, which means that A's own activity enters into the stimulus which is causing his activity." In every situation, therefore, "our own activity is part of the cause of our activity. We respond to stimuli which we have helped to make." *Dynamic Administration*, 194. See also Follett, *Creative Experience*, 62–63 and 133ff.

156   Simpleminded, binary. But capable of complicating itself—computers (which are modeled on the ego) are also binary. It is simpleminded in the sense that while we can grasp complex wholes intuitively in an instant, the ego must work it out laboriously through linear logic.

157   Those of any despot. *The Authoritarian Personality*, by Adorno, et al., described people who are *drawn* to authoritarian structures—people who are racist and highly dependent on authority. But many people who espouse liberal values and are not authoritarian in this sense are nonetheless dominated by despotic egos.

158   Harman points out. Harman, *Global Mind Change*, 75–79.

158   Establishing his dominion. A psychiatrist, Arnold Mandell, suggests that "mathematical pathology" (unpredictability) is health in physiology, while "mathematical health" is disease. Gleick, *Chaos*, 293–99. Some people argue that linear thinking is itself a kind of neurosis.

158   Nature's exuberance. This is exemplified in what we euphemistically call "landscaping." Professional gardeners today descend on a neighborhood like some kind of horticultural riot squad:

with goggles, headphones, nose-mask, helmets, and an array of evil-looking weaponry—mowers, chain saws, weed cutters, edgers, trimmers, leaf blowers, and various lethal chemicals. Their deafening machines alert civilians in the neighborhood that a war is in progress so they can take cover inside their homes. All things that grow come under attack—uprooted, clipped, poisoned, or hacked to death. All irregularity and variety is eliminated: hedges are hewn into the shape of warehouses; lawns are flattened and squared like parking lots; trees—with their messy habit of shedding leaves—are cut down altogether. The result is considered beautiful by the ego, for everything is under control and every hint of rebellion has been squashed. The new science of chaos, which deals with irregular, nonlinear, and unpredictable phenomena, seems to mark a détente in the ego mafia's war with nature. For while traditional science saw irregularity as error, chaos scientists are discovering the order within that disorder. They were rewarded with this vision the moment they decided that understanding was desirable even in the absence of predictability. Thus chaos theory is a kind of intellectual letting go—an implicit recognition of the ego's limits, a willingness merely to *see* rather than having to *control* nature. This is what happens to an individual when the ego's control is loosened—"democratized."

159   Refuses to allow contact. For more on the relationship between the ego's despotism and addiction, see Slater, *Wealth Addiction* (New York: Dutton, 1980), 114–30, 155–98.

160   A recent newspaper article. *San Jose Mercury*, 12 April 1989.

160   (Four of the top ten.) Bagdikian, *Media Monopoly*, 145.

160   A common failing. Gregory Bateson, *Steps to an Ecology of Mind* (New York: Ballantine Books, 1972), 309–37.

161   Bulimia. Hence also our fascination with vampire stories—tales of people who cannot survive on their own life-energy, but must borrow the blood of others in order to feel alive.

161   Alcohol nipples. *San Francisco Chronicle*, 26 August 1989. During the 1930s, tobacco and liquor companies induced film studios to have their stars smoke and drink in films, so that these activities would become symbols of sophistication for teenagers.

162   Compulsively to gobble up. See, for example, Bryan Burrough and John Helyar, *Barbarians at the Gate: The Fall of RJR Nabisco* (New York: Harper & Row, 1990).

162   H.L. Hunt. Stanley H. Brown, *H.L. Hunt* (Chicago: Playboy Press, 1976), 199.

162   Single-tracked. See Slater, *Wealth Addiction*, 71–102.

163   Fortune 500 executives. Jan Halper, *Quiet Desperation: The Truth about Successful Men* (New York: Warner Books, 1989).

163   Baby boomers. Ramon G. Mcleod, *San Francisco Chronicle*, 13 February 1989.

14: Stumbling toward Democracy

168   Forty-seven of the fifty. *San Francisco Chronicle*, 21 March 1989.

169   A 10 percent drop. Martin Tolchin, *New York Times*, 23 March 1989.

169   Deliberate policies. Tolchin.

169   Poverty-level wages. Tolchin.

169   Working mothers. *San Francisco Chronicle*, 24 March 1989.

169   Nation's *children*. *San Francisco Chronicle*, 27 April 1990.

169   World Bank report. *San Francisco Chronicle*, 19 December 1988.

169   Thrift industry. Kenneth Howe, *San Francisco Chronicle*, 27 February 1989.

171   Sued for $200,000. Eve Pell, *California Magazine*, 1989; based on a study by George Pring and Penelope Canan of University of Denver, "Strategic Lawsuits Against Public Participation." A chapter of my *Wealth Addiction*, dealing with eight famous billionaires, was heavily censored by the publisher's lawyers even though (a) all but one of the individuals named had been dead for some time; (b) most of the censored comments referred to the billionaires as a group and merely stated that most or many shared certain characteristics; and (c) *all of the censored material had been published before.* This indicates how much the First Amendment has been eroded through the legal buying power of the wealthy.

171   No room for war. For a thoughtful discussion of these issues, see John Kenneth Galbraith and Stanislav Menshikov, *Capitalism, Communism and Coexistence* (Boston: Houghton Mifflin, 1988).

171   "First strike capability." The U.S. position in disarmament talks was that only land-based missiles be scrapped—i.e., that the USSR would disarm while the U.S. (whose offensive capability is mostly sea-based) would not. George Bush maintained in 1980 that the U.S. could survive and "win" a nuclear war, and has shown a scrappy willingness to risk other people's lives ever since.

171   "War on drugs." A favorite tactic of authoritarian governments is to plant illegal drugs on well-known dissidents. When Eugene McCarthy began to attract wide grass-roots support in his campaign for the presidency in 1968, the White House planned to discredit his volunteers in this way, but the plot was discovered and exposed. Goodwin, *Remembering America*, 506.

172   Contain aggression. It is also argued that American interests are threatened, but these "interests" are merely corporate. Our over-

dependence on foreign oil has been obvious for over twenty years, yet the government has made no serious effort to develop alternative energy sources—the Reagan administration actually cut back on funds for this purpose.

172   Helped finance. Michael Wines, *New York Times*, 13 August 1990.

172   A new military crisis. Just as an alcoholic uses his hangover as a justification for more drinking, Operation Desert Shield is "the hair of the dog."

173   Numerical superiority. They forgot that authoritarians are brought up on the myth of the (armed) One Who Overcomes the (unarmed) Many.

173   Indistinguishable from slavery. Workers were paid a dollar and a half a day in scrip redeemable only at company stores charging extortionate prices, and they paid exorbitant rents to live in two-room company shacks from which they could be evicted with three days' notice. Even libraries and churches were company-monitored, and the company maintained a large, well-paid force of detectives, guards, and spies to prevent unionization. There was an "epidemic" of deaths and injuries from unsafe working conditions. Peter Collier and David Horowitz, *The Rockefellers: An American Dynasty* (New York: Holt, Rinehart and Winston), 109–16.

174   These goals were advanced. See, for example, Walter Karp, *Liberty Under Siege* (New York: Holt, 1988); and Tom Gervasi, *The Myth of Soviet Military Supremacy* (New York: Harper & Row, 1986).

174   Voter turnout. Frances Fox Piven and Richard A. Cloward, *Why Americans Don't Vote* (New York: Pantheon Books, 1988), 4–5.

175   Public servant's salary. From the Volcker Commission Report. See Walter A. Haas, Jr., *San Francisco Chronicle*, 24 December 1988.

175   Rich . . . overrepresented. Piven and Cloward, *Why Americans Don't Vote*, 4, 15.

175   Deliberate policy. Piven and Cloward, 78–94, 195–200.

175   "Affirmative obligation." Piven and Cloward, 17ff.

176   Elected by nonvoters. Piven and Cloward, 12–13.

176   *Block* registration. Piven and Cloward, 195–200. This is as true in New England and the Midwest as in the Deep South.

176   No one represents them. Piven and Cloward, 18–22.

177   Mumford once said. Lewis Mumford, "The Fallacy of Systems," *Saturday Review of Literature* 33, October 1949.

177   Follett. Metcalf and Urwick, *Dynamic Administration*, 194.

178   Follett. In *New State*, 99. "There is no result *of* process but only a moment *in* process." (Follett, *Creative Experience*, 60.)

178   Contradictory . . . approaches. Social systems are held in place by contradictions and can only be unlocked by them.

180   Cross-fertilization. See Craig Lambert, "Global Spin," *Harvard Magazine*, January/February 1990.

15: Self-Creating Coherence

182   Naisbitt. John Naisbitt, *Megatrends: Ten New Directions Transforming Our Lives* (New York: Warner Books, 1982).

182   "Self-creating coherence." Follett, in Metcalf and Urwick, *Dynamic Administration*, 200.

183   "We should see." Follett, *Creative Experience*, 262.

184   Emergence of oxygen. Lovelock, *Gaia*, 31.

184   Cold War is over. Except, perhaps, in Washington; the Soviet Union is decentralizing and ending its draft as well as reducing its military forces, declaring the need is no longer there. It is also relying more on the United Nations to deal with international crises, while we still respond to each situation with our own troops. For a thoughtful discussion of potential changes in policy, see Richard J. Barnet, "After the Cold War," *The New Yorker*, 1 January 1990, 65–76. See also Michael Shuman, Hal Harvey, and Daniel Arbess, *Alternative Security: Beyond the Controlled Arms Race* (New York: Hill and Wang, 1990).

184   Powerfully entrenched. Polls gave McCarthy no chance at all in the primary, and the Johnson forces thought they could run the campaign from Washington. In classic authoritarian fashion they had succeeded completely in insulating themselves from reality: since criticism was "unpatriotic," the critics were "just a few radicals." See Goodwin, *Remembering America*, 483–515.

185   The Bushmen. Sahlins, *Stone Age Economics*, 1–39.

186   Just to keep alive. Even now the volume of voluntary, unpaid labor in our society exceeds the volume of work done for pay, and is of greater social value. See Scott Burns, *Home, Inc.* (New York: Doubleday, 1975).

187   "Really fundamental changes." Harman, *Global Mind Change*, 155.

188   Something for everyone. Specific needs are suggested by the contents of the various chapters in Part II. There have also been many books published in the last decade or two suggesting mental and social pathways to democratization. In addition to those cited throughout this volume, I would like to call attention to Frances Moore Lappé, *Rediscovering America's Values* (New York: Ballantine Books, 1989); Charlene Spretnak and Fritjof Capra, *Green*

Politics (New York: Dutton, 1984), especially pp. 29ff. and 229ff.; Hazel Henderson, *The Politics of the Solar Age: Alternatives to Economics* (New York: Anchor, 1981); E.F. Schumacher, *Small Is Beautiful: Economics As If People Mattered* (New York: Harper & Row, 1973); Herman E. Daly and John B. Cobb, Jr., *For the Common Good: Redirecting the Economy Toward Community, the Environment, and a Sustainable Future* (Boston: Beacon Press, 1989); Gene Sharp, *Social Power and Political Freedom* (Porter Sargent, 1980).

188   "People give legitimacy." Harman, *Global Mind Change.*

189   "We ... create our ideals." Follett, *New State,* 52–53.

189   Fallows points out. Fallows, *More Like Us.*

190   Michael Lerner. Lerner was suggesting that the Democrats lost the 1988 election because they focused too exclusively on bread-and-butter issues. See "Liberals: Get Radical," *This World,* 20 November 1988.

191   "The essence of democracy." Follett, *New State,* 7.

Index

Adams, Walter, 19
Addiction, 159, 160–161; to alcohol and tobacco, social cost of, 65–66; to money, 161–163
AEC, 129
Afghanistan, 50, 57
Alaska, 65
"American Dream," 190
American Psychiatric Association, 127
Amnesty International, 47
Anticommunism, 50, 51, 52, 53–54
Apathy, public, 168, 174–176
Arbenz, Jacobo, 139, 140
Aristotle, 30, 101
Armies, inefficiency of bureaucratic, 48–49
Army, U.S., 49, 57
Association of American Universities, 132
Atrocities, 38–39
Authoritarianism: change and, 19; and constriction, 176–177; as dead weight, 28–29; decline of, 3, 29–30; and decline in position of women, 39–41, 85–95; defined, 25; democratization of, 2; different forms of, 3; and dualism, 97–98, 102; in education, 73–83 passim; and the enemy, 37–38; in family, 72–73; and freedom, 60–61; and God and religion, 116–123; and good and evil, 36–37; and higher and lower, 34–35, 98, 102; history of, 3, 25, 28; inefficiency of, 17, 18; and individualism, 151–152; and media, 138–149 passim; in medicine, 82; and myths, 105–109, 111–112, 113; origin of, 25; and patriotism, 58; as phase in human development, 24;

pillars of, 27–28; in power, tenacity of, 168, 172–173; presidential, 17; and road to atrocity, 38–39; and strong and weak, 36; vestiges of, 5; and war, 39, 171; in workplace, 66–68
Authority, 12, 13–14
Autocratic groups, 11
Automation, 67

Bagdikian, Ben, *The Media Monopoly*, 143, 144–145
Baritz, Loren, 13, 77, 130
Basics: advanced, 77–78; extracurricular, 76–77; return to, in authoritarian society, 74
Bateson, Gregory, 160
Batista, Fulgencio, 50, 51, 53, 140
Bavelas, Alex, 11
Bay of Pigs invasion, 50
Bell, John, 103
Benneke, Richard, 142
Bennis, Warren, 2
Benson, Ezra Taft, 122–123
Bettelheim, Bruno, 126
Bible, 101; Old Testament, 117, 121, 123
Bluestone, Barry, 61
Blumstein, Philip, 89
Boot camp training, 47–48
Brainwashing, 127
Brezhnev, Leonid, 144
Brock, James W., 19
Building-block model, of science, 100–102
Bush, George, 12, 54, 55, 129, 142

Cambodia, 16, 94, 140
Cameron, Ewen, 127

Capitalism, 50, 67; democracy and, 4, 60
Carnegie Foundation for the Advancement of Teaching, 75
Carter, Jimmy, 176
Casey, William, 142
Castro, Fidel, 50
Catholic Church, 122
CBS, 140
Ceausescu, Nicolae, 51
Censorship: by advertisers, 144; journalistic, 141
Change, fear of, 183
Chaos theory, 78, 103, 132, 183
Charisma, 146, 147
Chatwin, Bruce, *Utz*, 104
Chernobyl disaster, 129
Chiang Kai-shek, 53, 140
Child care, reducing support for, 174
Chile, 49, 50
China, 57, 172–173
Christianity, 118, 119–121, 122
CIA, 15, 55, 57, 129, 138, 142; covert operations of, 140; experimental use of drugs by, 127–128; and heroin trade, 143; media manipulation by, 139
Cincinnatus, 156
Civil rights movement, 123
Cloward, Richard A., 175, 176
Coetzee, J.M., *Waiting for the Barbarians*, 43
Cohen, Warren I., 129
Coherence, self-creating, 182
Cold War, 2, 50, 52, 55, 122, 130; end of, 171, 184
Communication, 134–135; opening, 187
Communism, 4, 10, 54, 55, 60, 67
Conflict, 29, 180; war as failure to deal with, 109, 184
Conquest myths, 107
Constitution, 57, 58, 168; First Amendment to, 171
Constriction, 176–177
Context, 145
Cooper, Marc, 143
Corporation for Enterprise Development, 168
Corporations: and authoritarian workplace, 66–68; freedom of multinational, 60–61; and "government waste," 64–66; many faces of, 61–64; secrecy in, 133–134, 135
Crucifixion, 120–121

Cuba, 57, 131–132
Cultural conditioning, 154, 159
Czechoslovakia, 57

Deaver, Michael, 141, 142
Decentralization, 18, 20, 60, 66, 67
Declaration of Independence, 168, 180
Defense, Department of, 49
Defense spending, increase in, 174
Deference, *see* Submissiveness
Deflection, authoritarianism and, 28
Demilitarizing, 184–185
Democracy: in America today, 22; avenues leading to, 183–188; and capitalism, 4, 60; criteria of, 19–21; demand for greater, 168; educational goals of, 73; efficiency of, 4, 10, 18, 19; as emerging megaculture, 4, 5; feminism and, 88; flexibility and, 17–18; heart of, 14; history of, 30; and individualism, 151; inevitability of, 2; and innovation, 18–19; misconceptions about, 4–5; as modern necessity, 10–11; obstacles to, 168–180; and participation, 21–22, 75, 76, 154, 188; and patriotism, 58; religion of, 123–124; and self-creating coherence, 182; sexism and, 85; U.S. retreat from, 2
Deng Xiaoping, 172–173
Deniability, principle of, 89
Devil, 37. *See also* Satan
Dictatorships, 2, 10, 51, 60–61, 152
DOE, 134
Dominator model, 25
Don Juan, myth of, 110–111
Double binds, 90
Double standards, 90–92
Drug(s): experimental use of, by CIA, 127–128; trafficking, 129; war on, 171
Dualism: authoritarian, 97–98, 102; decline of, in science, 102–103
Dulles, Allen, 55, 139, 140
Dulles, John Foster, 55, 139, 140

Eastern Europe, 50, 60, 179; democratization in, 2, 30, 51, 112
Economy, "basically healthy," 69–70
Edsel, 12
Education: authoritarianism in, 73–83 *passim*; reducing support for, 174; working toward improvements in, 186

Ego, 156–157, 163–164, 182–183; -despot, 157, 158, 163; and emptiness, 159; mafia, 158; techniques of, for maintaining control, 157
Eichmann, Adolf, 93, 99
Einstein, Albert, 99, 101, 103
Eisenhower, Dwight, 45, 55
Eisler, Riane, 28, 33, 39, 86; *The Chalice and the Blade*, 24–25
El Salvador, 69, 171
Emotion, power and, 93–94
Emptiness, 159
Enemy, 37–38
Environmental Protection Agency (EPA), 65
Equal Rights Amendment, 86
Evil, 36–37, 57. *See also* Triumph of Good over Evil, myth of
Executive power, increases in, 174
Exxon, 61, 65, 134

Fallows, James, 81, 82–83, 189
Family myth, authoritarian, 72–73
Farmer, Doyne, 103
Fascism, 10
FBI, 138, 140
FDA, 128
Films, *see* Movies
First strike capability, 171
Follett, Mary Parker, 74, 100, 114, 177, 183, 189; *Creative Experience*, 165; on democracy, 1, 14, 20, 73, 178, 182, 191; and individualism, 154–155; *The New State*, 1, 71
Ford, Henry, 54
Foreign policy, U.S., 51–52, 55, 130
Fortune 500: corporations, 143; executives, 163
Fosdick, Harry Emerson, 181
Fossil fuels, 132
Founding Fathers, wisdom of, 56–58
Fox, Matthew, 122
Franco, Francisco, 54
Freedom, corporate, 60–61
Freedom of Information Act, 127, 187
Free speech movement (Berkeley, 1964), 173
Fundamentalists, 121, 122
Future, providing for, 186

GAO, 134
Gender, 89; authoritarianism and, 86–88; gap, 95
Germany, 53, 99
Gibson, James, 18

Gilligan, Carol, 88, 95
Gimbutas, Marija, 24
Ginsberg, Allen, 143
Gleick, James, 78
God: authoritarian ideas of, 116–123; democratic concept of, 123–124
Goode, William, 19
Good/evil, 36–37. *See also* Triumph of Good over Evil, myth of
Goodman, Ellen, 147
Goodwin, Richard, 14–15, 16, 17, 57–58
Gorbachev, Mikhail, 56, 138
Government: secrecy in, 126–132, 174; waste, 64–66
Great Depression, 69
Greed, containing, 185–186
Greene, Graham, 54
Guatemala, 49, 69, 139–140

Haig, Alexander, 94
Hanford weapons facility, radioactive emissions from, 129
Hansen, James E., 132
Haraway, Donna, 99–100
Harman, Willis, 103, 158, 187, 188; *Global Mind Change*, 96
Harris, Richard L., 68
Harrison, Bennett, 61
Hazlitt, William, 59
Hegel, G.W.F., 31
Heisenberg, Werner, 101
Hell, 37, 121; concept of, 118
Helms, Richard, 127
Heroic Leader, myth of, 105, 106
Hertsgaard, Mark, 142–143; *On Bended Knee*, 137
Higher/lower, 34–35, 98, 102
Hitler, Adolf, 12, 39, 86, 93, 99, 146; "lesson of," 54–55, 172
Holocaust, 28
Honduras, 139
Hughes, Howard, 153
Human error, 134
Humphrey, Hubert, 15–16
Hungary, 57
Hunt, H.L., 162
Hunter-gatherers, 24, 25, 26, 35, 36, 105; ideas of God for, 116–117, 118; myths of, 111, 112–113; and tragedy, 111; world view of, 32–34, 102, 183
Hussein, Saddam, 54, 172, 184
Huxley, Elspeth, *The Red Rock Wilderness*, 23

Napoleon Bonaparte, 31
Narcissism, male, 19, 25, 92
NASA, Goddard Institute for Space
    Studies of, 132
National Assessment of Educational
    Progress, 75
National security, 129, 132
National Security Council, 57
Natural selection, 28, 32
Navy, U.S., 134
Nazis, 11–12, 17, 55, 86
Neruda, Pablo, 54
New York Times, The, 15, 143, 144
Nicaragua, 51, 139, 145–146
"Nightline," 143
Nixon, Richard, 12, 14, 94, 127, 130,
    131; and invasion of Cambodia, 16;
    media manipulation by, 140
Noriega, Manuel Antonio, 172
North, Oliver, 126
NRC, 134

Objectivity, mask of, in science,
    99–100
Office of Management and Budget, 132
One Who Overcomes the Many,
    myth of, 107–108, 146–148, 152
Oppression, systematic, and
    authoritarianism, 27, 28
Ourselves, freeing, 188
Overstreet, H.A., 131

Panama, 55, 171
Paranoia, 15, 55, 127
Participation, democracy and, 21–22,
    75, 76, 154, 188
Pascarella, Perry, 68
Patriotism, 5, 58
Paul, St., 120, 121
Peasants, authoritarian attitudes
    toward, 85
People magazine, 148
Permissiveness, 72
Personality defects, as virtues, 55–56
Peter, Laurence J., 9
Peters, Tom, 135; Thriving on
    Chaos, 67
Pilate, Pontius, 120
Piven, Frances Fox, 175, 176
Plato, 30
Poland, 57
Poor, see Rich and poor
Pot, Pol, 93
Power, 56, 57; emotion and, 93–94
Pravda, 138

Primogeniture, 19
Procter and Gamble, 144
Product, obsession with, 177–179
Prohibition Amendment, 98
Protestants, 122–123
Psychology Today, 89
Punishment, 118, 120
Pure Son Who Overthrows Bad
    Father, myth of, 106
Purism, 176–177

Quakers, 123

Radiation, exposure to, 129, 134
Ranking, obsession with, 77–78
Rationality, 99
Reagan, Ronald, 14, 54, 56, 65, 174,
    176; foreign policy of, 130; and gap
    between rich and poor, 69, 70; and
    Saddam Hussein, 172; and media,
    138, 140, 141, 142, 143; his obses-
    sion with secrecy, 129, 130–131,
    132, 138; social programs cut by,
    169; his war on violence, 97
Rebellions, harmless, 109–110
Regan, Donald, 64
Religion: authoritarian, 116–123;
    democratic, 123–124
Renaissance, American, 189–191
Repression, 157
Rich and poor, gap between, 68–70,
    168–171, 174, 185–186
Riesman, David, 147, 151
Rigidity, 11–12, 55, 94
Rilke, Rainer Maria, 84
Rockefeller, John D., 54
Rockefeller, John D., Jr., 173
Roosevelt, Franklin D., 56, 174
Rusk, Dean, 16

Satan, 117, 119, 121
Schwartz, Pepper, 89
Science: building-block model of,
    100–102; decline of dualism in,
    102–103; mask of objectivity in,
    99–100
Scola, Ettore, 179
Secrecy: authoritarianism and, 27–28,
    126; fascination of, for men, 126;
    in government, 126–132, 174; ineffi-
    ciency of, 135–136; patriotism and,
    58; in private sector, 133–134, 135
Self-creating, democracy as, 20
Self-governing, democracy as, 20
Sexism, 85, 86

Sexual equality, promoting, 186–187
Shah of Iran, 140
Shakespeare, William, 28; *Henry V*, 31
Shaw, George Bernard, 71
Slavery, abolishing of, 85–86
Slaying of Needy Mother, myth of, 106, 109
Smith, Hedrick, 14, 130
Smoking, cancer, heart disease, and, 144
Snow, C.P., 126
Socialism, 4, 67
Soley, Lawrence C., 143
Somoza, Anastasio, 51, 53, 140, 145–146
South Africa, 130
South Korea, 172
Soviet Union, 50, 57, 129, 144; arms talks with, 130; containment policy toward, 55; relations between U.S. and, 56
Stalin, Joseph, 93
State Department, 14, 129, 131–132
Stephens, William, 24
Stereotypes, 93, 108
Stone, I.F., 118
Strong/weak, 36
Submissiveness, authoritarianism and, 27, 28
Sulzberger, C.L., 143
Supply-side economics, 70

Taiwan, 61
Television: function of, 148–149; programming, quality of, 144. *See also* Media
Thermodynamics, Second Law of, 103
Thieu, Nguyen Van, 140
Third Reich, 17
Third World, 52, 66, 94
Thornburgh, Richard, 63
Thucydides, 55
Tragedy, uses of, 111
Trickle-down theory, 70
Triumph of Good over Evil, myth of, 105, 106, 107–108

Underdog, identification with, 108
Underlings, blaming, 89–90
UNESCO, 170
Union Carbide, 66
Unitarians, 123
United Fruit Company, 139–140
Universe, splitting, 32–34
Unmotivated Female Puppet-Ideal, myth of, 106

Valdez disaster, 134
Veblen, Thorstein, 10
Verticality, authoritarianism and, 27, 98
Victim, blaming, 134
Victory sham, 112
Vietnam War, 13, 14–17, 18, 49, 131, 172; atrocities in, 39; deceptions about, 128, 132; and Lyndon Johnson, 15–16, 55, 93–94, 127, 140
Voter turnout, 174–176
Vulnerability, renouncing of, 105–106, 107

War, 29, 33, 37–38; authoritarianism and, 39, 171; as failure to deal with conflict, 109, 184; first casualty of, 125; leadership and, 26; patriotism and, 58
Watergate, 12
Welch, Robert, 54
Whitman, Walt, *Democratic Vistas*, 115
"Whore-madonna complex," 92
Wilson, Woodrow, 181
Winning, obsession with, 179–180
Women: authoritarianism and decline in position of, 39–41, 85–95; oppression of, 25; role of, in hunter-gatherer societies, 32; social innovations and, 19
World Bank, 16, 169
World War I, 28, 113
World War II, 12, 28, 46, 50, 54, 113; dictators defeated in, 140

Yorke, James, 132